S0-BNG-611

Course Authors
Mrs. Rivkah Slonim
Rabbi Avrohom Y. H. Sternberg

JLI Course Development Team
Ms. Neria Cohen
Rabbi Mordechai Dinerman
Rabbi Naftali Silberberg
Dr. Chana Silberstein

Printed in the United States of America

The Rohr Jewish Learning Institute
822 Eastern Parkway, Brooklyn, NY 11213

(888) YOUR-JLI/718-221-6900
www.myJLI.com

Pinchak

FASCINATING FACTS

Exploring the **Myths** and **Mysteries** of JUDAISM

JEWISH LEARNING INSTITUTE

The **Rohr Jewish Learning Institute**
gratefully acknowledges
the pioneering support of

George and Pamela Rohr

SINCE ITS INCEPTION,
the **Rohr JLI** has been
a beneficiary of the vision, generosity,
care, and concern
of the **Rohr family**

In the merit of
the tens of thousands of hours of Torah study
by **JLI** students worldwide,
may they be blessed with health,
Yiddishe nachas from all their loved ones,
and extraordinary success
in all their endeavors

וּבְסֵפֶר חַיִּים בְּרָכָה וְשָׁלוֹם וּפַרְנָסָה טוֹבָה
יְשׁוּעָה וְנֶחָמָה

THIS COURSE IS DEDICATED
WITH LOVE AND APPRECIATION TO

Mr. Sami Rohr שי׳

and to his children

George & Pamela Rohr and family,
Shmuel & Evelyn Katz and family,
and **Moshe & Lillian Tabacinic** and family,

שיחיו לאורך ימים ושנים טובות

Their generosity has helped bring the light of Torah
to nearly every corner of the globe.

*May Hashem grant them unbounded blessing,
peace, health, happiness, and prosperity,
and much Yiddishe nachas from all their loved ones.*

Dedicated by
Rabbi Moshe Kotlarsky
Lubavitch World Headquarters

Endorsements for **Fascinating Facts**

"As a teacher of Jewish adults, my responsibility is not only to convey knowledge, but also to help students unlearn and rethink their Judaism. Doing this—through the study of this intriguing course—they can potentially transform themselves, their families, and their communities."

Betsy Dolgin Katz, Ed.D.
Adjunct Professor, Spertus Institute of Jewish Studies and Gratz College
Author of *The Adult Jewish Education Handbook* and *Reinventing Adult Jewish Learning*

"*Kol Hakavod* to the Rohr Jewish Learning Institute for this valuable addition to the curriculum. Jewish culture, with books being its oldest and foremost component, is rich in beautiful traditions. *Fascinating Facts: Exploring the Myths and Mysteries of Judaism* goes a long way toward enriching our understanding and clarifying the meaning of many of the traditions we hold dear. It will deepen the knowledge for the informed Jew and provide an entrée for those with less background."

Carolyn Starman Hessel
Director, Jewish Book Council

"The JLI series of courses continues to be of high caliber with a judicious use of Jewish primary texts to facilitate study and discussion. Each volume is a fascinating exploration of a theme, bringing the corpus of Jewish learning into the conversation from every generation of Jewish learning and spanning—literally—more than three thousand years. I salute Chabad for soliciting and dedicating extensive resources to create and promote Jewish Learning Institute, among the most significant Jewish adult and teen educational endeavors offered in our Jewish community."

Rabbi Eric M. Lankin, D.Min.
Chief, Institutional Advancement and Education
Jewish National Fund

"I commend the Rohr Jewish Learning Institute on its new curriculum *Fascinating Facts: Exploring the Myths and Mysteries of Judaism.* This highly professional curriculum offers much more than a collection of readings, explanations, and discussion points. In each sentence, it connects with each learner's inner spark of curiosity about the universe and about being Jewish and then opens up new and profound worlds of knowledge and experience from within the depths of Jewish tradition. Judaism is not presented here as a cute titillating riddle that challenges the Jewish learner to find a solution, but rather as a precious gift that is offered lovingly, sensitively, and joyfully for ongoing spiritual, social, and existential enrichment. The pedagogical approach here is itself an enactment of the Jewish values that the curriculum seeks to inspire in the learner."

Daniel Marom, Ph.D.
Academic Director, Mandel Leadership Institute
Jerusalem, Israel

"How often do we hear misconceptions about the rich Jewish tradition from people whose own Jewish background was limited to an elementary education? This wonderful approach to learning is designed to engage curious adults in exploring the basics of our tradition that are so often misconstrued and fills a much-needed void in the adult learning field. Raising the questions and providing accurate and thoughtful responses will encourage even greater learning in the future."

Paul A. Flexner, Ed.D.
Assistant Professor, Georgia State University
Department of Educational Psychology and
Special Education

"The JLI course *Fascinating Facts* is the sort of entertaining crash course we all wish we had stumbled upon years ago. For someone looking for a broadband download of millennia of wisdom, this is one of the best places to start."

Lawrence Kelemen
Professor of Education, Neve Yerushalayim
College of Jewish Studies for Women
Author of *Permission to Believe*
and *Permission to Receive*

Table of Contents

Lesson 1

The Story of Your Life

How to Read the Torah

Introduction

It's time for a new reading of the Bible. We will start by picking out the bad apples and end by discovering who shattered something whole to fix what was broken. In between, we'll face justice eye to eye, and find out what Jews did before they learned to quote chapter and verse.

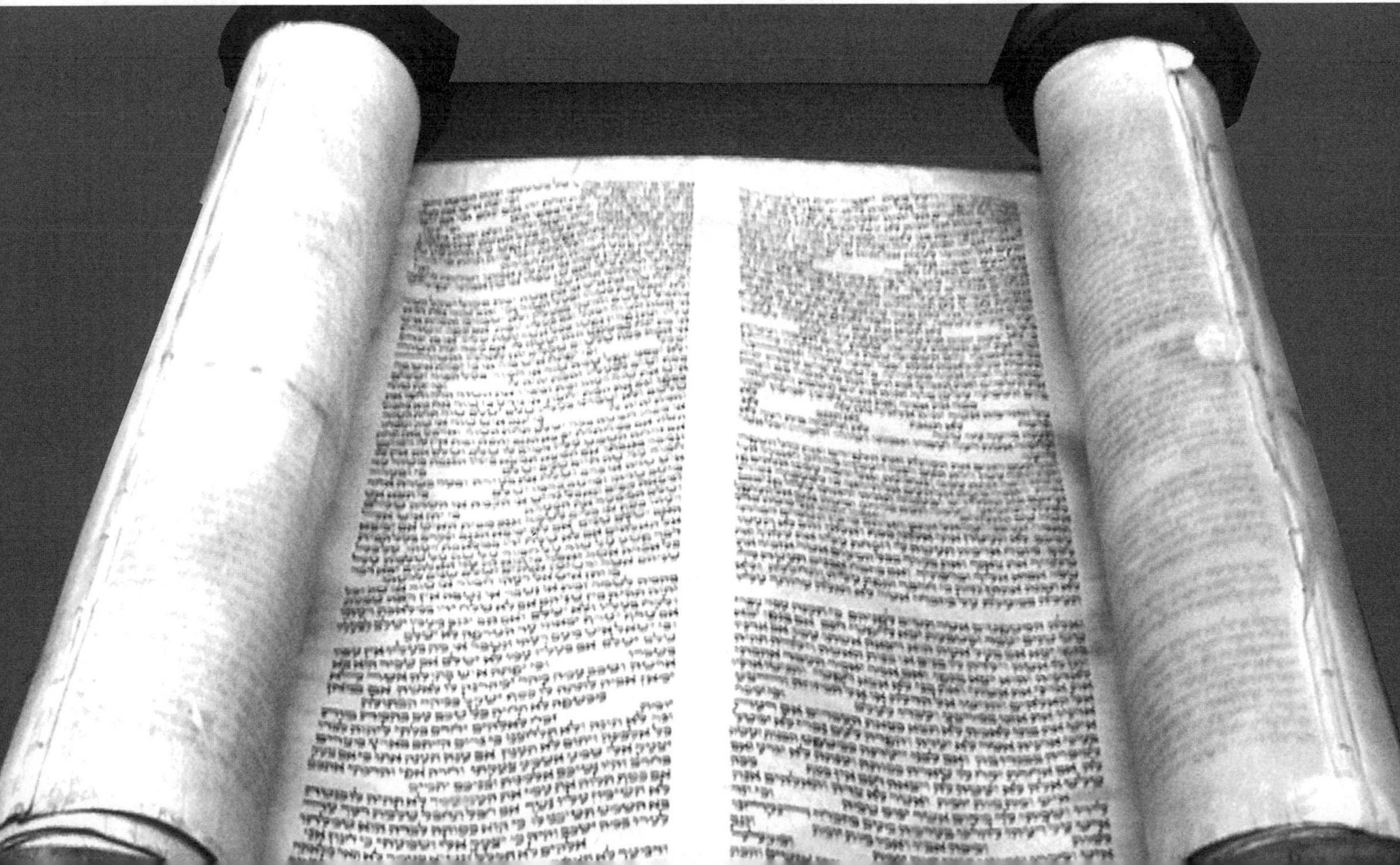

How to Read the Torah

Curious Omissions

Figure 1.1

Number of Chapters	Stories Related	Time Span Covered
11 (Genesis 1–11)	Story of Creation; Tree of Knowledge; Cain and Abel; Noah; first 70 years of Abraham's life	**Years 1–2018** 2,018 years
41 (Genesis 12–Exodus 2)	Lives of the Patriarchs and Matriarchs (Abraham, Isaac, Jacob, and their wives); 209 years of Egyptian slavery	**Years 2018–2447** 429 years
83 (Exodus 3–Numbers 19)	Moses at the burning bush; the Exodus from Egypt and events of the following year	**Years 2447–2449** 2+ years
—	Jews wandering in the desert	**Years 2449–2487** 38 years
52 (Numbers 20–Deuteronomy 34)	Miriam's passing until Moses' passing less than a year later	**Years 2487–2488** 11 months

Question for Discussion

Why would the Torah report historical events so unevenly?

Out of Order

The stories related in the Torah are not necessarily in chronological order. Thus, the first chapter of the Book of Numbers talks about a census that occurred "in the second month of the second year [following the Exodus]," while the ninth chapter of the same book discusses events that occurred a month earlier, "in the first month of the second year."

Though events *are* usually recounted in chronological order, the Torah makes exceptions in instances where there is a lesson to be derived from the reversal of order.

Text 1a

התורה מורה לאדם את הדרך, אשר בדרך ההוא יגיע אל תכליתו האחרון מה שאפשר לאדם להגיעו . . . ולכך ראוי לה דווקא לתורה שם תורה, שהוא לשון הוראה.

נתיבות עולם א, נתיב התורה א

The Torah guides people along the path they must take in order to reach their greatest potential. . . . It is therefore appropriately called "Torah," which implies guidance.

Rabbi Yehudah Loew, *Netivot Olam* 1, *Netiv HaTorah* 1

Rabbi Yehudah Loew (1525–1609). Talmudist and philosopher, also known as the Maharal of Prague. Descended from the Babylonian exilarchs, Maharal rose to prominence as leader of the famed Jewish community of Prague. He is the author of more than a dozen works of original philosophic thought, most notably *Tiferet Yisrael* and *Netsach Yisrael*. He also authored *Gur Aryeh*, a supercommentary on Rashi's biblical commentary, and a commentary on the Talmud. He is buried in the Old Jewish Cemetery of Prague.

Text 1b

וי להוא בר נש דאמר דהא אורייתא אתא לאחזאה ספורין בעלמא ומלין דהדיוטי . . .
אי לאחזאה מלה דעלמא, אפילו אינון קפסירי דעלמא אית בינייהו מלין עלאין יתיר,
אי הכי נזיל אבתרייהו ונעביד מנייהו אורייתא כהאי גוונא!

זוהר ג, קנב,א

Woe to the person who says that the Torah's objective is merely to relate stories and simplistic tales. . . . If the objective of the Torah were to relate historical matters, the rulers of the world have historical chronicles that are superior; let us utilize them and produce from them a [better] Torah!

Zohar 3:152a

A Tale of Two Trees

Text 2

וַיַּצְמַח ה׳ אֱלֹקִים מִן הָאֲדָמָה כָּל עֵץ נֶחְמָד לְמַרְאֶה וְטוֹב לְמַאֲכָל, וְעֵץ הַחַיִּים בְּתוֹךְ הַגָּן וְעֵץ הַדַּעַת טוֹב וָרָע . . .

וַיְצַו ה׳ אֱלֹקִים עַל הָאָדָם לֵאמֹר, "מִכֹּל עֵץ הַגָּן אָכֹל תֹּאכֵל. וּמֵעֵץ הַדַּעַת טוֹב וָרָע לֹא תֹאכַל מִמֶּנּוּ, כִּי בְּיוֹם אֲכָלְךָ מִמֶּנּוּ מוֹת תָּמוּת".

בראשית ב,ט-יז

And the Lord God caused to sprout from the ground every tree that was pleasant to see and good to eat, and, in the midst of the garden, the Tree of Life and the Tree of Knowledge of Good and Evil. . . .

And the Lord God commanded man, saying, "Of every tree of the garden you may freely eat. But of the Tree of Knowledge of Good and Evil you shall not eat, for you shall surely die on the day that you eat thereof."

Genesis 2:9–17

Text 3a

אילן שאכל ממנו אדם הראשון:
רבי מאיר אומר גפן היה . . .
רבי נחמיה אומר תאנה היתה . . .
רבי יהודה אומר חטה היתה.
תלמוד בבלי, ברכות מ,א

The tree from which Adam ate:

Rabbi Meir says it was a grapevine. . . .

Rabbi Nechemiah says it was a fig tree. . . .

Rabbi Yehudah says it was a wheat stalk.

Talmud, Berachot 40a

Text 3b

רבי עזריה ורבי יהודה בר סימון בשם רבי יהושע בן לוי אמר: ״חס ושלום! לא גלה הקדוש ברוך הוא אותו אילן לאדם, ולא עתיד לגלותו״.
בראשית רבה טו,ז

Rabbi Azariah and Rabbi Yehudah ben Simon said in the name of Rabbi Yehoshua ben Levi: "Heaven forbid! God never revealed the identity of the tree to any man, and He never will."

Midrash, *Bereishit Rabah* 15:7

Text 4a

וַיֵּרָא מַלְאַךְ ה' אֵלָיו בְּלַבַּת אֵשׁ מִתּוֹךְ הַסְּנֶה. וַיַּרְא, וְהִנֵּה הַסְּנֶה בֹּעֵר בָּאֵשׁ וְהַסְּנֶה אֵינֶנּוּ אֻכָּל.

שמות ג,ב

An angel of God appeared to [Moses] in the heart of a fire in the midst of the thornbush. He looked, and, behold, the thornbush was ablaze, but the thornbush was not consumed.

Exodus 3:2

Text 4b

מתוך הסנה, ולא אילן אחר, משום "עמו אנכי בצרה" (תהילים צא,טו).

רש"י, שם

From within the thornbush, and not any other type of tree, because "I am with [Israel] in their distress" (Psalms 91:15).

Rashi, ad loc.

Rabbi Shlomo Yitschaki (1040–1105). Better known by the acronym Rashi. Rabbi and famed author of comprehensive commentaries on the Talmud and Bible. Born in Troyes, France, Rashi studied in the famed *yeshivot* of Mainz and Worms. His commentaries, which focus on the simple understanding of the text, are considered the most fundamental of all the commentaries that preceded and followed. Since their initial printings, the commentaries have appeared in virtually every edition of the Talmud and Bible. Many of the famed authors of the *Tosafot* are among Rashi's descendants.

The Writing on the Wall

Many common English phrases originate in the Bible. For example, the source of the idiom "the writing's on the wall," which refers to an omen of an unpleasant fate, is in the Book of Daniel (ch. 5):

King Belshazzar made a great feast and asked that the vessels that his grandfather Nebuchadnezzar had taken from the Holy Temple be brought to the feast. When the king's wishes were fulfilled, the figure of a human hand emerged and wrote four Aramaic words on the wall of the palace: *Menei menei tekel ufarsin*. The king was terrified. Daniel was summoned to interpret their meaning, and in doing so, he prophesied the destruction of the kingdom:

Menei menei (to count)—God has counted and recounted the days of your kingdom and has brought it to an end.
Tekel (to weigh)—You were weighed on the scales and found wanting.
Ufarsin (to divide)—Your kingdom has been broken up and given to Media and Persia.

That very night, Belshazzar was assassinated, and Media and Persia conquered the Babylonian Empire.

Myths and Misconceptions
The Mystery of Matzah

Text 5a

וַיֹּאפוּ אֶת הַבָּצֵק אֲשֶׁר הוֹצִיאוּ מִמִּצְרַיִם עֻגֹת מַצּוֹת כִּי לֹא חָמֵץ, כִּי גֹרְשׁוּ מִמִּצְרַיִם וְלֹא יָכְלוּ לְהִתְמַהְמֵהַּ.

שמות יב,לט

They baked the dough that they had brought out of Egypt into matzah rounds, for it had not leavened—because they were driven out of Egypt and could not delay.

Exodus 12:39

Don't Watch the Movie—Read the Book!

In the 1998 film *The Prince of Egypt,* Moses' siblings, Aaron and Miriam, are depicted as slaves. Yet the Torah describes how Aaron accompanied Moses to the palace to ask Pharaoh to free the Jews. Why were they allowed to walk freely to the palace? In the Bible, there is no indication that *all* Jews were forced to work all the time. In particular, according to Jewish tradition, the tribe of Levi was never conscripted at all.

Text 5b

וְאָכְלוּ אֶת הַבָּשָׂר בַּלַּיְלָה הַזֶּה, צְלִי אֵשׁ וּמַצּוֹת עַל מְרֹרִים יֹאכְלֻהוּ.

שם, יב,ח

During this night, they shall eat the meat [of the Paschal Lamb]. It shall be roasted over fire and eaten with matzah and bitter herbs.

Ibid., 12:8

Text 5c

מה שנצטוו על המצות קודם לכן היה על שם העתיד, שהשם יודע העתידות ידע שהיה להם לצאת ממצרים בחפזון ואפילו אם היו רוצים לא היו יכולים להחמיץ בצקם, צוה לאכול הפסח על המצות.

אבודרהם, סדר ההגדה ופירושה

The [Jews] were commanded to eat matzah before [the Exodus] because of what would transpire afterwards. God, Who knows the future, knew that the [Jews] would need to leave Egypt in a hurry, and would not have time to bake leavened bread even if they wished to do so. He therefore commanded them to eat the Paschal Lamb together with matzah.

Rabbi David Abudraham, *Seder Hahagadah Upirushah*

Rabbi David ben Yoseph Abudraham (14th century), resided in Seville, Spain, and is famous for his work on Jewish prayers and blessings. The work—completed around the year 1340—is a commentary on the daily, Shabbat, and festival prayers and collects many customs and laws relating to them. He is believed to have been a disciple of Rabbi Ya'akov ben Asher, author of *Arba'ah Turim*.

Text 6

נגלה עליהם מלך מלכי המלאכים הקדוש ברוך הוא וגאלם.

הגדה של פסח

The supreme King of kings, the Holy One, blessed be He, revealed Himself unto [the Jews] and redeemed them.

Passover Haggadah

"Man, oh, Manischewitz"

Founded in 1888 by Lithuanian immigrants to America, the Manischewitz Company was the first to mass-produce machine-made matzah. By the 1920s, Manischewitz produced 1.25 million *matzot* per day. Their advertising slogan, "Man, oh, Manischewitz," became so well known that Apollo 17 astronaut Eugene Cernan actually exclaimed that phrase during a moonwalk in 1973.

U-Turn?

Why did the Jews cross the sea? To get to other side? Not according to commonly accepted Jewish tradition. Based on textual analysis, the sages deduced that the Jews entered the sea, made a semicircle, and came out on the same side as the one they had entered! What would be the purpose of coming out on the same side? The objective was not a navigational shortcut, but to annihilate the Egyptian army, so that the Jews would no longer live in dread of their erstwhile taskmasters.

Squaring the Tablets

Text 7a

והלוחות, ארכן ששה ורחבן ששה ועביין שלשה.

תלמוד בבלי, בבא בתרא יד,א

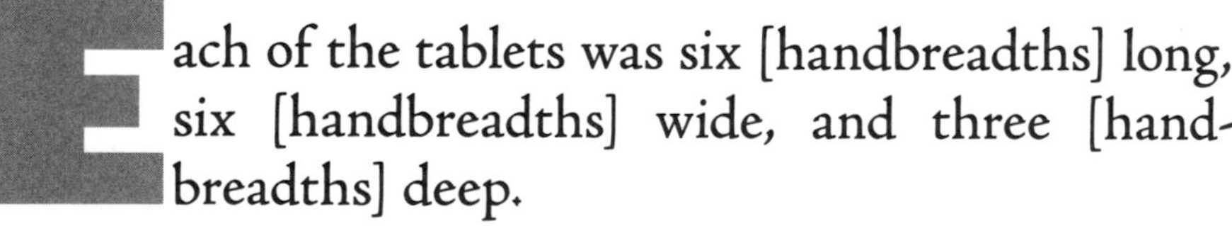

Each of the tablets was six [handbreadths] long, six [handbreadths] wide, and three [handbreadths] deep.

Talmud, Baba Batra 14a

Text 7b

הלוחות היו מרובעות, ששה טפחים באורך וששה טפחים ברוחב . . . ואם תשכיל עוד במדת הלוחות, בין אורך ורוחב ועובי תמצא כי היה בכל לוח ולוח מאה ושמונה טפחים.

רבינו בחיי, שמות לא,יח

The tablets were square: six handbreadths long and six handbreadths wide. . . . If you study the dimensions of the tablets—the height, width, and depth—you will find that each tablet contained 108 cubic handbreadths.

Rabbi Bachaye ben Asher, Exodus 31:18

Rabbi Bachaye ben Asher (ca. 1255–1340), author of a Torah commentary, *Midrash Rabbeinu Bachaye;* born in Saragossa, Spain. He is known for systemizing the four classic levels of exegesis: *peshat* (plain meaning), *remez* (allusive meaning), *derash* (homiletic exposition), and *sod* (kabbalistic meaning). He also authored a work on ethics, *Kad Hakemach*.

Figure 1.2

6 × 6 × 3= 108

The Menorah Angle

The tablets are not the only Jewish symbol that is often inaccurately represented; the common depiction of the Temple menorah with semicircular branches extending from its center is also erroneous. According to Maimonides and others, the menorah's branches were straight, extending outward on a diagonal from the middle branch.

Diagram of the Menorah drawn by Maimonides

Moses' Horns

Text 8a

וַיְהִי בְּרֶדֶת מֹשֶׁה מֵהַר סִינַי, וּשְׁנֵי לֻחֹת הָעֵדֻת בְּיַד מֹשֶׁה בְּרִדְתּוֹ מִן הָהָר, וּמֹשֶׁה לֹא יָדַע כִּי קָרַן עוֹר פָּנָיו בְּדַבְּרוֹ אִתּוֹ. וַיַּרְא אַהֲרֹן וְכָל בְּנֵי יִשְׂרָאֵל אֶת מֹשֶׁה וְהִנֵּה קָרַן עוֹר פָּנָיו, וַיִּירְאוּ מִגֶּשֶׁת אֵלָיו.

שמות לד,כט–ל

When Moses descended from Mount Sinai, the two tablets of the testimony were in his hand as he descended from the mountain. And Moses did not know that the skin of his face had become radiant (*karan*) when [God] spoke with him. Aaron and all the children of Israel saw Moses and, behold, the skin of his face was radiant, and they were afraid to approach him.

Exodus 34:29–30

Text 8b

And when Moses came down from Mount Sinai, he held the two tablets of the testimony, and he knew not that his face was horned from the conversation of the Lord.

Vulgate, Exodus 34:29

Jerome (ca. 337–420), the most learned student of the Bible among the Latin ecclesiastical writers, and, until modern times, the only Christian scholar able to study the Hebrew Bible in the original. His knowledge of Hebrew appears especially in his chief work, the Latin translation of the Bible from the Hebrew original, the Vulgate. No friend of the Jews, he often reproached them for being stiff-necked, dissented with their views in the strongest terms, and reveled in their misfortune.

Text 9

מקום שבעלי תשובה עומדין צדיקים גמורים אינם עומדין.
תלמוד בבלי, ברכות לד,ב

The spiritual heights achieved by those who repent cannot be attained even by those who are perfectly righteous.

Talmud, Berachot 34b

Family Matters

Sometimes you have to scratch your head and wonder: How did a certain myth gain such widespread circulation, when the Bible clearly states otherwise?

One such example is the common belief that Esther was Mordecai's niece, when actually they were first cousins. Here's what the second chapter of the Book of Esther says: "And [Mordecai] raised Hadassah, that is Esther, his uncle's daughter, for she was orphaned from her father and mother."

"An Eye for an Eye"

Text 10a

עַיִן תַּחַת עַיִן, שֵׁן תַּחַת שֵׁן, יָד תַּחַת יָד, רֶגֶל תַּחַת רָגֶל.
שמות כא,כג-כד

An eye for an eye, a tooth for a tooth, a hand for a hand, a foot for a foot.

Exodus 21:23–24

Text 10b

וְכִי יְרִיבֻן אֲנָשִׁים וְהִכָּה אִישׁ אֶת רֵעֵהוּ בְּאֶבֶן אוֹ בְאֶגְרֹף, וְלֹא יָמוּת וְנָפַל לְמִשְׁכָּב, אִם יָקוּם וְהִתְהַלֵּךְ בַּחוּץ עַל מִשְׁעַנְתּוֹ וְנִקָּה הַמַּכֶּה, רַק שִׁבְתּוֹ יִתֵּן וְרַפֹּא יְרַפֵּא.

שם, כא,יח-יט

If men quarrel and one strikes the other with a stone or with a fist, and [the victim] does not die but is confined to bed, if [the victim] then gets up and walks about outside unaided, the assailant shall be cleared; he shall only pay for [income lost due to the victim's enforced] idleness and his medical costs.

Ibid., 21:18–19

Text 10c

וּמַכֵּה נֶפֶשׁ בְּהֵמָה יְשַׁלְּמֶנָּה, נֶפֶשׁ תַּחַת נָפֶשׁ.

ויקרא כד,יח

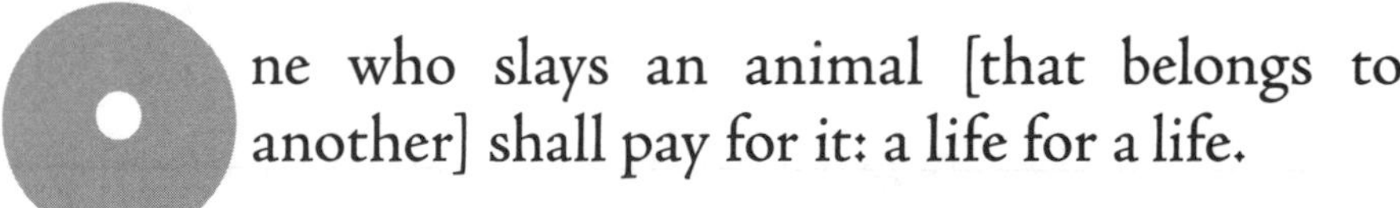

One who slays an animal [that belongs to another] shall pay for it: a life for a life.

Leviticus 24:18

The Oral Torah

Help Needed!

Learning Activity 1a

The following is a literal translation of a full, stand-alone section from the Torah (Numbers 5:5–10). Take a moment to read it and then—if you can—jot down your interpretation of the text.

And God spoke to Moses to say speak to the children of Israel a man or woman if they shall do of all the sins of man to act treacherously against God and that soul is guilty they shall confess the sin they committed and return his guilt in his head and its fifth he should add on it and give it to the one to whom he was guilty and if the man has no redeemer to whom to return the guilt the guilt that is returned to God to the priest besides the ram of atonements which he atones with him on him and every uplifting for all the holies of the children of Israel which they bring near to the priest shall be his a person his holies to him shall be which he gives to the priest shall be his.

Learning Activity 1b

The following paragraph is taken from the *Shema* (Deuteronomy 6:6–9). Immediately after we are commanded to love God with "all our heart, soul, and might," we are instructed:

And these words that I command you this day shall be upon your heart. You shall teach them to your sons and speak of them when you sit in your house, when you walk on the way, when you lie down, and when you rise up. And you shall bind them for a sign upon your hand, and they shall be for *totafot* between your eyes. And you shall inscribe them upon the doorposts of your house and upon your gates.

Divest yourself of any knowledge you may already have regarding the nature of the *mitzvot* referred to in this passage (which is all a product of the oral interpretation). Relying only on your careful reading of the text, try to answer these questions:

a. **What are "these words that I command you today"?**
b. **How do we place them on our heart?**
c. **How and where do we bind them to our hand?**
d. **How and where do we make them into *totafot* between our eyes?**
e. **How do we inscribe them on our doorposts and on our gates?**

At the Tender Age of . . . ?

In our mind's eye, we envision the characters of certain famous biblical stories as young children, when according to Jewish tradition they were well past their childhood years.

Two such examples: According to the Midrash, Isaac was 37 years old during the Binding of Isaac episode, and Jacob was 63 years old when he outsmarted his brother Esau to receive his father's blessing.

I Told You So!

Text 11a

וְזָבַחְתָּ מִבְּקָרְךָ וּמִצֹּאנְךָ אֲשֶׁר נָתַן ה׳ לְךָ כַּאֲשֶׁר צִוִּיתִךָ, וְאָכַלְתָּ בִּשְׁעָרֶיךָ בְּכֹל אַוַּת נַפְשֶׁךָ.

דברים יב,כ-כא

You shall slaughter, as I have commanded you, of your cattle and of your sheep that God has given you, and you may eat [meat] in your cities as per your hearts' desire.

Deuteronomy 12:20–21

Text 11b

זביחה זו האמורה בתורה סתם צריך לפרש אותה ולידע: באי זה מקום מן הבהמה שוחטין? וכמה שיעור השחיטה? ובאי זה דבר שוחטין? ומתי שוחטין? והיכן שוחטין? וכיצד שוחטין? ומה הן הדברים המפסידין את השחיטה? ומי הוא השוחט?

ועל כל הדברים האלו צונו בתורה ואמר, ״וזבחת מבקרך וגו׳ כאשר צויתיך ואכלת בשעריך וגו׳״, שכל הדברים האלו על פה צוה בהן כשאר תורה שבעל פה.

משנה תורה, הלכות שחיטה א,ד

The slaughter that the Torah mentions, without any elaboration, needs to be explained in order for us to know the following: Which place on the animal is [appropriate] for ritual slaughter? How large must the incision be? With what do we slaughter? When do we slaughter? Where do we slaughter? How do we slaughter? What factors disqualify the slaughter? Who can slaughter?

Regarding all these factors, the Torah instructs us: "You shall slaughter, as I commanded you, of your cattle. . . ." All of these laws were commanded to us orally, as is true with regard to the remainder of the Oral Law.

Maimonides, *Mishneh Torah*, Laws of Ritual Slaughter 1:4

Rabbi Moshe ben Maimon (1135–1204). Better known as Maimonides or by the acronym Rambam; born in Cordoba, Spain. After the conquest of Cordoba by the Almohads, he fled Spain and eventually settled in Cairo, Egypt. There, he became the leader of the Jewish community and served as court physician to the vizier of Egypt. His rulings on Jewish law are considered integral to the formation of halachic consensus. He is most noted for authoring the *Mishneh Torah,* an encyclopedic arrangement of Jewish law, and for his philosophical work, *Guide for the Perplexed.*

Chapter and Verse

Figure 1.3

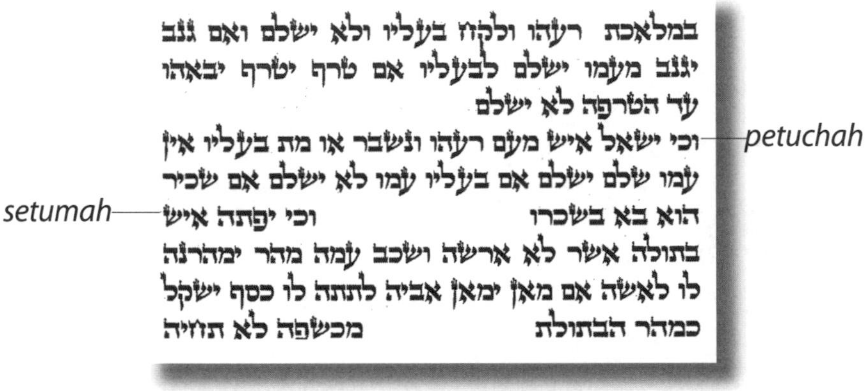

במלאכת רעהו ולקח בעליו ולא ישלם ואם גנב
יגנב מעמו ישלם לבעליו אם טרף יטרף יבאהו
עד הטרפה לא ישלם
וכי ישאל איש מעם רעהו ונשבר או מת בעליו אין — petuchah
עמו שלם ישלם אם בעליו עמו לא ישלם אם שכיר
setumah — הוא בא בשכרו וכי יפתה איש
בתולה אשר לא ארשה ושכב עמה מהר ימהרנה
לו לאשה אם מאן ימאן אביה לתתה לו כסף ישקל
כמהר הבתולת מכשפה לא תחיה

Text 12

Rabbi Shlomo Luria (1510–1574). Known by the acronym "Maharshal" or "Rashal"; born in Posen, Poland, to a prestigious rabbinic family. A renowned Ashkenazic rabbi, his rulings in Jewish law are integral to modern Halachah. Author of *Yam Shel Shlomo,* a work of Jewish law and Talmudic commentary, and *Chochmat Shlomo,* a work mostly dedicated to establishing the proper text of the Talmud and its primary commentaries. After serving as rabbi in various Lithuanian towns, Rabbi Luria succeeded Rabbi Shalom Shachna as head of the famed yeshivah in Lublin, Poland. He is buried in Lublin.

פתוחה אין לה חבור עם מה שלמעלה, והוא עניין חלוק בפני עצמו וכאילו התחיל פה. וסתומה מחוברת וסתום לדברים שלפניה.

שאלות ותשובות מהרש"ל לז

A *petuchah* has no connection to that which precedes it; it is the opening of a new concept. A *setumah* is connected to the preceding words.

Rabbi Shlomo Luria, *Responsa Maharshal* 37

Text 13

ראיתי לחלק כל ספר וספר מהם אל פרשיות, אבל לא יהיו ארוכות וגדולות . . . וגם לא יהיו קטנות וקצרות כמו שעשאם החכם גירונימ״ו אשר העתיק ספרי הקדש לנוצרים, שעשה בספר יהושע כ״ד פרשיות, ובספר שופטים כ״א פרשיות, ובספר שמואל ל״ה.

אברבנאל, הקדמה לנביאים ראשונים

I decided to divide each book into sections. However, they will not be very long . . . nor will they be very short chapters, like [the chapters of] the scholar Hieronymus, who translated the holy Scriptures for the Christians and divided the book of Joshua into 24 chapters, the book of Judges into 21 chapters, and the book of Samuel into 35 chapters.

Rabbi Don Yitschak Abarbanel, Introduction to the Early Prophets

Rabbi Don Yitschak Abarbanel (1437–1508). Born in Lisbon, Portugal; rabbi, scholar, and statesman. Abarbanel served as a minister in the court of King Alfonso V of Portugal. After intrigues at court led to accusations against him, he fled to Spain, where he once again served as a counselor to royalty. It is claimed that Abarbanel offered King Ferdinand and Queen Isabella large sums of money for the revocation of their Edict of Expulsion of 1492, but to no avail. After the expulsion, he eventually settled in Italy where he wrote a commentary on Scripture, as well as other venerated works. He is buried in Padua.

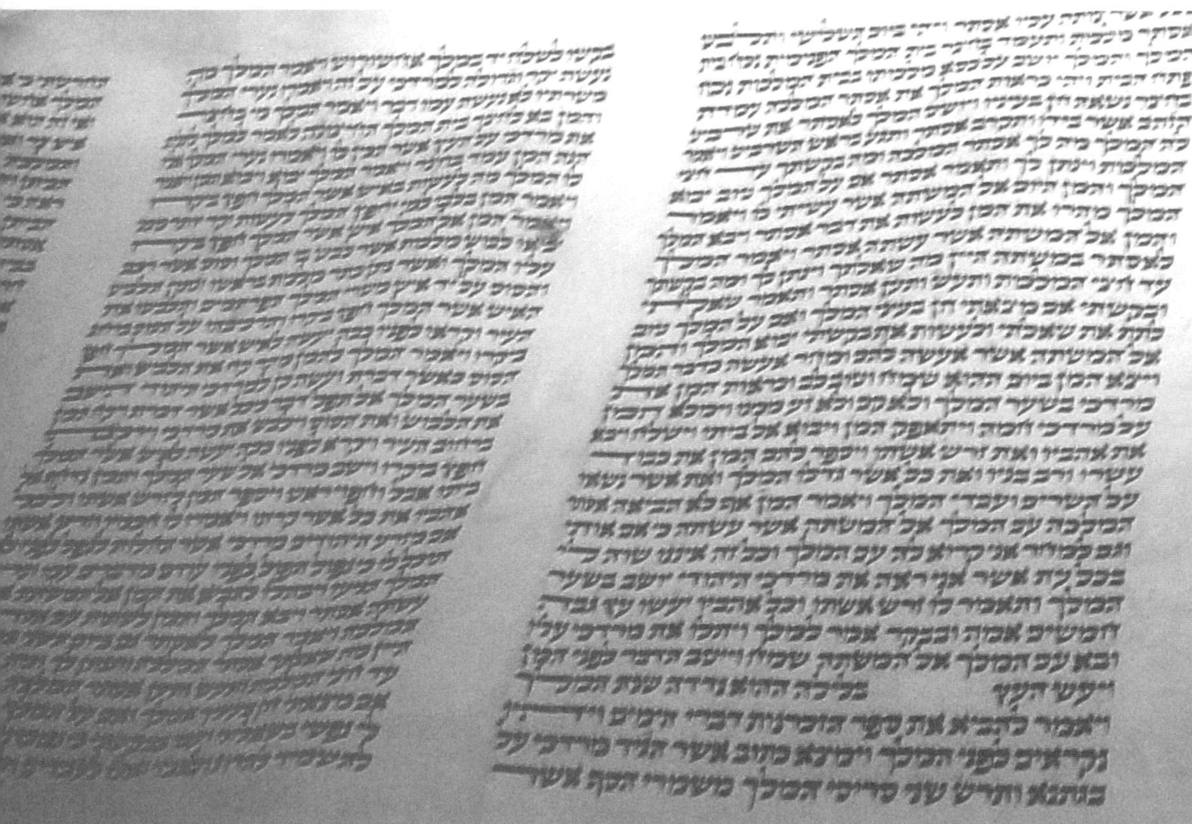

The Parting Lesson

Learning Activity 2

What was Moses' greatest feat, his most defining achievement?

a. Splitting the Red Sea

b. Transmitting the Torah to the Jews

c. Breaking the tablets

d. Leading the conquest of the territories on the east bank of the Jordan River

e. Other ______________________________

Text 14a

וְלֹא קָם נָבִיא עוֹד בְּיִשְׂרָאֵל כְּמֹשֶׁה אֲשֶׁר יְדָעוֹ ה׳ פָּנִים אֶל פָּנִים, לְכָל הָאֹתוֹת וְהַמּוֹפְתִים אֲשֶׁר שְׁלָחוֹ ה׳ לַעֲשׂוֹת בְּאֶרֶץ מִצְרָיִם לְפַרְעֹה וּלְכָל עֲבָדָיו וּלְכָל אַרְצוֹ, וּלְכֹל הַיָּד הַחֲזָקָה וּלְכֹל הַמּוֹרָא הַגָּדוֹל אֲשֶׁר עָשָׂה מֹשֶׁה לְעֵינֵי כָּל יִשְׂרָאֵל.

דברים לד,י-יב

There has never arisen another prophet in Israel like Moses, who communicated with God face to face; [who executed] all the signs and wonders that God sent him to perform in the land of Egypt upon Pharaoh and all his servants, and to all his land; and for all the strong hand and great awesomeness performed by Moses before the eyes of all of Israel.

Deuteronomy 34:10–12

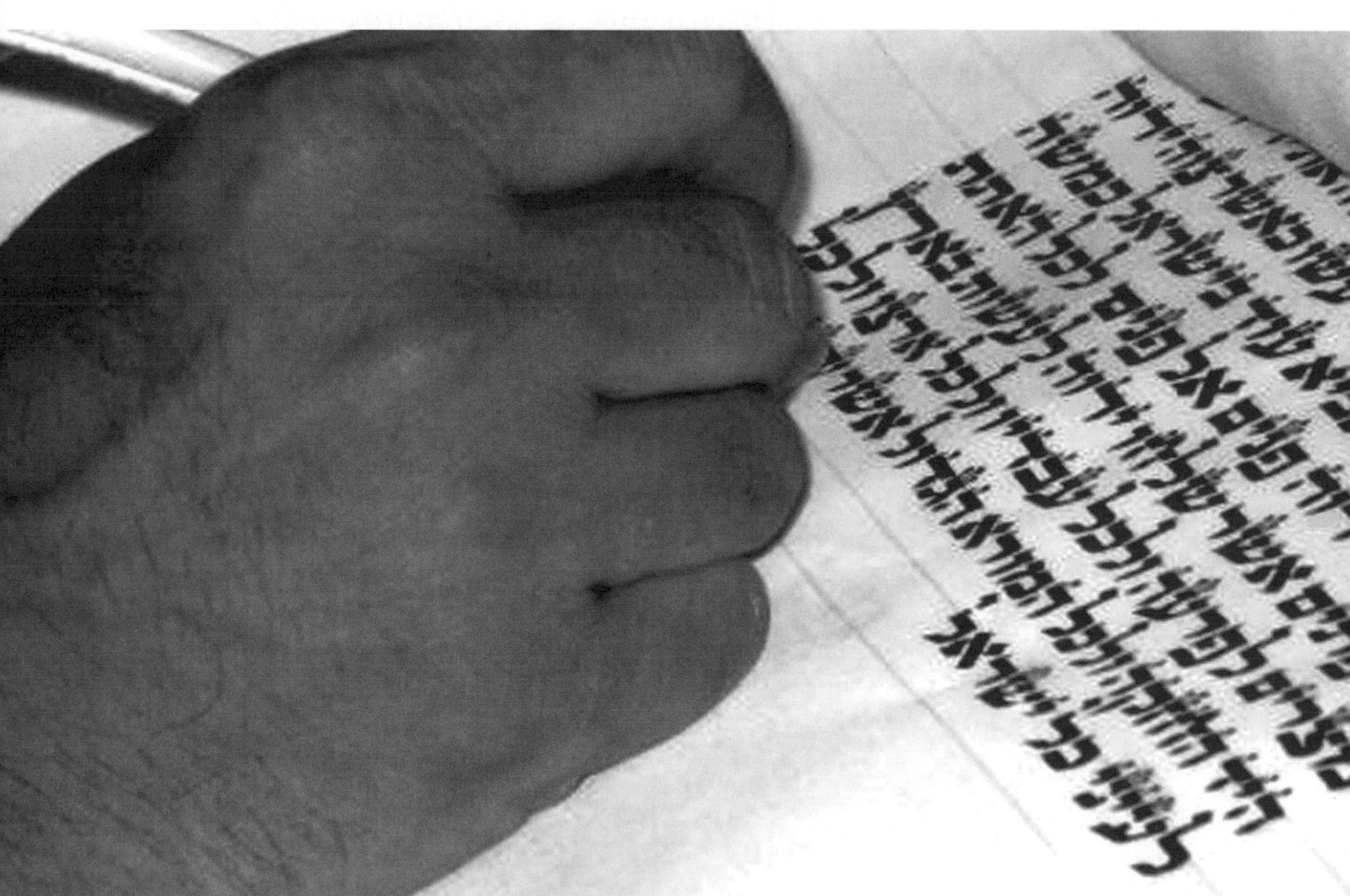

Text 14b

שנשאו לבו לשבור הלוחות לעיניהם, שנאמר (דברים ט,יז), "ואשברם לעיניכם".
רש"י, שם

This expression alludes to the incident in which [Moses] was inspired to smash the tablets before [Israel's] eyes, as is stated (Deuteronomy 9:17), "And I shattered them before your eyes."

Rashi, ad loc.

Questions for Discussion

Why is the breaking of the tablets considered a monumental achievement? Of all of Moses' aforementioned accomplishments, how can this act possibly be construed as his greatest moment?

Text 15

למה הדבר דומה, למלך ששלח לקדש אשה עם הסרסור, הלך הסרסור לעשות שליחות
המלך וקלקלה עם אחה. הסרסור שהיה נקי מה עשה? נטל את כתובתה מה שנתן לו
המלך לקדשה, וקרעה. אמר, "מוטב שתדון כפנויה ולא כאשת איש".
כך עשה משה, כיון שעשו ישראל אותו מעשה נטל את הלוחות ושיברן.
שמות רבה מג,א

This is like a king who sent an agent to betroth a woman on his behalf. The agent executed the king's order, and the [now-betrothed] woman proceeded to engage in an adulterous affair. What did the agent do? He ripped up the betrothal contract that the king had given him. "Better," he reasoned, "that she should be judged as an unbetrothed woman, and not as a betrothed one."

Moses did the same: When the Jews committed that terrible act, he took the tablets and broke them.

Midrash, *Shemot Rabah* 43:1

Text 16a

משל למלך בשר ודם שיש לו בנים ועבדים הרבה בתוך ביתו, ויש לו למלך עבד זקן ביניהם שהוא מלמד את בניו דרכים נאים ומעשים טובים. ובכל יום ויום כשנכנסין בניו ועבדיו לפניו מניח המלך את כולם ואוהב את העבד הזקן שיש לו בתוך ביתו.

ואמרו לו עבדיו, "למה אהבת את העבד הזקן יותר מן הכל?"

ואמר להם המלך, "אלמלא עבד זקן זה שהוא מלמד את בני דרכים נאים ונעימים ומעשים טובים, מה יהיה עליהן?"

כך דברי תורה, הואיל ומכריעין את ישראל לכף זכות ומחנכין אותן במצות ומביאין אותן לחיי עולם הבא, לפיכך חביבין דברי תורה עליו על הקדוש ברוך הוא.

תנא דבי אליהו רבה יד

A parable:

There was a king who had many children and servants in his court. [Among them was] one old servant who mentored the king's children and taught them to behave in a beautiful manner. Every day, when the children and servants would enter, the king would shower affection on the old servant.

"Why do you love this old servant above all?" the other servants asked.

"If not for his teaching my children beautiful ways and manners," the king replied, "what would become of them?"

The same is true regarding Torah. It causes Israel to be meritorious, teaches them the *mitzvot*, and brings them to merit life in the World to Come. Therefore, the words of Torah are precious to God.

Midrash, *Tana Devei Eliyahu Rabah* 14

Text 16b

When Moses saw the people standing below reveling in their worship of a golden calf, two options lay before him. On the one hand, Torah; on the other, his people. But he could not have both. Because if his people would receive the Torah in the state to which they had descended, they would be destroyed.

Moses threw down the tablets and saved his people.

Meaning that there is something about these people that is present even when they are committing the gravest sin. Something that makes them more valuable than even the Torah, than G-d's innermost wisdom.

It would seem, then, that the soul is greater than the Torah.

Yet, how do we know that this is so? How do we know the value of any human life? Only because the Torah tells us this story. Without the Torah, we would not know the greatness of the soul and of the people.

So, we have two sides of the coin: The soul cannot realize its greatness without the Torah; and the Torah cannot be fathomed to its depths until it is shattered for the sake of the people.

Rabbi Tzvi Freeman, "Broken and Whole," www.chabad.org

Rabbi Tzvi Freeman (1955–) left a career as a classical guitarist and composer to study Talmud and Jewish mysticism. A published expert consultant and lecturer in the field of educational technology, Freeman held posts at the University of British Columbia and Digipen School of Computer Gaming. Rabbi Freeman is the author of *Bringing Heaven Down to Earth*; *Heaven Exposed*; *Men, Women & Kabbalah* and *Trembling with Joy*. He is a senior editor at Chabad.org.

Key Points

1. The Torah is not a history book. The English word "Bible" means "book," but the Hebrew word "Torah" suggests instruction and guidance—it is an instruction manual for life.

2. A deeper exploration of the details of the Torah's narratives uncovers meaning and personal relevance that speak to our lives today.

3. The Torah does not name the fruit from the Tree of Knowledge that was eaten by Adam and Eve in order to teach us a lesson about guarding the honor of another person.

4. There are many popular myths, misconceptions, and misunderstandings of certain narratives and facts in the Torah.

5. Matzah was not first created when the Jews left Egypt in haste. On the night *before* the Exodus, the Jewish people ate matzah. This represents two stages of humility that are experienced when one moves from a place of enslavement to a place of freedom.

6. The fact that Moses' face began to glow only after he received the second set of tablets teaches us that it is from our failures that we can experience the most profound growth.

7. It is clear from within the Bible that "an eye for an eye" refers to monetary compensation and is not meant to be taken literally.

8. It is not possible to understand the Torah without the explanation of the oral tradition.

9. The closing words of the Torah suggest that Moses' defining moment was the destruction of the tablets. This incident highlighted the fact that without the people, the Torah has no value.

Additional Readings

What's the Truth about... the Translation of Yam Suf?

by **Rabbi Dr. Ari Zivotofsky**

MISCONCEPTION: Upon leaving Egypt, the Jews crossed the Yam Suf, which is translated as the Red Sea. This translation, however, is an error. Red Sea is a corruption of the correct Old English (OE) translation, Reed (Rede) Sea. (Rede is a legitimate spelling of reed in OE.)

FACT: The notion that the Yam Suf is the modern-day Red Sea predates any English translation of the Bible by well over a thousand years. In fact, it seems that until the late eighteenth century no one questioned the translation and identification of Yam Suf with the Red Sea.[1]

Red Sea is the ancient and preferred translation of Yam Suf. While some believe that *suf* refers to reed-like plants growing in or near the sea and that literal translations of proper nouns in the Bible are preferable, Reed Sea remains a questionable translation at best. Unfortunately, the notion that Yam Suf should be translated as "Reed Sea" and not "Red Sea" seems to be gaining in popularity.[2]

BACKGROUND: Determining the "correct" translation of Yam Suf is not simply a matter of ascertaining the meaning of the words. Rather, several issues need to be addressed: Is the body of water that is today called the Red Sea the one that was split for the Israelites to pass through? Irrespective of the location, is Reed Sea an accurate translation of Yam Suf? Assuming Reed Sea *is* the literal translation of Yam Suf, does that make it the *correct* translation? Every one of these separate but inter-dependent questions needs to be looked at, although not every question has a complete and satisfactory answer.

The name Yam Suf appears in Tanach a total of twenty-three times.[3] However, most people associate Yam Suf with the body of water the Israelites crossed while fleeing Egypt. Many of the sources that translate Yam Suf as Red Sea indicate that literally it means "Sea of Reeds or Rushes" (see, for example, *The Interpreter's Dictionary of the Bible*[4] [1962, vol. 4, pp. 19-21]). In Exodus 13:18, when describing the Jews fleeing Egypt, the Torah states: "God took the people in a roundabout path . . . to the Yam Suf." ArtScroll's Stone Edition Chumash translates Yam Suf as Sea of Reeds and includes a note stating that what is today known as the Red Sea is situated too far south for the Jews to have crossed it upon fleeing Egypt. The Jewish Publication Society Tanakh simply calls it the Sea of Reeds, and the Koren Chumash calls it the Sea of Suf with no attempt at translation or identification.

In order to determine which body of water Yam Suf is referring to, it is important to look for parallels in Tanach. The Hebrew word spelled *samach-vav-peh* can be read either as *suf* or as *sof*, i.e., the Sea of Suf or the Sea of Sof,[5] depending upon whether the vav is vocalized as a *shuruk* (*suf*) or a *cholam* (*sof*). Ibn Ezra (Exodus 13:18) states that some read the word as *sof* and explain that it is called Yam Sof because it lies at the end of the world[6]; however, he claims, that this is a "big error"

---

1 See *Encyclopeda Mikrait*, vol. 3, 695-699, s.v. Yam Suf.

2 See e.g., *Schottenstein Edition Talmud Bavli, Sotah* 11a, no. 36, 39 and 61.

3 For example: Exodus 13:18; 15:4; 15:22; 23:31; Numbers 14:25; 21:4; 33:10; 33:11; Deuteronomy 1:40; 2:1; 11:4; Joshua 2:10; 4:23; 24:6; Shoftim 11:16; I Kings 9:26; Psalms 106:7, 9, 22; 136:13, 15; Nechamiah 9:9; and Jeremiah 49:21.

4 The translators of this work are so convinced of the accuracy of this translation, they wrote (p. 20): "Luther, who relied on the Hebrew, rendered *Yam Sûph* correctly by calling it *Schilfmeer*, 'Sea of Reeds.'"

5 In Judges 11:16, the Septuagint (Manuscript B) has Yam Siph.

6 That the world has an "end" is not a strange idea. See e.g., Daniel 4:8: "that its sight was to the end (*sof*) of the earth."

because "the Yam Sof is not at the end [of the world]; the Atlantic Ocean is at the end." The correct reading, he asserts, is *suf*. Rashi (Exodus 13:18) explains that *suf* in Yam Suf is similar to *"agam,"* which means a pond, in that it has reeds (*kanim*) growing in it. Expounding on Rashi, Siftei Chachamim explains that lest one think it is read as *sof* and means "end of the sea," Rashi is clarifying that it means a sea full of reeds. Despite the controversy among the commentators, it is clear that according to the Masoretic tradition, the word is read as *suf*. Any *ba'al koreh* will confirm this.

How was Yam Suf[7] understood in antiquity?[8] The Septuagint (second to third century BCE) translated Yam Suf into Greek as *Erythra Thalassa* or Red Sea—that is, neither "end" nor "reed!"[9] Thus, 2,200 years ago, long before the Bible was translated into Old English, the Septuagint identified the Yam Suf the Israelites crossed as the Red Sea. Josephus (*Antiquities* 2:15:3) identifies the Yam Suf as the Red Sea as well. This translation was carried over into the Latin when the fourth-century Latin Vulgate translated Yam Suf in Exodus 13:18 as *Mare Rubrum*, and in other places it translates Yam Suf as Mare Erythrae, both of which mean Red Sea.

Early English translations of the Bible, such as the 1611 *King James Version*, continued to translate Yam Suf as the Red Sea. Evidently, the theory that Red Sea is a corruption of the correct Old English (OE) translation, Reed (Rede) Sea, is unfounded.

Another important authoritative work maintains the tradition of identifying Yam Suf as Red Sea. In his commentary on the Bible, known as *Tafsir*, Rabbi Sa'adia Gaon (d. 942 CE), who lived in Egypt and Israel as well as in Baghdad, translated Yam Suf as *Bahr al Qulzum*, the Arabic name used for the Red Sea till this very day. Thus, it is clear that Jews at the time of the Geonim took it for granted that the Yam Suf in the Bible refers to the modern-day Red Sea.[10]

Another fascinating piece of evidence comes from a tribe in India that claims to be descended from the Lost Tribe of Menashe. Author Hillel Halkin[11] cites evidence in support of this claim, such as a "Red Sea Song." The song contains many Biblical details regarding the Exodus: cloud by day, fire by night, water split in two, miraculous water from a rock, Divine delivery of quail, et cetera. It also calls the sea that was parted the Red Sea. While the exact age of the song is unknown, it is purported to be ancient.

The Hebrew word *suf* does not mean red literally. So where did the name "Red Sea" come from? There are various suggestions. Let's first look at the other places where Yam Suf is mentioned in the Bible and is translated as "Red Sea." In I Kings (9:26) it states that King Solomon based his navy on the Yam Suf near Eilat. This Yam Suf was probably not the one crossed by the Israelites[12] and may have been termed "red" after the inhabitants of the surrounding mountains, the people of Edom (see Genesis 25:30), which means red. Or the Sea might have been named so due to the reddish coral in the vicinity. (This is also probably why the country Eritrea is called so; Eritrea, whose name is a rendition of the ancient Greek name *Erythraía*, or the "Red Land," is located on the southwestern shore of the Red Sea.) Or it may be that the mineral-rich red mountain ranges and desert sands surrounding the sea inspired mariners of antiquity to name the sea *Mare Rostrum*, Red Sea. Rabbi Aryeh Kaplan (*The Living Torah*, Exodus 2:3, p. 260) suggests that the name Red Sea is based on the fact that in

---

7 It may even be possible to read it as *suf* and have it mean end. A similar word, such as in Esther 9:28 *"vezichram lo yasuf mizaram*, nor the memory of them shall cease from their descendents," with *ya-suf* having a meaning akin to end.

8 The most important ancient translator, from a Jewish perspective, is the first to second-century Onkelos. Unfortunately, he does not contribute to this discussion because he translates, or more accurately transliterates, Yam Suf as Yama Suf. However, the transliterated name is sometimes the most accurate "translation." For example, no one translates New York into Hebrew as "York Ha'chadash" but rather as "New York."

9 For references to the Red Sea, see also: 1 Maccabees 4:9; Wisdom of Solomon 10:18, 19:7 and Judith 5:12.

10 I thank Rabbi Dr. Seth Mandel for the information in this paragraph.

11 *Across the Sabbath River: In Search of a Lost Tribe of Israel* (New York, 2002), p. 222 and related notes on 377-378; p. 347 and related notes on 386-387.

12 A recent theory proposes that the crossing did indeed take place at the Gulf of Aqaba; there are even claims of material evidence to prove this.

the language spoken in Ethiopia, *supho* denotes a red-topped kind of plant. Alternate possibilities (*The Living Torah*, Exodus 10:19, p. 304-5) include that its name derived from the ancient nation Erythria, so named because its inhabitants painted their faces red; or that it's based on the seasonal blooms of the red-colored *Trichodesmium erythraeum* near the water's surface. The author of the column "Philologos," in the *Forward* (April 14, 2000, p. 12) suggests that the Gulf of Aqaba, which flows past ancient Edom and into Eilat, was once known as Yam Edom, which can mean the Sea of Edom or the Red Sea. He suggests that this name was eventually transferred, erroneously, to the other side of the Sinai, where it stuck.

Those who translate Yam Suf as Sea of Reeds do so because they prefer to translate it literally. But literal translations do not work all the time. This is especially true in this case since the precise definition of *suf* is unclear. Rashi (Exodus 2:3) identifies it as *"rosel"* in Old French (possibly *"roseau"* in modern French), which means a kind of flexible rhizome found along the edges of shallow, usually stagnant ponds. Like reeds, this is freshwater vegetation, which is not found at the edge of a salt sea such as the Red Sea. Rashi, based on *Sotah* 12b, finds a parallel in Isaiah 19:6, *kaneh vesuf ka'mailu*– the reeds and *suf* will dry up. From this verse it is clear that *suf* may be a plant that is similar to, but not synonymous with, *kaneh*, reed. Thus, Reed Sea is not even an accurate literal translation! Rashi elsewhere (*Sotah* 12b) identifies *suf* as a thin *aravah*, willow. Rabbi Kaplan suggests (*The Living Torah*, Exodus 2:3, p. 260) that *suf* is from *thuf*, the ancient Egyptian word for uncut papyrus. (Indeed the Latin translation of the Bible translates *suf* in Exodus 2:5 as papyrus.) He compares it to other places in Tanach (Exodus 2:3, 5) where *suf* seems to mean a type of reed (Isaiah 19:6; Jonah 2:6). Professor Yehuda Feliks (*Chai Vetzome'ach B'Torah*, 5744, p. 215) identifies the *suf* as the cattail or bulrush (genus *Typha*). This is not the same as *kaneh*, reed, which he identifies (*Hatzome'ach VeHa'Chai B'Mishnah*, 5743, p. 146) as being from the *Gramineae* (*Poaceae*, grasses) family and one of two species: *Arundo donax* (giant cane or giant reed) and *Phragmites communis* (*Phragmites australis*, the common reed).

The Exodus Route

This discussion also bears on what route the fleeing Israelites took. If Yam Suf is a sea with reeds, it rules out identifying it as either the Red Sea or the Mediterranean. The Red Sea is a long saltwater inlet separating the Arabian Peninsula from the east coast of Egypt. The sea with reeds would have to be freshwater, or at least brackish, in order for reeds to flourish at its shore. This lends credence to the theory that Yam Suf was one of the shallow, marshy, bitter lakes east of the Nile Delta, such as a shallow spot connecting the Great and Little Bitter Lakes. Rabbi Kaplan (*The Living Torah*, Exodus 13:18, p. 321) cites sources that the Yam Suf was located at the mouth of the Nile, possibly identified with Lake Manzaleh. Other Biblical passages, in which Yam Suf refers to a body of water in a context other than the Exodus, indicate that its location was well known in Biblical times and that it was likely near Eilat and the Gulf of Aqaba, and not near the Bitter Lakes region of the Nile Delta (e.g., Exodus 23:31; Numbers 21:4; Deuteronomy 2:1; Judges 11:17-17; I Kings 9:26; and Jeremiah 49:21).

Three basic routes for the Exodus have been proposed by modern scholars who reject the Red Sea theory. Some propose a northern route whereby the Israelites went north to the coast and then eastward, and the "sea" they crossed was part of Lake Sirbonis, an arm or bay of the Mediterranean, and they then turned south into the Sinai Peninsula. Others, suggesting a central route, claim that the body of water crossed was a shallow lake north of the Red Sea called the Reed Sea. Indeed some of the lakes north of the Red Sea are abundant with reed-like plants. Finally, there are those who suggest a southern route and translate Yam Suf as the "sea at the end of the world."[13] Da'at Mikra (Shemot 13:18) finds support for his claim that the body of water crossed was at the northern end of the Gulf of Suez from Isaiah 11:15, which speaks about the "tongue of the Sea of Egypt."

Place names in the Bible, particularly those that sound similar or seem to refer to an equivalent

13 See Bernard F. Batto, "Red Sea or Reed Sea," *Biblical Archaeology Review* (July-August 1984): 57-63, who argues that the correct pronunciation is Yam Sof and the meaning is the "distant, southern sea, at the end of the land."

location, can cause further confusion. Is the location called simply Suf (Deuteronomy 1:1) identical to Yam Suf, as many suggest? Might Sufa (Numbers 21:14) be the name of a place, even Yam Suf?

In other Biblical references, Yam Suf unequivocally refers to what is today called the Red Sea or its arms, the Gulf of Suez and Gulf of Aqaba. In I Kings 9:26 it states: "King Solomon also built a fleet of ships at Ezion Geber, which is near Eilat on the shore of the Red Sea [Yam Suf], in the land of Edom." If this were a marshy lake close to Egypt, this would certainly be a strange place for King Solomon to build his great fleet. The assumption is that the Eilat in Kings is the port at the northernmost end of the Gulf of Aqaba, the same location of modern-day Eilat.

Another reference indicating that it is the modern Red Sea is the list of encampments of the Israelites in the desert, as found in Numbers 33: 8-10. The Torah states that after the Israelites crossed "the Yam,"[14] they camped in Marah, then Elim and then "they camped by the Yam Suf." How could they have crossed the Sea of Reeds and, after many days of travel, still camped by that same Sea of Reeds? No body of water in the region except the Red Sea is large enough for them to have traveled for so long and still be close to its coast. Other references that support the identification of Yam Suf with Red Sea are Numbers 21:4, Deuteronomy 1:40, 2:1 and Jeremiah 49:21.

It is likely that the name Yam Suf and/or Red Sea was applied in the ancient world to more than one location. Professor Nahum M. Sarna (*Exploring Exodus* [New York, 1986], 106-110) says that Yam Suf is used in the Torah to refer to both the Gulf of Suez (between Egypt and the Sinai) and the Gulf of Aqaba (between the Sinai and Saudi Arabia). This is also supported by one of the Dead Sea Scrolls, known as the Genesis Apocryphon.[15] In a section of this Aramaic text (1Q20, column 21, lines 17-18; see Michael Wise, trans., *Dead Sea Scrolls Reader*, Brill ed., vol. 3, p. 31) Abraham describes his travels up the Gichon River, to the Mediterranean and beyond. He states, ". . . until I came to the Euphrates River. I journeyed along the Euphrates until I reached the Red Sea in the east, whence I followed the coast of the Red Sea until I came to the tongue of the Yam Suf, jutting out from the Red Sea." This indicates that the Red Sea branches off of Yam Suf. A tributary can easily be called after the main body; thus, it would not be strange to identify the Yam Suf as the Red Sea. In recounting the story of Genesis, Josephus (*Antiquities* I:1:39) says that the Euphrates and Tigris end in the Erythraean Sea, literally the Red Sea.

In summary, Yam Suf in the Bible refers to multiple places, many of which were translated by the ancients as Red Sea. Similarly, specific bodies of water were referred to by multiple names, such as the Mediterranean Sea, which seems to have at least three names: Yam Plishtim (Exodus 23:32), Yam Hagadol (Numbers 34:6, 7) and Yam Ha'acharon (Deuteronomy 34:2). This leaves a translator in a serious quandary. But it is important to remember that translations are not always meant to be literal but rather to inform the reader of the target language what was intended in the source language. Thus, in general, Yam Hagadol is translated in English as Mediterranean Sea and not as Great Sea; Moshe is called Moses and not "drawn forth," Yam Hamelach is referred to as Dead Sea and not as Salt Sea,[16] and Sha'ar Ha'ashpot is translated as Dung Gate and not Refuse Gate.

Thus, it is possible that the name Yam Suf has nothing to do with *suf* and was simply the name of

---

[14] The body of water crossed is also referred to simply as *ha'yam* in Exodus 14:9, 21, 22.

[15] See N. Avigad and Y. Yadin, *A Genesis Apocryphon* (Jerusalem, 1956); Maurice Copisarow, "The Ancient Egyptian, Greek, and Hebrew Concept of the Red Sea," *Vetus Testamentum* XII (1962); Joseph A. Fitzmyer, *The Genesis Apocryphon of Qumran Cave I: A Commentary* (Rome, 1966); and Eliezer Segal, "Red Sea, Reed Sea...and the Persian Gulf," (Jewish Free Press, March 1991, also at http://people.calgary.ca/~elsegal/Shokel/9 10329_Red_Sea.html).

[16] One has to credit ArtScroll for being consistent in its policy of translating places literally. It translates Yam Hamelach as Salt Sea (Genesis 14:3, Numbers 34:2 and 34:12) and Yam Hagadol as Great Sea (Numbers 34:6, 7). In truth, while the Yam Suf translation may be justifiable because of the ArtScroll policy of translating according to Rashi, the other two translations cited are inexplicable. Even ArtScroll does not translate Abraham's two sons as "He is rejoicing" and "May God listen."

the body of water.[17] The name need not have any meaning beyond that, similar to other names of locations (there are not and have never been buffalo in Buffalo, New York, and Beit Lechem, a hilly region, is not known for either its bread or its wheat). While no one today can state definitively which body of water God split so that the Israelites could pass, the most ancient translations translate Yam Suf in the Exodus story as Red Sea. I would argue that despite the fact that reeds cannot grow in the Red Sea, we should accept the tradition of the Septuagint and of the Geonim and translate Yam Suf as the Red Sea. For those who cannot tolerate anything but a literal translation, they can always simply refer to Yam Suf as the Cattail Sea.

Jewish Action 70, no. 3 (2010):62-65
Reprinted with permission of *Jewish Action*, the magazine of the Orthodox Union

17 This is, in fact, the subject of a Tannaic dispute. In the context of the infant Moshe story, Rabbi Shmuel bar Nachmani says that *suf* refers to a marsh with reeds and willows. But Rabbi Elazar opines that *suf* was shorthand for Yam Suf, and the Torah was not describing the physical surroundings but the actual location (*Shemot Rabbah* 1:21; *Sotah* 12a-b).

Lesson 2

Sunrise, Sunset

Exploring the Jewish Life Cycle

Introduction

Life is unpredictable, but it certainly is exciting. In this lesson, you will learn why life is like a wedding feast, and why a wedding is like a three-ring circus. You will find out how a dead body is like a Torah scroll, and discover a celebration that many people attend but no one is ever invited to.

Introduction

Learning Activity 1

a. Below are some metaphors for life. Underline the one that resonates most with you, or add a metaphor of your own. Be prepared to explain your choice.

"Life is a roller coaster, just gotta ride it."
—Ronan Keating (song, 2000)

"My Mama always said: 'Life is like a box of chocolates: you never know what you are going to get.'"
—Forrest Gump (motion picture, 1994)

"Life is a great big canvas, and you should throw all the paint on it you can."
—Danny Kaye

"Life is like a coin. You can spend it any way you wish, but you only spend it once."
—Lillian Dickson

"Life is just a bowl of cherries."
—Popular song (1931)

My metaphor:

Life!

b. Does the Torah have a metaphor for life? It does indeed:

אמר ליה שמואל לרב יהודה, ״שיננא, חטוף ואכול חטוף ואישתי,
דעלמא דאזלינן מיניה כהלולא דמי״.
תלמוד בבלי, עירובין נד,א

Shmuel said to Rav Yehudah, "Clever one, hurry and eat, hurry and drink, because the world from which we must depart is like a wedding feast."

Talmud, Eiruvin 54a

Why do you think life is like a wedding? Be prepared to share your answer.

Life is like a wedding because . . .

Rabbi Menachem Mendel Schneerson (1902–1994). Known as "the Lubavitcher Rebbe," or simply as "the Rebbe." Born in southern Ukraine. Rabbi Schneerson escaped from the Nazis, arriving in the U.S. in June 1941. The towering Jewish leader of the 20th century, the Rebbe inspired and guided the revival of traditional Judaism after the European devastation, and often emphasized that the performance of just one additional good deed could usher in the era of Mashiach.

Text 1

דנשמה וגוף הם דוגמת איש ואשה . . . "האי עלמא כבי הילולא דמיא", שהחיבור והיחוד דנשמה הרוחנית עם הגוף הגשמי (האי עלמא) הוא בדוגמת יחוד חתן וכלה (הילולא, חתונה).

ספר המאמרים מלוקט ה, ע׳ פו-פז

Man and woman are compared to a soul and body. . . . "This world is like a wedding feast" because the fusion of the spiritual soul and the physical body ("this world") is similar to the union of bride and groom ("a wedding feast").

Rabbi Menachem Mendel Schneerson, *Sefer Hama'amarim Melukat* 5:86–87

Birth
The Launching Pad

Text 2a

ומלמדין אותו כל התורה כולה . . . וכיון שבא לאויר העולם, בא מלאך וסטרו על פיו,
ומשכחו כל התורה כולה.
תלמוד בבלי, נדה ל,ב

The fetus is taught the entire Torah. . . . As it enters this world, an angel approaches and slaps it on its mouth and causes it to completely forget the entire Torah.

Talmud, Nidah 30b

Rabbi Joseph B. Soloveitchik (1903–1993), spent his formative years studying Torah in Lithuania and Belorussia. In 1926, he commenced his studies at the University of Berlin and wrote his dissertation on the epistemology and metaphysics of Hermann Cohen. In 1937, he founded the first Jewish day school in the New England area. In 1941, he became professor of Talmud at RIETS—Yeshiva University. In this capacity, he ordained more rabbis that anyone else in Jewish history. A remarkable orator, his annual Torah discourse, delivered on his father's *yahrtzeit*, attracted thousands of listeners. Among his published works are *Halakhic Man* and *Lonely Man of Faith*.

Text 2b

Every Jew comes into the world with a natural responsiveness to Torah teaching. Every Jew begins with a share in Torah that was vested in him before his birth, and though he is made to forget it, it is preserved in the deep recesses of his soul, waiting to be awakened by study and a favorable environment.

Rabbi Joseph B. Soloveitchik, *Reflections of the Rav* [Hoboken, N.J.: Ktav Pub. House, 1989], 1:60–61

Text 3a

רבי יהושע בן חנניה—אשרי יולדתו.

משנה, אבות ב,ט

Fortunate is the woman who gave birth to Rabbi Yehoshua ben Chananyah!

Mishnah, Avot 2:9

Text 3b

Rabbi Eliyahu of Vilna (1720–1797). Known as the Gra or the Vilna Ga'on; one of the greatest scholars of his day. In addition to Talmud, he excelled in all aspects of Torah study, including Kabbalah, and was proficient in secular subjects as well. He left a tremendous legacy, both from his writings on the Tanach, Talmud, and Shulchan Aruch, and from the many students that he inspired to Torah and scholarship.

רבי יהושע אשרי יולדתו, כי תיכף כשנתעברה אמו לא זזה מבית המדרש, כדי שישמע תמיד תורה.

פירוש הגר"א, שיר השירים א,ח

Fortunate is she who gave birth to Rabbi Yehoshua—because from the time when she conceived, she did not budge from the study hall, so that he would constantly hear words of Torah.

Rabbi Eliyahu of Vilna, Song of Songs 1:8

Heartfelt Nourishment

In the ethical will of Rabbi Yehudah the Pious, he advises that a mother nursing her newborn child for the very first time should begin with the left breast, so that the baby's first meal comes from the place that is closest to the heart.

Blast Off!

Birth and Birthday

Some Jewish Birthday Customs

- During the course of the day, make some alone-time and think about the past year: what went right, what went not-so-right, and what can be fixed.
- Take your life to a new level with a new mitzvah.
- Give some extra charity.
- Spend more time in prayer. Take some extra time for Torah study. Share what you learn with friends.
- Every year of your life has a corresponding chapter in the book of Psalms: your age +1 (i.e., if you are turning 32, your psalm is chapter 33). Recite your psalm today and continue to recite it each day for the coming year.
- Gather with friends and publicly thank God for the gift of life. This is an opportune time to encourage each other to strive for spiritual growth.
- Eat a new seasonal fruit on your birthday so that you can say the special *Shehecheyanu* blessing, thanking God for granting you life.
- For men: Arrange to receive an *aliyah* on the Shabbat before your birthday. If the Torah is read on your birthday, arrange to receive an *aliyah* on that day too.

Text 4

Rabbi Yosef Chaim of Baghdad (1834–1909). Leading halachist and kabbalist, successful orator, poet, author of more than 50 works; succeeded his father as chief rabbi of Baghdad in 1859. Best known as author of his halachic work, *Ben Ish Chai*, by which title he is also known. Also popular is his commentary on the homiletical sections of the Talmud, called *Ben Yehoyada*.

יש נוהגים לעשות בכל שנה את יום הלידה ליום טוב וסימן יפה הוא וכן נוהגים בביתנו.
בן איש חי, חלק ההלכות, שנה א, פרשת ראה יז

Some people have a custom to annually celebrate their birthday in a festive manner. This is an auspicious custom, and such is the custom in our household.

Rabbi Yosef Chaim of Baghdad, *Ben Ish Chai, Chelek Hahalachot, Shana Aleph, Parashat Re'eh* 17

Birthday Holidays?

Two of the major holidays we celebrate are actually birthdays of sorts. The first one is Rosh Hashanah. According to Jewish tradition, Adam and Eve were created on Rosh Hashanah. Thus, Rosh Hashanah is the collective birthday of humankind.

Passover is referred to as the birthday of the Jewish nation. The Exodus is described in Ezekiel (16:4) as "our birth, the day we were born."

Circumcision

Text 5

אשה כמאן דמהילא דמיא.
תלמוד בבלי, עבודה זרה כז,א

woman is considered circumcised.

Talmud, Avodah Zarah 27a

This Party Needs No Invitation

Have you ever gone to a party uninvited? If you have attended a traditional *brit,* chances are that the answer is yes. But don't worry; this is not a breach of etiquette. Traditionally, we do not invite friends to attend a *brit,* but simply notify them of the proper time and place. This is because, given the holiness of the occasion, it would be considered a sign of spiritual insensitivity to turn down such an invitation.

Naming

Text 6

Rabbi Shne'ur Zalman of Liadi (1745–1812). Chasidic rebbe and founder of the Chabad movement, also known as "the Alter Rebbe" and "the Rav." Born in Liozna, Belarus, he was among the principal students of the Magid of Mezeritch. His numerous works include the *Tanya*, an early classic containing the fundamentals of Chasidism; *Torah Or; Likutei Torah*; and *Shulchan Aruch HaRav*, a reworked and expanded code of Jewish law. He is interred in Hadiach, Ukraine, and was succeeded by his son, Rabbi Dovber of Lubavitch.

הנה הנשמה עצמה קודם בואה בגוף אינה נקראת בשם כלל . . . נמצא השם אינו לבחינת הנשמה עצמה, והרי גם לגוף עצמו אין השם מועיל, אך השם מקשר הנשמה בגוף, והחיות הנמשך מהנשמה ומחיה הגוף הוא נשרש בהשם.

לקוטי תורה, בהר מא,ג

Before a soul enters the body, it has no name.... The soul itself has no need for a name, nor does a lifeless body have any use for a name. Rather, the function of the name is to join the soul with the body; the vitalizing energy that emanates from the soul to give life to the body is rooted in the name.

Rabbi Shne'ur Zalman of Liadi, *Likutei Torah, Behar* 41c

Change That Name!

There is an age-old Jewish custom to give a new name to a person who is critically ill or who has suffered a great misfortune. This custom is based on the biblical account of God's changing the names of the childless Abram and Sarai to Abraham and Sarah, thereby conferring upon them a new destiny, allowing them to give birth to children.

The common custom is to add an additional name to the ill person's existing name. The new name is added in the synagogue during the course of a public Torah reading.

Learning Activity 2

Do you know the source of your Jewish name, or the name of a loved one? Share your name story with a partner.

For Whom Are You Named?

There is a long-standing Jewish tradition to name children after their forebears. Jews of Ashkenazic descent name only after people who are already deceased, while Sefardic Jews consider it a great honor to give a child the name of a living relative, such as a grandparent.

Text 7

כאשר נולד האדם וקוראים לו אביו ואמו שם אחד העולה בדעתם, אינו באקראי ובהזדמן, כי אם הקדוש ברוך הוא משים בפיו השם ההוא המוכרח אל הנשמה ההיא.

ספר הגלגולים, הקדמה כג

When a father and mother choose a name for their newborn child, [the name] is not random or arbitrary. Rather, God places in [their] mouth the name that is needed for that soul.

Rabbi Chaim Vital, *Sefer Hagilgulim*, Introduction 23

Rabbi Chaim ben Yosef Vital (1542–1620). Born in Israel, lived in Safed, Jerusalem, and later Damascus. Vital was the principal disciple of Arizal, though he studied under him for less than two years. Before his passing, Arizal authorized Vital to record his teachings. Acting on this mandate, Vital began arranging his master's teachings in written form, and his many works constitute the foundation of the Lurianic school of Jewish mysticism, which was later universally adopted as the kabbalistic standard. Thus, Vital is one of the most important influences in the development of Kabbalah. Among his most famous works are *Ets Chayim*, and *Sha'ar Hakavanot*.

Pidyon Haben

Text 8a

וַיְהִי כִּי הִקְשָׁה פַרְעֹה לְשַׁלְּחֵנוּ וַיַּהֲרֹג ה׳ כָּל בְּכוֹר בְּאֶרֶץ מִצְרַיִם . . .
עַל כֵּן אֲנִי זֹבֵחַ לַה׳ כָּל פֶּטֶר רֶחֶם הַזְּכָרִים וְכָל בְּכוֹר בָּנַי אֶפְדֶּה.
שמות יג,טו

When Pharaoh stubbornly refused to send us out, God slew every firstborn in the land of Egypt. . . . Therefore, I bring as a sacrifice all male [cattle and sheep] that open the womb, and all firstborn of my sons I will redeem.

Exodus 13:15

Text 8b

למה ציוה התורה לפדות בכור זכר ולא בכורה נקיבה, הלא במצריים הוכה גם הנקיבות? . . . דזכרים טעונין פדיון . . . לפי שגם הם היו חייבין, כמבואר במדרשים בכלל ישראל שטען שר של מצריים, "הללו עובדי עבודה זרה והללו עובדי עבודה זרה", ובכורי ישראל בכלל. אם כן גם הם היו ראוין ללקות כמו המצריים, לכך טעונין פדיון . . . על שהציל אותם הקדוש ברוך הוא בחסדו.

מה שאין כן הנקבות, דאיתא בסוטה (יא,ב), "בזכות נשים צדקניות שבאותו הדור נגאלו", ואם כן הדין נותן שלא ילקו, לכך אינם צריכים . . . פדיון.
מעשה רוקח, מסכת בכורות

Why did the Torah command us to redeem the firstborn sons and not the firstborn daughters? After all, God also smote the Egyptian [firstborn] daughters. . . .

The [Jewish] sons require redemption . . . because they, too, were deserving of punishment [in Egypt]. As the Midrash recounts, the archangel of Egypt argued [before God], "If the [Egyptians] are idolaters [worthy of punishment], so are the [Jews]!" Thus, the male Israelite firstborn—like the Egyptians—were worthy of being smitten, and because God kindly spared them, they need to be redeemed. . . .

Not so with the females. The Talmud (Sotah 11b) states, "The Jews were redeemed [from Egypt] in the merit of the righteous women of that generation." They were never deserving of punishment, and therefore they require no . . . redemption.

Rabbi Elazar Roke'ach, *Ma'aseh Roke'ach*, Tractate Bechorot

Rabbi Elazar ben Shmuel Roke'ach (1665–1741). Presided over the rabbinical courts in various cities in Poland, most notably Brody. Later in life, he moved to Amsterdam, where in 1740 he published his *Ma'aseh Roke'ach*, a kabbalistic commentary on the Mishnah. He emigrated to the Holy Land and resided in Safed. He is an ancestor of the rebbes of the chasidic dynasty of Belz.

Bar and Bat Mitzvah

Question for Discussion

In what way does Judaism consider a 13-year-old boy and a 12-year-old girl to be full-fledged adults?

Marriage
Whose Choice?

Text 9a

אסור לאדם שיקדש את האשה עד שיראנה.
תלמוד בבלי, קדושין מא,א

A man may not betroth a woman whom he has not seen [and of whom he has not approved].

Talmud, Kidushin 41a

Text 9b

וַיֹּאמְרוּ, "נִקְרָא לַנַּעֲרָ וְנִשְׁאֲלָה אֶת פִּיהָ".

בראשית כד,נז

nd they said, "Let us summon the maiden and ask her."

Genesis 24:57

Text 9c

מכאן שאין משיאין את האשה אלא מדעתה.

רש"י, שם

e learn from this verse that a woman may only be married with her consent.

Rashi, ad loc.

Rabbi Shlomo Yitschaki (1040–1105). Better known by the acronym Rashi. Rabbi and famed author of comprehensive commentaries on the Talmud and Bible. Born in Troyes, France, Rashi studied in the famed *yeshivot* of Mainz and Worms. His commentaries, which focus on the simple understanding of the text, are considered the most fundamental of all the commentaries that preceded and followed. Since their initial printings, the commentaries have appeared in virtually every edition of the Talmud and Bible. Many of the famed authors of the *Tosafot* are among Rashi's descendants.

The Three-Ring Circle

Text 10a

מנהג ישראל שלוקחים את החתן ואת הכלה אל החופה, ותחת החופה סובבת הכלה את החתן, והחתן נותן לה טבעת ומקדשה בטבעת זו . . .

הכלה סובבת את החתן—הוא ענין המקיף שנותנת הכלה, שזוהי ההתמסרות שלה מצד בחינת המקיף לבנות בית בישראל על יסודי התורה ומצוות.

החתן נותן טבעת (עגולה) לכלה—הוא ענין המקיף שנותן החתן, שזוהי ההתמסרות שלו מצד בחינת המקיף לבנות בית בישראל על יסודי התורה ומצוות.

תורת מנחם ג, ע׳ 293

According to Jewish tradition, the bride and groom are escorted to a *chupah*; there the bride circles the groom and the groom betroths her with a ring. . . .

The bride's encircling of the groom represents her contribution of a transcendent dimension—her absolute commitment to building a Jewish home based on the foundation of the Torah and *mitzvot*.

Likewise, the groom giving the round ring to his bride represents his contribution of a transcendent dimension—his absolute commitment to building a Jewish home based on the foundation of the Torah and *mitzvot*.

Rabbi Menachem Mendel Schneerson, *Torat Menachem* 3:293

Text 10b

ובתור נתינת כח להחתן והכלה שיוכלו להתמסר מצד בחינת המקיף שלהם לבנות בית בישראל על יסודי התורה ומצוות, מוליכים את החתן והכלה אל החופה, שהוא ענין המקיף שנותן הקדוש ברוך הוא, בחינת מקיף העליון שלמעלה מסדר השתלשלות.

תורת מנחם, שם

To enable the bride and groom to tap into their essential soul levels, the couple is led to the *chupah,* whose encompassing shade represents God's transcendent energy.

Rabbi Menachem Mendel Schneerson, ibid.

Figure 2.1

Life-Cycle Event	Soul Milestone
Birth	Soul enters body.
Circumcision and Naming	Soul starts fusing with body.
Bar/Bat Mitzvah	Deepening of soul-body fusion results in the ability to take responsibility for one's decisions.
Marriage	Soul reaches completion by uniting with its partner.

Sinai Reenacted

Text 11a

"ביום חתונתו" (שיר השירים ג,יא), זו מתן תורה.

משנה, תענית ד,ח

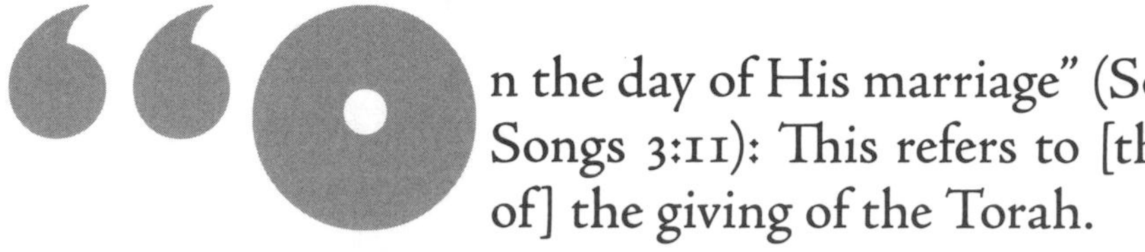

"On the day of His marriage" (Song of Songs 3:11): This refers to [the day of] the giving of the Torah.

Mishnah, Ta'anit 4:8

Text 11b

״השמים שמים לה׳ והארץ נתן לבני אדם״ (תהלים קטו,טז). משל למה הדבר דומה, למלך שגזר ואמר, ״בני רומי לא ירדו לסוריא ובני סוריא לא יעלו לרומי״. כך כשברא הקדוש ברוך הוא את העולם גזר ואמר, ״השמים שמים לה׳ והארץ נתן לבני אדם״. כשבקש ליתן התורה בטל גזירה ראשונה ואמר, ״התחתונים יעלו לעליונים והעליונים ירדו לתחתונים, ואני המתחיל״. שנאמר (שמות יט,כ), ״וירד ה׳ על הר סיני״, וכתיב (שם כד,א), ״ואל משה אמר עלה אל ה׳״.

שמות רבה יב,ג

"The heavens belong to God; the earth He bequeathed to man" (Psalms 115:16). To what can this be compared? To a king who decreed: "Roman citizens shall not go down to Syria, and Syrians shall not go up to Rome."

Similarly, upon creating the world, God decreed: "The heavens belong to God; the earth He bequeathed to man." As He was about to give the Torah, God rescinded the decree, and He said, "The inhabitants of the lower realms may now ascend to the higher realms, and those of the upper realms may now descend to the lower realms—and I will be the first to do so!" Hence, it says, "And God descended upon Mount Sinai" (Exodus 19:20), and, "To Moses He said, 'Go up to God'" (ibid. 24:1).

Midrash, *Shemot Rabah* 12:3

Rabbi Shimshon ben Tsadok (13th–14th centuries). Author of *Tashbets Katan*—a halachic work. Most of the work is dedicated to documenting the rulings of his teacher, Maharam of Rothenburg. It is an important source for the halachic rulings of Ashkenazic Judaism. His work was cited extensively by later halachists and serves as the basis for many laws in the Shulchan Aruch.

Text 12

נקוט האי כללא בידך: כל המנהגים של חתן ושל כלה אנו למדין ממתן תורה, שה׳ היה מראה עצמו כחתן נגד כלה שהם ישראל.

תשב״ץ קטן תסה

The general rule is that all the customs regarding the bride and groom are learned from the giving of the Torah, when God appeared as a groom before His bride, Israel.

Rabbi Shimshon ben Tsadok, *Tashbets Katan* 465

Text 13

It is also taught that the Torah itself was like the "wedding ring" with which God married Israel. The revelation at Sinai, where God gave the Torah to Israel, is said to be like a wedding. The Torah is like a ring; it is endless, and as soon as one finishes, one must begin again. Each time one studies a Torah lesson, one gains new insights. The Torah is therefore like a wedding ring, a circle without beginning or end.

Rabbi Aryeh Kaplan, *Made in Heaven: A Jewish Wedding Guide* [New York: Moznaim Pub. Corp., 1983], p. 47

Rabbi Aryeh Kaplan (1934–1983). Noted American rabbi and prolific author. During his short life, he authored over 50 volumes on Torah, Talmud, Jewish mysticism and philosophy, many of which have become modern-day classics. He is best known for his popular translation and elucidation of the Bible, *The Living Torah*, and his translation of the Ladino biblical commentary, *Me'am Lo'ez*.

Figure 2.2

Jewish Wedding Tradition	Parallel at Mount Sinai

Matches are arranged by a *shadchan*.	Moses was the intermediary between God and Israel.
The wedding is held in the bride's hometown.	The Torah was given here on earth, on "our" turf.
Escorts of the bride and groom hold candles.	Lightning was seen at the giving of the Torah.
The groom breaks a glass beneath the wedding canopy.	Moses broke the Tablets.
The bride and groom are entertained with summersaults.	That which was up came down; that which was down went up.
Marriage is effected through a ring.	God betrothed us with the Torah, which is akin to a ring.

Text 14

כִּי יִקַּח אִישׁ אִשָּׁה חֲדָשָׁה לֹא יֵצֵא בַּצָּבָא וְלֹא יַעֲבֹר עָלָיו לְכָל דָּבָר, נָקִי יִהְיֶה לְבֵיתוֹ שָׁנָה
אֶחָת וְשִׂמַּח אֶת אִשְׁתּוֹ אֲשֶׁר לָקָח.
דברים כד,ה

When a man weds a new wife, he shall not go out in the army, nor shall he be conscripted to any [war] effort. He shall remain free to attend to his home for one year and delight his wife whom he has taken.

Deuteronomy 24:5

Continuing the Cycle of Life

Learning Activity 3

True or False?

Only men are required to endeavor to marry and procreate; women are absolved from these obligations.

Rabbi Moshe ben Maimon (1135–1204). Better known as Maimonides or by the acronym Rambam; born in Cordoba, Spain. After the conquest of Cordoba by the Almohads, he fled Spain and eventually settled in Cairo, Egypt. There, he became the leader of the Jewish community and served as court physician to the vizier of Egypt. His rulings on Jewish law are considered integral to the formation of halachic consensus. He is most noted for authoring the *Mishneh Torah,* an encyclopedic arrangement of Jewish law, and for his philosophical work, *Guide for the Perplexed.*

Text 15a

האיש מצווה על פריה ורביה אבל לא האשה.

משנה תורה, הלכות אישות טו,ב

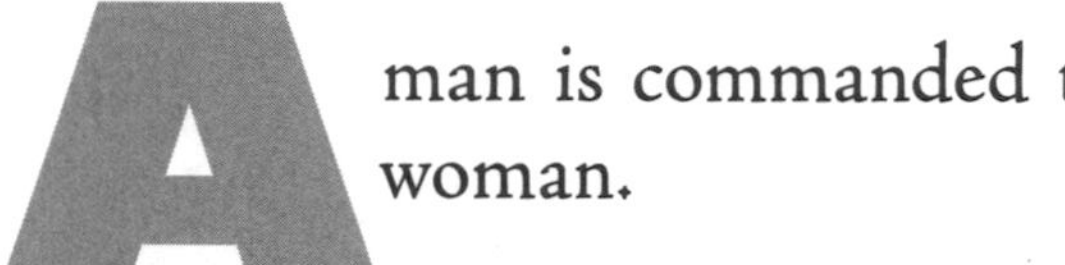

A man is commanded to procreate; not so a woman.

Maimonides, *Mishneh Torah,* Laws of Marriage 15:2

Text 15b

הא שפטרה התורה נשים מפריה ורביה וחייבה רק אנשים, כי משפטי ה׳ ודרכיו דרכי נועם וכל נתיבותיה שלום, ולא עמסה על הישראלי מה שאין ביכולת הגוף לקבל . . . ואם כן נשים שמסתכנות בעיבור ולידה, ומשום זה אמרו, ״מיתה שכיחא״ . . . לא גזרה התורה לצוות לפרות ולרבות על אשה . . .

רק לקיום המין עשה בטבעה שתשוקתה להוליד עזה משל איש . . . ומצאנו לרחל שאמרה, ״הבה לי בנים ואם אין מתה אנכי״ (בראשית ל,א).

משך חכמה, בראשית ט,ז

God's statutes and ways are "ways of pleasantness and all its pathways are peaceful" (Proverbs 3:17). Pregnancy and birth entail a degree of mortal danger for women, as the sages said [regarding childbirth], "death is common." Hence, since the Torah does not burden us with directives that the body cannot [reasonably] tolerate, the Torah only obligates men to procreate, and absolves women from this mitzvah.

In order, then, to ensure the perpetuation of the species, God created women with a powerful desire to have children, more so than men. . . . So we find that Rachel [told Jacob], "Give me children, otherwise I am [as if] dead" (Genesis 30:1).

Rabbi Meir Simchah Hakohen of Dvinsk, *Meshech Chochmah*, Genesis 9:7

Rabbi Meir Simchah Hakohen of Dvinsk (1843–1926). Served as rabbi of Dvinsk for nearly 40 years. He is renowned for two works: *Or Same'ach*, a commentary on Maimonides' *Mishneh Torah*, and *Meshech Chochmah*, a profound commentary on the Bible. In the latter work, Rabbi Meir Simchah demonstrates the unity between the Written and Oral Laws and presents original interpretations of biblical and Talmudic passages. In 1906, he was offered the position of rabbi of Jerusalem but bowed to the entreaties of the city folk to remain in Dvinsk.

Prayer for Mother and Newborn Baby

There is an ancient custom for the birthing woman to take a copy of psalm 121—often referred to by the first words of the psalm, *"Shir Lama'alot"*—into delivery, and to place it under her pillow or some other covered place in her vicinity. A copy of this psalm is also placed in the bassinet with the newborn baby.

מזל טוב

שיר למעלות אשא עיני אל ההרים מאין
יבוא עזרי. עזרי מעם יי עשה שמים
והארץ. אל יתן למוט רגלך אל ינום שמרך.
הנה לא ינום ולא ישן שמר ישראל. יי שמרך יי
צלך על ידי ימינך. יומם השמש לא יככה וירח
בלילה. יי ישמרך מכל רע ישמר את נפשך.
יי ישמר צאתך ובואך מעתה ועד עולם.

שדי

מכשפה לא תחיה
לא תחיה מכשפה
מכשפה תחיה לא
לילית וכל כת

אדם
אברהם
יצחק
יעקב

תחיה לא מכשפה
לא מכשפה תחיה
מכשפה תחיה לא

בשם ה' אלהי ישראל, מימיני מיכאל, ומשמאלי גבריאל, מלפני
אוריאל, ומאחורי רפאל, ועל ראשי שכינת אל.

Death and Bereavement

Text 16a

העומד על המת בשעת יציאת נשמה חייב לקרוע. הא למה זה דומה לספר תורה שנשרף.
תלמוד בבלי, מועד קטן כה,א

One who is present at the time of a person's passing is required to rend his clothing. This is because [a person's passing] is likened to the burning of a Torah scroll.

Talmud, Mo'ed Katan 25a

Questions for Discussion

We see from the preceding text that a person is compared to a Torah scroll, and that his or her death is akin to the burning of a Torah scroll. Why the comparison between a person and a Torah scroll? What commonality do they share?

Text 16b

והרמב"ן ז"ל פירש, שהנפש בגוף כאזכרות בגוילין.
ריטב"א, שם

Nachmanides, of blessed memory, explains that the soul in the body is like the parchment of a Torah scroll that is inscribed with God's names.

Rabbi Yom Tov ben Avraham Asevilli, ad loc.

Rabbi Yom Tov ben Avraham Asevilli (1250–1330). Spanish rabbi and author, know by the acronym Ritva; born in Seville; famous for his commentary on the Talmud. A student of the Rashba and Re'ah, he later assumed the rabbinate and became famous among Spanish Jewry. His commentary on the Talmud is extremely clear, and to this day is among the commentaries most frequently quoted and used.

Text 16c

כל מתעסק במת צריך לדעת שיש לו עסק עם דבר קדוש: גופו של אדם הוא לא רק נרתיק של קדושה ששמש לנשמה העילאית, אלא שהוא עצמו נתקדש גם בקדושה עצמית, בדומה לספר תורה.
גשר החיים ה,א

All those who handle the dead must be aware that they are involved with a holy entity. The human body is not only the "container" that served the exalted soul, but has itself become sanctified with an independent holiness, similar to a Torah scroll.

Rabbi Yechiel Michel Tucazinsky, *Gesher Hachayim* 5:1

Rabbi Yechiel Michel Tucazinsky (1874–1955). Born in Lithuania, his father died when he was still young. In 1882, his family settled in Israel and he studied in the Ets Chayim Yeshivah, where he eventually became the dean. Throughout the years he published many books and articles on halachic issues, including *Hayomam Bekadur Ha'arets,* an effort to locate the halachic dateline. He was the first to publish an annual calendar that specified the laws and customs observed on each day.

Rabbi Yosef Caro (1488–1575). Born in Spain, fled the country with his family during the expulsion in 1492, and eventually settled in Safed, Israel. Also known as "the Beit Yosef," after the title of his commentary on the *Arba'ah Turim,* and Maran ("our master") for his status as a preeminent authority on Jewish law. Author of 10 works on Jewish law and the Torah, including the *Beit Yosef, Kesef Mishneh,* and a mystical work, *Magid Meisharim.* Rabbi Caro's magnum opus, the Shulchan Aruch (Code of Jewish Law), has been universally accepted as the basis for modern Jewish law.

Text 17a

מת בעיר כל בני העיר אסורין במלאכה.

שולחן ערוך, יורה דעה שמג,א

hen a person dies, all the inhabitants of the city are forbidden to work.

Rabbi Yosef Caro, Shulchan Aruch, *Yoreh De'ah* 343:1

Text 17b

ואם יש חבורות בעיר שכל אחת מתעסקת במתים ביומה, מותר ביום שאינה יומה.

שולחן ערוך, שם

If there are shifts in the city, with every shift tending to the dead on its designated day, then on their off-days, the members of the other shifts may work [even if there is a deceased person that needs to be cared for].

Rabbi Yosef Caro, ibid.

Text 18

שמירת המת היא . . . משום כבודו.
שאם יניחוהו לבדו הרי זה כאלו עזבוהו ככלי אין חפץ עוד בו.
גשר החיים ה,ד

We maintain a watch over the dead . . . out of respect. For if we were to leave the body alone, it would appear as if we abandoned it like a utensil that is no longer desired.

Rabbi Yechiel Michel Tucazinsky, *Gesher Hachayim* 5:4

Text 19

דכי בצלם אלהים עשה את האדם . . . אין חילוק בין ספר תורה שלם לאות אחת ממנו,
והוא הדין נמי עצם מעצמות הקדושים שנבראו בצלם אלהים אסור לנהוג בהם מנהג בזיון.
שאלות ותשובות חתם סופר, יורה דעה שנג

Man was created in God's image. . . . Just as there is no difference between a complete Torah scroll and one letter from a Torah scroll [as both must be treated with utmost respect], it is forbidden to accord disrespect to even a single bone from sacred bodies that were created in God's image.

Rabbi Moshe Sofer, *Responsa Chatam Sofer, Yoreh De'ah* 353

Rabbi Moshe Sofer (1762–1839). Also known by the title of his works, *Chatam Sofer*. One of the leading rabbinical authorities of the 19th century, his policies and decisions helped shape Austro-Hungarian Jewry. Born in Frankfurt am Main, Germany, he entered the yeshivah of Rabbi Natan Adler at the age of 9. After declining various offers for the rabbinate, he ultimately accepted a position in Pressburg (now Bratislava), Slovakia. Serving as rabbi, and head of the yeshivah he established, Rabbi Sofer maintained a strong traditionalist perspective, fighting all deviations from tradition.

Next of Kin

While many people, family and friends alike, are deeply affected by the death of a loved one, only next of kin sit *shivah*. One sits *shivah* only upon the passing, God forbid, of a parent, spouse, child, or sibling.

Text 20a

Rabbi Yosef Shaul Natanson (1808–1875). Born in Berezhany, Poland; rabbi and authority on Jewish law. In 1857, he was elected rabbi of Lvov where he officiated for 18 years. His rulings, including his decision permitting machine-made matzah, are still widely cited. A wealthy man, Rabbi Natanson was also known for his activity as a philanthropist. He authored nine works on Jewish law and the Talmud, including *Me'irat Einayim* and *Sho'el Umeshiv*, a collection of his responsa. He is buried in Lvov.

כתוב בעבודה זרה (דף יח) דשאלו תלמידים "מה אתה רואה?" ואמר להם, "גוילין נשרפים ואותיות פורחות באויר" . . .
דהגויל הגשמי נשרף, והאותיות שהן רוחני פורחות למעלה . . .
והנה האדם מורכב מחומר וצורה, ובמות האדם לא מת רק חלק החומרי והגופני, והנשמה פורחת למעלה למקום אהלה שהיה שם בתחלה.

יד שאול, יורה דעה שמ,ה

It is related in the Talmud (Avodah Zarah 18a) that the students [of Rabbi Chananyah ben Teradyon] asked, "What do you see?" and he responded, "The parchment is burning and the letters are flying up in the air." . . . The physical parchment burned, and the letters, which are spiritual, flew up to heaven. . . .

A person, too, is comprised of matter and spirit. When a person dies, only the corporeal body dies, while the soul ascends to the place it originally inhabited.

Rabbi Yosef Shaul Natanson, *Yad Shaul, Yoreh De'ah* 340:5

Text 20b

צדיק אבד, לדורו אבד. משל לאדם שאבדה לו מרגלית, כל מקום שהיא מרגלית שמה. לא אבדה אלא לבעלה.

תלמוד בבלי, מגילה טו,א

When a righteous person is lost, he is lost to his generation. This can be compared to a person who lost a diamond. The diamond is lost to its owner; yet the diamond, wherever it may be, remains a diamond.

Talmud, Megilah 15a

Torn with Grief

One of the most enduring symbols of mourning in Jewish law is *keri'ah*, the tearing of the clothes by the next of kin (usually done right before the funeral). The mourners then wear this torn garment throughout the *shivah*. The mourner tears the right lapel of his or her jacket or shirt. After the passing of a parent, however, the left lapel is torn, closer to the heart, symbolizing the special honor and respect one must harbor for a parent.

Text 21a

המקום ינחם אתכם בתוך שאר אבלי ציון וירושלים.

נוסח ניחום אבלים

ay God comfort you among the other mourners of Zion and Jerusalem.

Traditional text for comforting mourners

Text 21b

נקודת נחמה אפילו באסון גדול כהאמור, ועוד יותר מנקודה, מתבטאת בנוסח המסורתי והמקודש על ידי עשיריות דורות של תורה ומסורה של עמנו—המקום ינחם אתכם בתוך שאר אבלי ציון וירושלים . . .

כמו שבנוגע לציון וירושלים שלטה יד הרומים, וקודם לכן יד הבבלים, רק בבית המקדש הבנוי מעצים ואבנים כסף וזהב, אבל בית המקדש הפנימי שבלב כל אחד ואחת של ישראל אין יד האומות יכולה לשלוט בו ונצחי הוא,

כך הוא גם בנוגע לאבל היחיד, אשר יד המות שולטת אך ורק בהגוף ועניניו, אבל הנשמה נצחית היא רק שעלתה לעולם האמת.

אגרות קודש כ״ק אדמו״ר זי״ע כה, ע׳ ד-ה

Even in such a great tragedy, a modicum of solace—and even more than a modicum—is expressed in our traditional text of consolation to mourners, "May the Almighty comfort you among the other mourners of Zion and Jerusalem." . . .

The Romans—and the Babylonians before them—were able to destroy the Holy Temple of wood and stone, of gold and silver, but no nation can lay a hand on the inner "Holy Temple" in the heart of every Jew, for it is eternal.

The same applies to every personal loss. The hand of death can only touch the body and its concerns, but the soul is eternal; it has simply ascended to the World of Truth.

Rabbi Menachem Mendel Schneerson, *Igrot Kodesh* 25:4–5

Text 21c

כמו שבודאי ובודאי יבנה השם חרבות ציון וירושלים ויקבץ נדחי ישראל מכל קצוי תבל על ידי משיח צדקנו ויביאם ברנה לראות בשמחתה של ציון וירושלים, כך הוא ללא ספק בנוגע לאבל היחיד, אשר יקיים ה׳ דברו והקיצו ורננו שוכני עפר, ותגדל השמחה, שמחה אמתית, בהפגשם כולם יחד בעת תחית המתים.

אגרות קודש, שם

We have perfect confidence that God will rebuild the ruins of Zion and Jerusalem; He will gather the dispersed remnants of Israel from the ends of the earth through our righteous Mashiach, and He will bring them in gladness to witness the joy of Zion and Jerusalem. We are equally confident that God will fulfill His promise that "those that dwell in the dust shall awake and rejoice" (Isaiah 26:19). Great indeed will be the happiness and rejoicing then, when all will meet together after the Revival of the Dead.

Rabbi Menachem Mendel Schneerson, ibid.

Mourning Reflections

In the *shivah* house, all mirrors are taken down or covered in order to avoid personal vanity during moments of tragedy and to diminish the usual over-concern with one's appearance. Another explanation of this custom is that man was created in the image of God, and that divine image—reflected in the mirror—has been diminished by the recent death. This is also the reason why all photographs of people are covered or removed.

Key Points

1. Like a wedding, life is an opportunity to make the most of every moment.

2. The fetus is taught Torah *in utero* so that the Torah will naturally resonate with the soul throughout life.

3. The fusion of body and soul that occurs for a baby boy at the time of circumcision occurs for a baby girl at the time of naming.

4. At the age of bar or bat mitzvah, the child has the capacity to tell right from wrong and to act on this knowledge, though maturity of judgment will continue to develop for a long time to come.

5. Neither man nor woman may be married without consent.

6. Many customs of the wedding mirror that which occurred when the Torah was given at Sinai.

7. Only men are required to marry and have children.

8. The body that housed the soul in life must continue to be treated with respect even after the soul has departed.

9. The soul is eternal and continues to exist even after life has ended.

Additional Readings

Fetal Psychology

by **Janet L. Hopson**

Behaviorally speaking, there's little difference between a newborn baby and a 32-week-old fetus. A new wave of research suggests that the fetus can feel, dream, even enjoy *The Cat in the Hat*. The abortion debate may never be the same.

The scene never fails to give goose bumps: the baby, just seconds old and still dewy from the womb, is lifted into the arms of its exhausted but blissful parents. They gaze adoringly as their new child stretches and squirms, scrunches its mouth and opens its eyes. To anyone watching this tender vignette, the message is unmistakable. Birth is the beginning of it all, ground zero, the moment from which the clock starts ticking.

Not so, declares Janet DiPietro. Birth may be a grand occasion, says the Johns Hopkins University psychologist, but "it is a trivial event in development. Nothing neurologically interesting happens."

Armed with highly sensitive and sophisticated monitoring gear, DiPietro and other researchers today are discovering that the real action starts weeks earlier. At 32 weeks of gestation—two months before a baby is considered fully prepared for the world, or "at term"—a fetus is behaving almost exactly as a newborn. And it continues to do so for the next 12 weeks.

As if overturning the common conception of infancy weren't enough, scientists are creating a startling new picture of intelligent life in the womb. Among the revelations:

By nine weeks, a developing fetus can hiccup and react to loud noises. By the end of the second trimester it can hear.

Just as adults do, the fetus experiences the rapid eye movement (REM) sleep of dreams.

The fetus savors its mother's meals, first picking up the food tastes of a culture in the womb.

Among other mental feats, the fetus can distinguish between the voice of Mom and that of a stranger, and respond to a familiar story read to it.

Even a premature baby is aware, feels, responds, and adapts to its environment.

Just because the fetus is responsive to certain stimuli doesn't mean that it should be the target of efforts to enhance development. Sensory stimulation of the fetus can in fact lead to bizarre patterns of adaptation later on.

The roots of human behavior, researchers now know, begin to develop early—just weeks after conception, in fact. Well before a woman typically knows she is pregnant, her embryo's brain has already begun to bulge. By five weeks, the organ that looks like a lumpy inchworm has already embarked on the most spectacular feat of human development: the creation of the deeply creased and convoluted cerebral cortex, the part of the brain that will eventually allow the growing person to move, think, speak, plan, and create in a human way.

At nine weeks, the embryo's ballooning brain allows it to bend its body, hiccup, and react to loud sounds. At week ten, it moves its arms, "breathes" amniotic fluid in and out, opens its jaw, and stretches. Before the first trimester is over, it yawns, sucks, and swallows, as well as feels and smells. By the end of the second trimester, it can hear; toward the end of pregnancy, it can see.

Fetal Alertness

Scientists who follow the fetus' daily life find that it spends most of its time not exercising these new abilities but sleeping. At 32 weeks, it drowses 90 to 95% of the day. Some of these hours are spent in deep sleep, some in REM sleep, and some in an indeterminate state, a product of the fetus' immature brain that is different from sleep in a baby, child, or adult. During REM sleep, the fetus' eyes move back and forth just as an adult's eyes do, and many researchers believe that it is dreaming. DiPietro speculates that fetuses dream about what they know—the sensations they feel in the womb.

Closer to birth, the fetus sleeps 85 or 90% of the time: the same as a newborn. Between its frequent naps, the fetus seems to have "something like an awake alert period," according to developmental psychologist William Filer, Ph.D., who with his Columbia University colleagues is monitoring these sleep and wakefulness cycles in order to identify patterns of normal and abnormal brain development, including potential predictors of sudden infant death syndrome. Says Filer, "We are, in effect, asking the fetus: 'Are you paying attention? Is your nervous system behaving in the appropriate way?'"

Fetal Movement

Awake or asleep, the human fetus moves 50 times or more each hour, flexing and extending its body, moving its head, face, and limbs and exploring its warm, wet compartment by touch. Heidelise Als, Ph.D., a developmental psychologist at Harvard Medical School, is fascinated by the amount of tactile stimulation a fetus gives itself. "It touches a hand to the face, one hand to the other hand, clasps its feet, touches its foot to its leg, its hand to its umbilical cord," she reports.

Als believes there is a mismatch between the environment given to preemies in hospitals and the environment they would have had in the womb. She has been working for years to change the care given to preemies so that they can curl up, bring their knees together, and touch things with their hands as they would have for weeks in the womb.

Along with such common movements, DiPietro has also noted some odder fetal activities, including "licking the uterine wall and literally walking around the womb by pushing off with its feet." Laterborns may have more room in the womb for such maneuvers than first babies. After the initial pregnancy, a woman's uterus is bigger and the umbilical cord longer, allowing more freedom of movement. "Second and subsequent children may develop more motor experience in utero and so may become more active infants," DiPietro speculates.

Fetuses react sharply to their mother's actions. "When we're watching the fetus on ultrasound and the mother starts to laugh, we can see the fetus, floating upside down in the womb, bounce up and down on its head, bum-bum-bum, like it's bouncing on a trampoline," says DiPietro. "When mothers watch this on the screen, they laugh harder, and the fetus goes up and down even faster. We've wondered whether this is why people grow up liking roller coasters."

Fetal Taste

Why people grow up liking hot chilies or spicy curries may also have something to do with the fetal environment. By 13 to 15 weeks a fetus' taste buds already look like a mature adult's, and doctors know that the amniotic fluid that surrounds it can smell strongly of curry, cumin, garlic, onion and other essences from a mother's diet. Whether fetuses can taste these flavors isn't yet known, but scientists have found that a 33-week-old preemie will suck harder on a sweetened nipple than on a plain rubber one.

"During the last trimester, the fetus is swallowing up to a liter a day" of amniotic fluid, notes Julie Mennella, Ph.D., a biopsychologist at the Monell Chemical Senses Center in Philadelphia. She thinks the fluid may act as a "flavor bridge" to breast milk, which also carries food flavors from the mother's diet.

Fetal Hearing

Whether or not a fetus can taste, there's little question that it can hear. A very premature baby entering the world at 24 or 25 weeks responds to the sounds around it, observes Als, so its auditory apparatus must already have been functioning in the womb. Many pregnant women report a fetal jerk or sudden kick just after a door slams or a car backfires.

Even without such intrusions, the womb is not a silent place. Researchers who have inserted a hydrophone into the uterus of a pregnant woman have picked up a noise level "akin to the background noise in an apartment," according to DiPietro. Sounds include the whooshing of blood in the mother's vessels, the gurgling and rumbling of her stomach and intestines, as well as the tones of her voice filtered through tissues, bones, and fluid, and the voices of other people coming through the amniotic wall. Fifer has found that fetal heart rate slows when the mother is speaking, suggesting that the fetus not only hears and recognizes the sound, but is calmed by it.

Fetal Vision

Vision is the last sense to develop. A very premature infant can see light and shape; researchers presume that a fetus has the same ability. Just as the womb isn't completely quiet, it isn't utterly dark, either. Says Filer: "There may be just enough visual stimulation filtered through the mother's tissues that a fetus can respond when the mother is in bright light," such as when she is sunbathing.

Japanese scientists have even reported a distinct fetal reaction to flashes of light shined on the mother's belly. However, other researchers warn that exposing fetuses (or premature infants) to bright light before they are ready can be dangerous. In fact, Harvard's Als believes that retinal damage in premature infants, which has long been ascribed to high concentrations of oxygen, may actually be due to overexposure to light at the wrong time in development.

A six-month fetus, born about 14 weeks too early, has a brain that is neither prepared for nor expecting signals from the eyes to be transmitted into the brain's visual cortex, and from there into the executive-branch frontal lobes, where information is integrated. When the fetus is forced to see too much too soon, says Als, the accelerated stimulation may lead to aberrations of brain development.

Fetal Learning

Along with the ability to feel, see, and hear comes the capacity to learn and remember. These activities can be rudimentary, automatic, even biochemical. For example, a fetus, after an initial reaction of alarm, eventually stops responding to a repeated loud noise. The fetus displays the same kind of primitive learning, known as habituation, in response to its mother's voice, Fifer has found.

But the fetus has shown itself capable of far more. In the 1980s, psychology professor Anthony James DeCasper, Ph.D., and colleagues at the University of North Carolina at Greensboro, devised a feeding contraption that allows a baby to suck faster to hear one set of sounds through headphones and to suck slower to hear a different set. With this technique, DeCasper discovered that within hours of birth, a baby already prefers its mother's voice to a stranger's, suggesting it must have learned and remembered the voice, albeit not necessarily consciously, from its last months in the womb. More recently, he's found that a newborn prefers a story read to it repeatedly in the womb—in this case, *The Cat in the Hat*—over a new story introduced soon after birth.

DeCasper and others have uncovered more mental feats. Newborns can not only distinguish their mother from a stranger speaking, but would rather hear Mom's voice, especially the way it sounds filtered through amniotic fluid rather than through air. They're xenophobes, too: they prefer to hear Mom speaking in her native language than to hear her or someone else speaking in a foreign tongue.

By monitoring changes in fetal heart rate, psychologist JeanPierre Lecanuet, Ph.D., and his colleagues in Paris have found that fetuses can even tell strangers' voices apart. They also seem to like certain stories more than others. The fetal heartbeat will slow down when a familiar French fairy tale such as "La Poulette" ("The Chick") or "Le Petit Crapaud" ("The Little Toad"), is read near the mother's belly. When the same reader delivers another unfamiliar story, the fetal heartbeat stays steady.

The fetus is likely responding to the cadence of voices and stories, not their actual words, observes Fifer, but the conclusion is the same: the fetus can listen, learn, and remember at some level, and, as with most babies and children, it likes the comfort and reassurance of the familiar.

Fetal Personality

It's no secret that babies are born with distinct differences and patterns of activity that suggest individual temperament. Just when and how the behavioral traits originate in the womb is now the subject of intense scrutiny.

In the first formal study of fetal temperament in 1996, DiPietro and her colleagues recorded the heart rate and movements of 31 fetuses six times before birth and compared them to readings taken twice after birth. (They've since extended their study to include 100 more fetuses.) Their findings: fetuses that are very active in the womb tend to be more irritable infants. Those with irregular sleep/wake patterns in the womb sleep more poorly as young infants. And fetuses with high heart rates become unpredictable, inactive babies.

"Behavior doesn't begin at birth," declares DiPietro. "It begins before and develops in predictable ways." One of the most important influences on development is the fetal environment. As Harvard's Als observes, "The fetus gets an enormous amount of 'hormonal bathing' through the mother, so its chronobiological rhythms are influenced by the mother's sleep/wake cycles, her eating patterns, her movements."

The hormones a mother puts out in response to stress also appear critical. DiPietro finds that highly pressured mothers-to-be tend to have more active fetuses—-and more irritable infants. "The most stressed are working pregnant women," says DiPietro. "These days, women tend to work up to the day they deliver, even though the implications for pregnancy aren't entirely clear yet. That's our cultural norm, but I think it's insane."

Als agrees that working can be an enormous stress, but emphasizes that pregnancy hormones help to buffer both mother and fetus. Individual reactions to stress also matter. "The pregnant woman who chooses to work is a different woman already from the one who chooses not to work," she explains.

She's also different from the woman who has no choice but to work. DiPietro's studies show that the fetuses of poor women are distinct neurobehaviorally—less active, with a less variable heart rate—from the fetuses of middle-class women. Yet "poor women rate themselves as less stressed than do working middle-class women," she notes. DiPietro suspects that inadequate nutrition and exposure to pollutants may significantly affect the fetuses of poor women.

Stress, diet, and toxins may combine to have a harmful effect on intelligence. A recent study by biostatistician Bernie Devlin, Ph.D., of the University of Pittsburgh, suggests that genes may have less impact on IQ than previously thought and that the environment of the womb may account for much more. "Our old notion of nature influencing the fetus before birth and nurture after birth needs an update," DiPietro insists. "There is an antenatal environment, too, that is provided by the mother."

Parents-to-be who want to further their unborn child's mental development should start by assuring that the antenatal environment is well nourished, low-stress, drug-free. Various authors and "experts" also have suggested poking the fetus at regular intervals, speaking to it through a paper tube or "pregaphone," piping in classical music, even flashing lights at the mother's abdomen.

Does such stimulation work? More importantly: Is it safe? Some who use these methods swear their children are smarter, more verbally and musically inclined, more physically coordinated and socially adept than average. Scientists, however, are skeptical.

"There has been no defended research anywhere that shows any enduring effect from these stimulations," asserts Filer. "Since no one can even say for certain when a fetus is awake, poking them or sticking speakers on the mother's abdomen may be changing their natural sleep patterns. No one would consider poking or prodding a newborn baby in her bassinet or putting a speaker next to her ear, so why would you do such a thing with a fetus?"

Als is more emphatic. "My bet is that poking, shaking, or otherwise deliberately stimulating the fetus might alter its developmental sequence, and anything that affects the development of the brain comes at a cost."

Gently talking to the fetus, however, seems to pose little risk. Fifer suggests that this kind of activity may help parents as much as the fetus. "Thinking about your fetus, talking to it, having your spouse talk to it, will all help prepare you for this new creature that's going to jump into your life and turn it upside down," he says—once it finally makes its anti-climactic entrance.

Psychology Today 31, no. 5 (1998):44
Reprinted with permission of the publisher

Get a Life!

by **Rabbi Yanki Tauber**

We Jews are a funny people. We celebrate the weirdest things. Everyone's heard of end-of-the-school-year parties, graduation parties, retirement parties. But who ever throws a get-to-work party?

Let me explain. Imagine that you have this dream job that's the envy of all your friends. Then, one day you receive a summons to the boss's office. The conversation goes something like this:

Boss: "Have a seat."

You: "Thank you."

Boss: "You've been here—what is it, twelve years now?"

You: "Yeah, it's almost that already. You guys take such good care of me . . . "

Boss: "We pay you a comfortable living wage, plus full health benefits, free day care and spa privileges, 31 days annual paid vacation . . . "

You: "Yes. I'm truly thankful."

Boss: "And what are your duties and responsibilities?"

You: "Nothing. Nada. Zilch. I've no duties or responsibilities."

Boss: "You don't even have to come to work, if you don't want to."

You: "Oh, but I do. Lots of times. It's fun. I hang around the office, see how things are done. Sometimes they even let me help out. You'd be surprised at how much I've learned. And I participate in all the company banquets and outings. I wouldn't miss those for anything . . . "

Boss: "Well, young lady, the party's over."

You: "W-what do you mean?"

Boss: "The party's over. Here, take this manual. It spells out your obligations . . . "

You: "Uh, it's sorta big and heavy. There must be almost a thousand pages in this book . . . "

Boss: "Actually, what you're holding in your hand is a very basic summary. The rest is in the library downstairs . . . "

You: "Oh, I know the library. There are tens of thousands of volumes there . . . "

Boss: "Well, we're doing important work here. And, starting tonight at sundown, you're going to be expected to be doing your part. You'll begin by following instructions, but to do your job right, you'll also need to understand the whys and the hows behind those instructions . . . You've picked up quite a bit in your time here, but we have guys who've been here all their adult lives and are still learning. Anyway, congratulations and good luck. I'll be watching your progress over the next 108 years . . . "

You: " . . . a hundred and eight years?"

Boss: "At least. Hopefully longer. Oh, by the way, don't forget to pick up your new ID tag at the front office on your way out."

After a conversation like that, would you run home and throw a party to celebrate? My daughter did. This week, she celebrated her Bat Mitzvah, the day that she became twelve years old.

A Bat Mitzvah is not an oversized birthday party. Leah's had eleven of those already. This is very different. What she celebrated was the fact that on the eve of her twelfth birthday she became *bat mitzvah* —a person who under Torah law is commanded, obligated and responsible to fulfill the mitzvot of the Torah.

She celebrated the fact that the Boss had called her into the office and told her that the party was over. Until now, she'd received everything her heart desired from Above and was not required to give anything in return. She was in learning mode—hanging around the office, picking up knowledge, getting a feel for how things are done. Now, she's a full-fledged employee, with a long list of duties and responsibilities. More than that—she's been made a partner in the company, fully responsible to make the enterprise work.

She's delighted. She threw a sumptuous party for her friends and family. We feasted, sang and danced and celebrated the event as the happiest day of her life to date.

It may be that life as a free lunch has its attractions. Very quickly, though, it becomes tedious and meaningless, forcing the free luncher to work harder and harder at all the contrivances that pump artificial meaning into life. But the fun leaks out faster than the most vigorous pumper can pump, leaving one deflated and defeated.

That's why we Jews don't throw retirement parties. Instead, we celebrate the day that we're handed the big fat book filled with duties and obligations and the ID tag that reads "Fully Responsible Member." Because we know that there is nothing more gratifying than being given a life that is truly our own.

Reprinted with permission of The Judaism Website, Chabad.org

A Jewish Wedding in 1787

by **Dr. Yitzchok Levine**

Dr. Benjamin Rush (1745-1813), a physician and a signer of the Declaration of Independence, "was the most striking, the most impressive, and the most controversial figure in North American medicine of his day. Brilliant and well educated, he was a restless soul, impatient and impulsive, quick to make decisions and to defend them against all disagreement. Nor did he confine his attention, solely to medicine: he was interested in every phase of life about him; and he was an ardent proponent of inoculation, and later, of vaccination, against smallpox. His work on mental illnesses was the standard for a half century."[1]

Dr. Rush was a prolific letter writer[2], and his letters give us keen insight into life during colonial times and after the Revolutionary War.

In 1787 Dr. Rush, who lived in Philadelphia, treated the family of Rebecca (Machado) and Jonas Phillips. On the morning of Tuesday, June 27, 1787, Mr. and Mrs. Phillips invited Dr. Rush, who was not Jewish, to attend the wedding of their daughter, Rachel, to Michael Levy, who was from Virginia. After attending the wedding Dr. Rush wrote a letter[3] to his wife, Julia, describing the *chasuna*. The reader will no doubt find it interesting to contrast the *chasuna* Dr. Rush attended with the *chasunas* of today:

> I accepted the invitation with great pleasure, for you know I love to be in the way of adding to my stock of ideas upon all subjects. At 1 o'clock the company, consisting of 30 or 40 men, assembled in Mr. Philips' common parlor, which was accommodated with benches for the purpose. The ceremony began with prayers in the Hebrew language, which were chanted by an old rabbi and in which he was followed by the whole company. As I did not understand a word except now and then an Amen or Hallelujah, my attention was directed to the haste with which they covered their heads with their hats as soon as the prayers began, and to the freedom with which some of them conversed with each other during the whole time of this part of their worship.

---

1 http://dodd.cmcvellore.ac.in/hom/21%20-%20Benjamin.html

2 *Letters of Benjamin Rush,* volumes I and II, edited by L. H. Butterfield, Volume I, 1761-1792, (Princeton, NJ: American Philosophical Society of Princeton University Press, 1951).

3 Ibid., pp, 429-432.

As soon as these prayers were ended, which took up about 20 minutes, a small piece of parchment was produced, written in Hebrew, which contained a deed of settlement to which the groom subscribed in the presence of four witnesses. In this deed he conveyed a part of his fortune to his bride, by which she was provided for after his death in case she survived him.

This ceremony was followed by the erection of a beautiful canopy composed of white and red silk in the middle of the floor. It was supported by four young men (by means of four poles), who put on white gloves for the purpose. As soon as this canopy was fixed, the bride, accompanied with her mother, sister, and a long train of female relations, came downstairs. Her face was covered with a veil which reached halfway down her body. She was handsome at all times, but the occasion and her dress rendered her in a peculiar manner a most lovely and affecting object. I gazed with delight upon her. Innocence, modesty, fear, respect, and devotion appeared all at once in her countenance.

She was led by her two bridesmaids under the canopy. Two young men led the bridegroom after her and placed him, not by her side, but directly opposite to her. The priest now began again to chaunt a Hebrew prayer, in which he was followed by part of the company. After this he gave to the groom and bride a glass full of wine, from which they each sipped about a teaspoonful. Another prayer followed this act, after which he took a ring and directed the groom to place it upon the finger of his bride in the same manner as is practised in the marriage service of the Church of England. This ceremony was followed by handing the wine to the father of the bride and then a second time to the bride and groom. The groom, after sipping the wine, took the glass in his hand and threw it upon a large pewter dish which was suddenly placed at his feet. Upon its breaking into a number of small pieces, there was a general shout of joy and a declaration that the ceremony was over. The groom now saluted his bride, and kisses and congratulations became general through the room.

I asked the meaning, after the ceremony was over, of the canopy and of the drinking of the wine and breaking of the glass. I was told by one of the company that in Europe they generally marry in the open air, and that the canopy was introduced to defend the bride and groom from the action of the sun and from rain. Their mutually partaking of the same glass of wine was intended to denote the mutuality of their goods, and the breaking of the glass at the conclusion of the business was designed to teach them the brittleness and uncertainty of human life and the certainty of death, and thereby to temper and moderate their present joys.

Mr. Phillips pressed me to stay and dine with the company, but business and Dr. Hall's departure, which was to take place in the afternoon, forbade it. I stayed, however, to eat some wedding cake and to drink a glass of wine with the guests. Upon going into one of the rooms upstairs to ask how Mrs. Philips did, who had fainted downstairs under the pressure of the heat (for she was weak from a previous indisposition), I discovered the bride and groom supping a bowl of broth together. Mrs. Phillips apologized for them by telling me they had eaten nothing (agreeably to the custom prescribed by their religion) since the night before.

Upon my taking leave of the company, Mrs. Phillips put a large piece of cake into my pocket for you, which she begged I would present to you with her best compliments. She says you are an old New York acquaintance of hers.

During the whole of this new and curious scene my mind was not idle. I was carried back to the ancient world and was led to contemplate the Passovers, the sacrifices, the jubilees, and other ceremonies of the Jewish Church. After this, I was led forward into futurity and anticipated the time foretold by the prophets when this once-beloved race of men shall again be restored to the divine favor.

The Jewish Press, August 2, 2006
Reprinted with permission of *The Jewish Press*

Handle with Care

by **Devorah Leah Mishulovin**

Today I helped prepare Phyllis to meet her Creator.

"It is better to know us and not need us,
Than to need us and not know us."

That is what the plaque on the funeral home office door read. I thought that to be extremely strange. I can see this kind of philosophy at, say, a hospital or doctor's office. But at a funeral home?! It is inevitable; everyone is going to need them . . .

Oh well. I had some time to spare, and would have inquired about it within the office, but it was closed.

I sat on a bench instead, soaking in the peacefulness while waiting for the other volunteers to arrive.

Preparation of the dead for burial is undertaken by a community organization called the *chevrah kadisha*, the "Sacred Society." The volunteers of the Sacred Society quietly and privately wash, purify and dress the deceased, while simultaneously reciting lyrical prayers and Psalms.

We were a group of five women, eager to fulfill this mitzvah. This was my first time and I was a tad anxious. But this was something I had *wanted* to volunteer for, so I came with a positive attitude.

We walked into the room where the deceased woman lay completely covered. Her name, Phyllis, was scribbled on the wall-board.

Her name and the fact that she was Jewish were the only things I knew about her. Nothing else mattered.

The little bit of nervousness that I had felt dissipated when Tova, the leader of our group, uncovered Phyllis' face and remarked, "Oh, wow, she was a beautiful woman."

The atmosphere in the room was serene. There was a calm, a composure, a holiness.

There was a task to be done and our concern was accomplishing it with utmost dignity and care for the deceased, and of course according to the letter of the law.

Since I was the most inexperienced of the group, I chose to be the one to recite the special prayers as needed. However, as Tova began to guide us through the procedures, I felt myself able and willing to help hands-on.

There are many details involved in preparing and purifying the body before its burial. Laws and customs with symbolism and meaning; so special, so sacred. There is a system and order for every stage of the process. From the washing through to the dressing, from the preparing of the casket to placing the body inside. It is truly amazing how many details and beautiful rituals are involved in preparing the body for its next phase. From the sprinkling of soil from the Land of Israel, to the tying of the ribbons in the shape of a *shin*, (signifying G-d's name)—it is all a holy experience.

Again and again we were reminded to handle the body with gentleness, care and utmost dignity. Every movement was infused with such reverence, gentleness, it was awe-inspiring. I felt comforted knowing that I too, some day, will be treated with such respect.

This concept is what touched me so—the absolute honor given to the deceased. Keeping the body covered whenever possible. Moving the body gently and as little as possible. For example, when dressing the body in *tachrichim* (shrouds) we encountered some difficulty pulling down the shirt in the back. We wanted to lift the body, but Tova pointed out that we will be able to smooth everything out when we put the top shirt (*kittel*) on, and that way she will only be moved once.

It was a challenging task, after Phyllis was all dressed, to lift her off the table and to carefully place her into the *aron* (casket). Thank G-d through the team effort we managed without incident.

Lying peacefully in the *aron*, dressed in white, face covered, she was an awesome sight to behold, so pure, so holy, so ready to greet her Maker.

I felt comforted knowing that I too, some day, will be treated with such respect. After the *aron* was closed, we each apologized to Phyllis, in case we had moved her too quickly, a tad too roughly, or if by chance we mishandled or offended her in any way. I later learned that an annual fast day was established for the volunteers of this Sacred Society, as a form of repenting, if, G-d forbid, we had failed to handle with appropriate care.

So much care and attention to avoid hurting a *body*. The emphasis and caution to guard against offending someone who can no longer feel really altered my perceptions.

Made me think . . . more aware.

How we need to be ever so careful in treating our friends, neighbors and even total strangers who are alive. People with feelings, with sensitivities, troubles. Not because they can hurt you back, but because they are part of G-d.

If the Torah teaches us, with lots of intricate details, how to treat a body without a soul—without G-d's holy spark that gives it life, shouldn't we be so much more cautious and careful when relating to a human being *with* a soul?

"Phyllis the daughter of . . . . We ask forgiveness of you if we did not treat you respectfully.

May you be an advocate for all of Israel.

Go in peace, rest in peace, and arise in your turn at the end of days."

Lesson 3

Under the Influence
Angels, Blessings, and Evil Eyes

Introduction

You know about gravity, electricity, and other forces that are invisible but real. In this lesson, we will explore a few more. We'll find out why ideas are contagious and how words can kill. We will also take a look at why it is forbidden to stand next to a fully ripe pumpkin patch and how angels are like translation software. (Hint: It's not because you can't understand a word they say.)

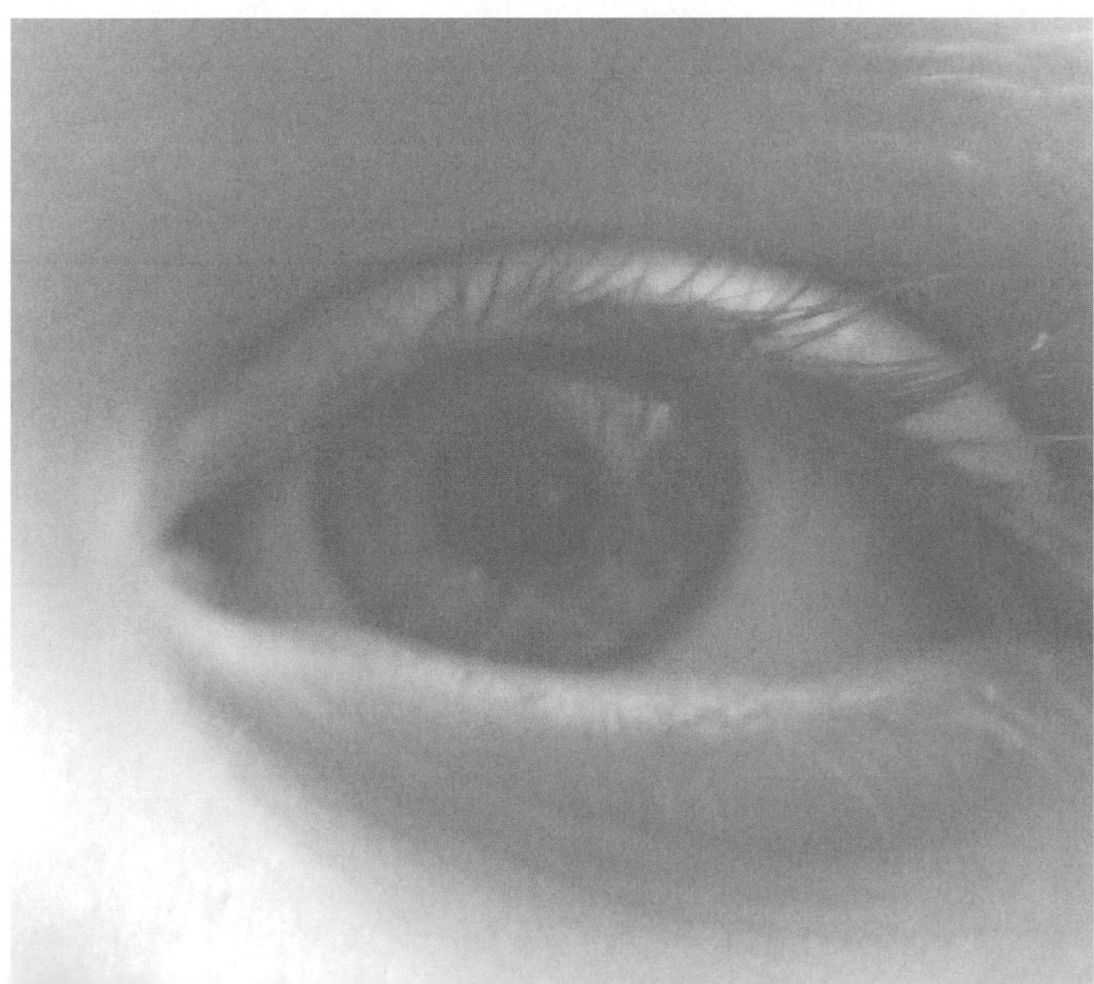

Mythical or Mystical?

Learning Activity 1

Circle the number that best describes your belief.

1. Do miracles happen?

1	2	3	4	5
Definitely Not	Likely Not	Not Sure	Likely Yes	Definitely Yes

2. Can people be harmed by an "evil eye"?

1	2	3	4	5
Definitely Not	Likely Not	Not Sure	Likely Yes	Definitely Yes

3. Do people have guardian angels?

1	2	3	4	5
Definitely Not	Likely Not	Not Sure	Likely Yes	Definitely Yes

4. Can negative speech (such as curses and ill wishes) cause negative outcomes?

1	2	3	4	5
Definitely Not	Likely Not	Not Sure	Likely Yes	Definitely Yes

Believe It or Not!

According to a 2005 Gallup poll, three out of four Americans profess at least one paranormal belief.

Text 1

עיקר הצווי בעבודת כוכבים שלא לעבוד אחד מכל הברואים, לא מלאך ולא גלגל ולא כוכב ולא אחד מארבעה היסודות ולא אחד מכל הנבראים מהן, ואף על פי שהעובד יודע שה׳ הוא האלקים.

משנה תורה, הלכות עבודת כוכבים ב,א

The essence of the commandment [forbidding] idolatry is the prohibition against worshipping any of the creations: not an angel, sphere, or star, none of the four fundamental elements nor any entity created from them. This is true even if the worshipper acknowledges that God is the [ultimate] authority.

Maimonides, *Mishneh Torah*, Laws of Idolatry 2:1

Rabbi Moshe ben Maimon (1135–1204). Better known as Maimonides or by the acronym Rambam; born in Cordoba, Spain. After the conquest of Cordoba by the Almohads, he fled Spain and eventually settled in Cairo, Egypt. There, he became the leader of the Jewish community and served as court physician to the vizier of Egypt. His rulings on Jewish law are considered integral to the formation of halachic consensus. He is most noted for authoring the *Mishneh Torah,* an encyclopedic arrangement of Jewish law, and for his philosophical work, *Guide for the Perplexed.*

Text 2a

עלמא תתאה קיימא לקבלא תדיר . . .
ועלמא עלאה לא יהיב ליה אלא כגוונא דאיהו קיימא. אי איהו קיימא בנהירו דאנפין מתתא כדין הכי נהרין ליה מעילא, ואי איהו קיימא בעציבו יהבין ליה דינא בקבליה. כגוונא דא "עבדו את ה׳ בשמחה" (תהלים ק,ב), חדוה דבר נש משיך לגביה חדוה אחרא עלאה.

זוהר ב, קעט,ב

The lower world is always ready to receive [the spiritual flow that emanates from above]. . . .

And the upper world provides in accordance with the state [below]. If the state [below] is radiant, then radiance shines down upon it from above; but if the state below is gloomy, then the radiance is constricted.

Likewise, "Serve God with gladness" (Psalms 100:2), because human gladness draws a corresponding supernal gladness.

Zohar 2:179b

Text 2b

דע מה למעלה ממך.

משנה, אבות ב,א

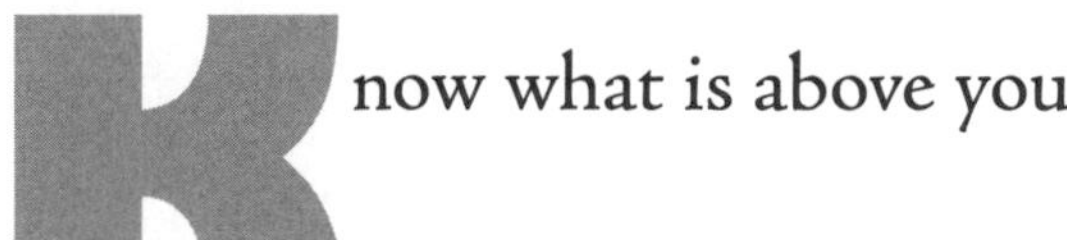

Know what is above you.

Mishnah, Avot 2:1

Text 2c

דע כל מה שלמעלה, הכל הוא ממך.
מגיד דבריו ליעקב, לקוטי אמרים קצח

Know that all that is above is dependent on you.

Rabbi Dov Ber of Mezeritch, *Magid Devarav LeYa'akov, Likutei Amarim* 198

Rabbi Dov Ber "the Magid" of Mezeritch (d. 1772). Was the primary disciple and eventual successor of the Ba'al Shem Tov. Amongst his disciples were the founders of various chasidic dynasties, including Rabbi Nachum of Chernobyl, Rabbi Levi Yitschak of Berditchev, and Rabbi Shne'ur Zalman of Liadi. His teachings, recorded by his students, appear in various volumes including the *Magid Devarav LeYa'akov.*

Text 3a

וַיֹּאמֶר אֱלֹקִים, "נַעֲשֶׂה אָדָם בְּצַלְמֵנוּ כִּדְמוּתֵנוּ".
בראשית א,כו

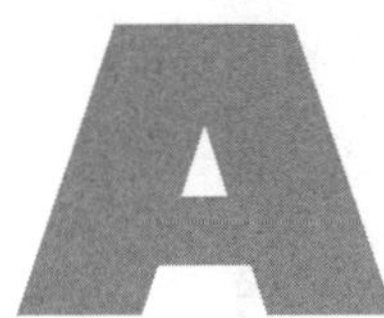

And God said, "Let us make man, in our image, after our likeness."

Genesis 1:26

Text 3b

אמר באדם ״נעשה״, כלומר, אני והארץ הנזכרת נעשה אדם, שתוציא הארץ הגוף מיסודיה כאשר עשתה בבהמה ובחיה, כדכתיב (להלן ב,ז), ״וייצר ה׳ אלקים את האדם עפר מן האדמה״, ויתן הוא יתברך הרוח מפי עליון, כדכתיב (שם), ״ויפח באפיו נשמת חיים״.

ואמר ״בצלמנו כדמותנו״, כי ידמה לשניהם. במתכונת גופו, לארץ אשר לוקח ממנה, וידמה ברוח לעליונים, שאינה גוף ולא תמות.

ואמר בכתוב השני ״בצלם אלקים ברא אותו״, לספר הפלא אשר נפלא בו משאר הנבראים.

רמב״ן, שם

Rabbi Moshe ben Nachman (1194–1270). Also known as Nachmanides, or by the acronym Ramban. Nachmanides authored a classic commentary on the Pentateuch that includes everything from critical examination of the text to kabbalistic insights. He also authored numerous other works, including a commentary on the Talmud. Born in Spain, he served as leader of Iberian Jewry. In 1263, he was summoned by King James of Aragon to a public disputation with Pablo Cristiani, a Jewish apostate. Though he was the clear victor of the debate, resulting persecution led to his expulsion from Spain. Settling in Israel, Nachmanides helped reestablish communal life in Jerusalem.

When creating man, God said, "Let *us* make": I will create man *together* with the aforementioned earth. The earth will produce the [human] body from its elements, as it did in the creation of the animals and beasts. As it is written (Genesis 2:7), "God formed man from the earth." And God will imbue the body with a soul that emanates from the divine utterance. As it is written (ibid.), "God blew into his nostrils the breath of life."

And God said [that man will be] "in our likeness and in our image" [that is, in the image and likeness of both God and earth]. For man is similar to both. His body is similar to the earth from which it was taken. And his soul is similar to the higher realms, for it is immortal and non-corporeal.

The following verse concludes, "In the image of God He created him," emphasizing the wondrous exaltedness of man in comparison to the rest of creation.

Nachmanides, ad loc.

Reaching for Angels
The Anatomy of Angels

Question for Discussion

Can you identify some biblical stories in which angels figure prominently?

The Role of Angels

The Right Angel for the Right Task

Angels are unidimensional creatures, programmed for a specific mission. One angel is not charged with two different types of missions, nor are two angels charged with the identical mission.

Text 4

עשה אדם מצוה אחת, מוסרים לו מלאך אחד; עשה שתי מצות, מוסרין לו שני מלאכים; עשה כל המצות, מוסרין לו מלאכים הרבה, שנאמר (תהלים צא,יא), "כי מלאכיו יצוה לך". ומי הן המלאכים אלו? שמשמרים אותו מן המזיקין.

מדרש תנחומא, משפטים יט

A person who does one mitzvah, is given one angel. One who does two *mitzvot,* is given two angels. One who does all the *mitzvot,* is given many angels—as it says, "He will assign His angels to you" (Psalms 91:11). Who are these angels? They are the ones who guard the person against harm.

Midrash, *Tanchuma, Mishpatim* 19

Text 5

אין גן עדן דערהערט מען די טייערקייט פון עולם הזה . . . מלאכי השרת . . . וואלטען אלץ אוועקגעגעבען פאר א אמן יהא שמיה רבא פון א אידען, אז ער זאגט בכל כחו כפירושו בכל כוונתו.

היום יום, יז אדר א

In the upper worlds, the preciousness of this world is well appreciated. The ministering angels . . . would forego everything for one *"Amen, yehei shemeih raba"* said by a Jew with full concentration.

Rabbi Shne'ur Zalman of Liadi, cited in *Hayom Yom*, 17 Adar I

Rabbi Shne'ur Zalman of Liadi (1745–1812). Chasidic rebbe and founder of the Chabad movement, also known as "the Alter Rebbe" and "the Rav." Born in Liozna, Belarus, he was among the principal students of the Magid of Mezeritch. His numerous works include the *Tanya*, an early classic containing the fundamentals of Chasidism; *Torah Or; Likutei Torah*; and *Shulchan Aruch HaRav*, a reworked and expanded code of Jewish law. He is interred in Hadiach, Ukraine, and was succeeded by his son, Rabbi Dovber of Lubavitch.

The Power of Speech

Questions for Discussion

"A word is dead when it is said some say,
I say it just begins to live that day."
—Emily Dickinson

In what way is a word "dead when it is said"? In what way does it "begin to live that day"?

Text 6

מורי זלה״ה היה נוהג כשנפלה לו איזה השגה במוחו היה אומרה בפה אף שלא יבינו השומעים כל כך, שהיה מדברה רק כמו בפני עצמו כו׳. והטעם לזה הוא בכדי להמשיך את ההשגה שנפלה לו בזה העולם בבחינת יציאת הדיבור כשמדברה בפיו, על ידי זה שמדברה בצירופי אותיות הדיבור ממשיכה לעולם הזה.
ואזי כשימשיכנה לעולם הזה, יוכל אחר, אף שהוא בסוף העולם, להשיגה על ידי יגיעתו בתורה ועבודה . . . אבל אם לא היה ממשיכה לעולם הזה על ידי הדיבור כו׳, אף שייגע אחר הרבה לא ישיגנה במוחו, שאינה נמצאת בזה העולם, שהיא בשמים.

מאמרי אדמו״ר הזקן הקצרים ע׳ 474

Whenever my master [Rabbi Dov Ber of Mezeritch], conceived an original [Torah] thought, he would voice it aloud, although those present could not understand him. He would speak as if to himself. By articulating the idea, he would draw it into this world.

Once the idea was present in this world, it could occur to another person—even one at the other end of the world—who was laboring in the study of Torah and the service of God. . . . Had it not been drawn into this world, even if the other were to toil mightily, he would not arrive at this idea—for it would still be in heaven.

Rabbi Shne'ur Zalman of Liadi, *Ma'amarei Admur Hazaken Haketsarim*, p. 474

Text 7

ואמר רבי אלעזר אמר רבי חנינא: לעולם אל תהי ברכת הדיוט קלה בעיניך, שהרי שני גדולי הדור ברכום שני הדיוטות ונתקיימה בהן, ואלו הן: דוד ודניאל. דוד, דברכיה ארונה, דכתיב (שמואל ב, כד,כג), "ויאמר ארונה אל המלך ה' אלקיך ירצך". דניאל, דברכיה דריוש, דכתיב (דניאל ו,יז), "אלקך די אנת פלח לה בתדירא הוא ישיזבינך". ואמר רבי אלעזר אמר רבי חנינא: אל תהי קללת הדיוט קלה בעיניך, שהרי אבימלך קלל את שרה, "הנה הוא לך כסות עינים" (בראשית כ,טז), ונתקיים בזרעה, "ויהי כי זקן יצחק ותכהין עיניו" (שם כז,א).

תלמוד בבלי, מגילה טו,א

Rabbi Elazar said in the name of Rabbi Chanina: Let not the blessing of an ordinary man be unimportant in your eyes, for two great men, David and Daniel, received blessings from ordinary men and they were fulfilled. David was blessed by Araunah, as it is written, "And Araunah said to the king, 'May God your God favor you'" (II Samuel 24:23). Daniel was blessed by Darius, as it is written, "Your God whom you continually serve will deliver you" (Daniel 6:17).

Rabbi Elazar further said in the name of Rabbi Chanina: Let not the curse of an ordinary man be unimportant in your eyes, because Abimelech cursed Sarah, saying, "Behold, this is to you a covering of the eyes" (Genesis 20:16), and this was fulfilled in her progeny, [as it says,] "And it came to pass when Isaac was old and his eyes dimmed" (ibid., 27:1).

Talmud, Megilah 15a

Text 8

מות וחיים ביד לשון.

משלי יח,כא

eath and life are in the hands of the tongue.

Proverbs 18:21

Text 9a

לא תקלל חרש.

ויקרא יט,יד

ou shall not curse a deaf person.

Leviticus 19:14

Text 9b

שמנענו ה׳ מהזיק בפינו לזולתינו כמו שמנענו מהזיק להם במעשה . . .
שיש כח בדברי פי אדם.

ספר החינוך, מצוה רלא

God commanded us to refrain from harming another with our words, just as He commanded us not to harm another with our actions. . . . For a person's words have power.

Sefer Hachinuch, Mitzvah 231

Sefer Hachinuch is a work on the 613 commandments, arranged in the order of the *mitzvot's* appearance in the Torah. Four aspects of every mitzvah are discussed in this work: the definition of the mitzvah and its sources in the Written and Oral Torah; ethical lessons which can be deduced from the mitzvah; basic laws pertaining to the observance of the mitzvah; and who is obligated to perform the mitzvah and when. The work was composed in the 13th century by an anonymous author who refers to himself in the introduction as "the Levite of Barcelona." It has been widely thought that this referred to Rabbi Aharon HaLevi of Barcelona (Re'ah); however, this view has been contested.

Text 10a

לישנא תליתאי קטיל תליתאי: הורג לאומרו, ולמקבלו, ולאומרין עליו.

תלמוד בבלי, ערכין טו,ב

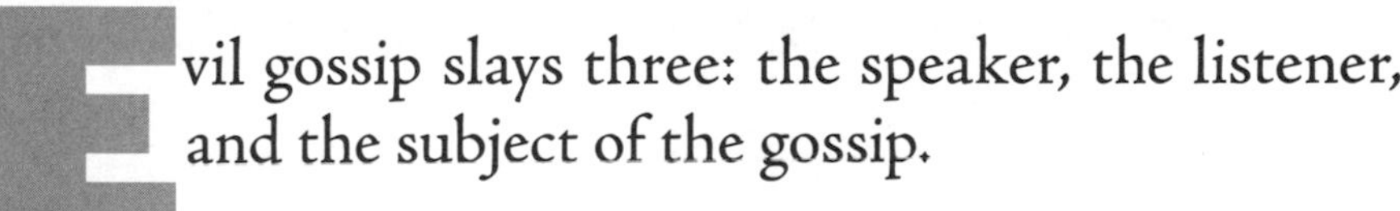

Evil gossip slays three: the speaker, the listener, and the subject of the gossip.

Talmud, Arachin 15b

Text 10b

The nature of speech is that of revealing something that was previously concealed in thought. Thus, when another's evil is revealed through speech, it has the capacity to do spiritual harm to the person about whom the evil is spoken; were this evil not to have been revealed through speech, it may well have remained dormant and not elicited the unfortunate ensuing results of its revelation.

It is axiomatic that "positive actions have a greater degree of efficacy than negative actions." If speaking of another's evil qualities and traits harms that individual, surely speaking of the other's good qualities and traits has a positive influence upon the person so praised.

Rabbi Sholom B. Wineberg, *The Chassidic Dimension* [Brooklyn N.Y.: Kehot Publication Society, 2003], 5:145 (adapted from discourses of the Lubavitcher Rebbe)

Learning Activity 2

Think of a loved one and a quality you appreciate about him or her. What words can you say to bring this quality to the fore?

Thoughts and Attitudes
Good Eye vs. Evil Eye

Text 11

בראותו חבירו בטוב עין הוא יברך וישפיע טוב לחבירו וגם יבורך, ולהיפך להיפך בר מינה, דכתיב (משלי כב,ט), "טוב עין הוא יְבֹרָךְ", וקרי יְבָרֵךְ.

ספר חרדים סו,צ

When one views another with a good eye, he blesses and draws good upon his friend, and he too is blessed. The opposite is true as well. As it is stated, (Proverbs 22:9), "One with a good eye shall be blessed," and [using alternate vocalization, it can be] read, "[one with a good eye] shall bless."

Rabbi Elazar Azikri, *Sefer Charedim* 66:90

Rabbi Elazar ben Moshe Azikri (1533–1600). Kabbalist, poet, and author, born in Safed to a Sefardic family that settled in the Holy Land after the expulsion from Spain. Rabbi Elazar studied Torah under Rabbi Yosef Sagis and Rabbi Ya'akov Berab and is counted with the greatest rabbis and intellectuals of his time. Rabbi Elazar authored the *Sefer Charedim*, a work focused on ethics, morals, and personality development. It was printed after his death in 1600. He composed the ode *Yedid Nefesh*, traditionally sung in many communities before *Kabalat Shabbat* and/or at the third Shabbat meal.

Text 12

יהי רצון מלפניך ה' אלקי ואלקי אבותי, שתצילני היום ובכל יום . . . מעין הרע.

סידור תהלת ה', ברכות השחר

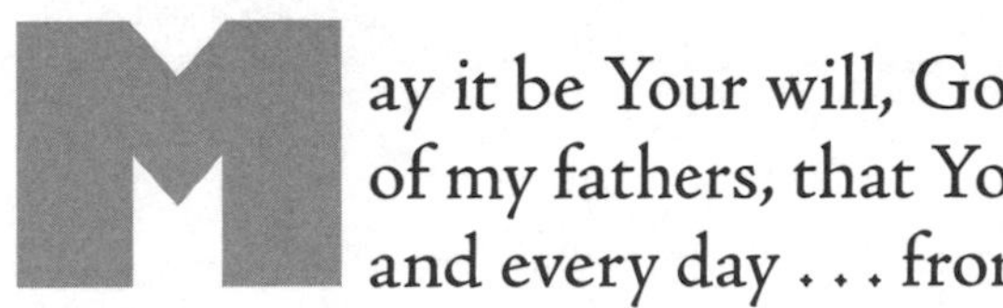

May it be Your will, God, my God, and God of my fathers, that You protect me this day and every day . . . from an evil eye.

Sidur Tehilat Hashem, Morning Blessings

Text 13

המספר שבח אדם בחכמה או עושר או בנים וכיוצא חייב לברכו שלא ישלוט בו עין הרע.

צפורן שמיר קעב

One who praises another regarding wisdom, wealth, children, and the like, should also offer a blessing that he not be affected by the evil eye.

Rabbi Chaim Yosef David Azulai, *Tsiporen Shamir* 172

Rabbi Chaim Yosef David Azulai (1724–1806). Commonly known by the acronym Chida; rabbi, Talmudist, and noted bibliophile. Born in Jerusalem, scion to a prominent rabbinic family, he studied under Rabbi Chaim ibn Atar. A prolific writer on various Jewish topics, his *Shem Hagedolim,* which provides short biographies of Jewish authors with overviews of their works, is particularly famous. He traveled extensively in Europe to raise funds on behalf of the Jewish community in the Land of Israel, and died in Italy.

Text 14a

אסור לו לאדם שיעמוד על שדה חבירו בשעה שעומדת בקמותיה.

תלמוד בבלי, בבא מציעא קז,א

It is forbidden to stand near another's field when the crop is ready for harvest.

Talmud, Bava Metsi'a 107a

Text 14b

יכולים לקרות שני אחים זה אחר זה והבן אחר האב. ואין מניחים אלא בשביל עין הרע.

שולחן ערוך, אורח חיים קמב,ו

In principle, two brothers or a father and son can be called up to receive consecutive *aliyot*. This is not done, however, to prevent the evil eye.

Rabbi Yosef Caro, Shulchan Aruch, *Orach Chayim* 142:6

Rabbi Yosef Caro (1488–1575). Born in Spain but fled the country with his family during the expulsion in 1492, and eventually settled in Safed, Israel. Also known as "the Beit Yosef," after the title of his commentary on the *Arba'ah Turim*, and Maran ("our master") for his status as a preeminent authority on Jewish law. Author of 10 works on Jewish law and the Torah, including the *Beit Yosef, Kesef Mishneh*, and a mystical work, *Magid Meisharim*. Rabbi Caro's magnum opus, the Shulchan Aruch (Code of Jewish Law), has been universally accepted as the basis for modern Jewish law.

Protecting Against the Evil Eye

Modesty

Text 15

שאין הברכה מצויה . . . אלא בדבר הסמוי מן העין.

תלמוד בבלי, תענית ח,ב

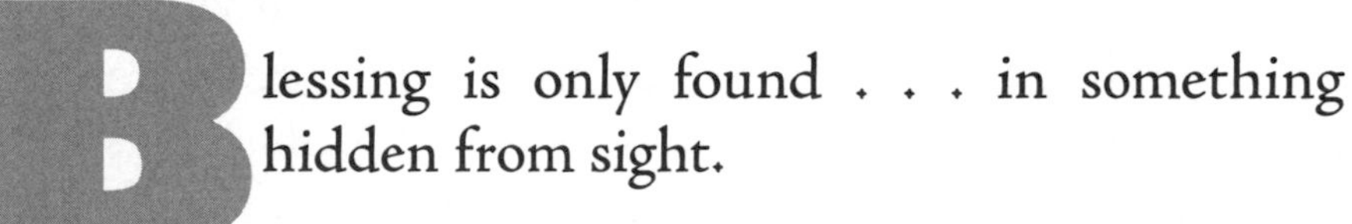

Blessing is only found . . . in something hidden from sight.

Talmud, Ta'anit 8b

עין טובה

A Good Eye

Text 16

מי שהוא נדיב ועין טובה אין שולט בו עין הרע.
דבש לפי, מערכת ע׳, ערך עין טובה

One who is generous and possesses a good eye is not affected by the evil eye.

Rabbi Chaim Yosef David Azulai, *Devash Lefi, Ma'arechet Ayin*, entry *Ayin Tovah*

Mitzvah Performance

Rabbi Eliezer Papo (1785–1826). Famed author on the topics of Jewish ethics, morals, and personality development. Born in Sarajevo, Rabbi Papo became an outstanding rabbinic scholar, noted for his piety and spirituality. He served as rabbi of the community of Selestria (today in Bulgaria). In spite of the brevity of his life, Rabbi Papo achieved remarkable depth and breadth in his rabbinic scholarship, and left to posterity a significant literary legacy—most notably, his work *Pele Yo'ets*.

Text 17

לא ימנע מעשות מצוה מפני חשש עין הרע, כגון להביא עני לביתו או לדרוש ברבים ללמוד דעת את העם, כי ״שומר מצוה לא ידע דבר רע״ (קהלת ח,ה), ומצוה אגוני מגינא והיא מגן וצנה.
פלא יועץ, ערך עין הרע

One should not abstain from performing a mitzvah for fear of incurring the evil eye. For example, [one should not hesitate] to invite a pauper into his home or to teach [Torah] in public. For "one who observes the *mitzvot* will know no evil" (Ecclesiastes 8:5). The mitzvah protects; it is a shield and armor.

Rabbi Eliezer Papo, *Pele Yo'ets*, entry *Ayin Hara*

Don't Worry!

Text 18

בענין עין הרע ודאי יש לחוש, אבל אין להקפיד הרבה, כי בדברים כאלו הכלל "מאן דלא קפיד לא קפדינן בהדיה".

אגרות משה, אבן העזר ג,כו

With regard to the evil eye, while it is certainly a matter to take into account, one mustn't be overly concerned. For regarding all such matters, the general principle is: "One who is not troubled by it will not be troubled by it."

Rabbi Moshe Feinstein, *Igrot Moshe, Even Ha'ezer* 3:26

Rabbi Moshe Feinstein (1895–1986). Rabbi and leading halachic authority of the 20th century. Born near Minsk, Belarus; he became rabbi of Luban in 1921; immigrated to the U.S. in 1937 and became the dean of Metivta Tiferet Yerushalayim in New York. Rabbi Feinstein became the leading halachic authority of his time and his rulings are always considered. His halachic decisions have been published in a multi-volume collection titled *Igrot Moshe*. He also published works on the Talmud and was known for his fine character traits.

Key Points

1. Although Judaism acknowledges the existence of metaphysical energies that affect our universe, it does not ascribe independent power to these energies, which are no more than the mechanisms through which God interacts with the universe.

2. A person can play an active role in directing these energies through his or her choices.

3. Angels are purely spiritual beings, each created to fulfill a particular mission.

4. A primary role of angels is to serve as a conduit for connecting the physical and spiritual realms.

5. Just as the physical world follows rules of nature, the metaphysical realms also follow certain rules.

6. Words, simply by being uttered, can bring a quality that was only present in a potential state into a manifest, actual state. Thus, people can be affected by good or bad words even if they do not actually hear what is said.

7. One who has an "evil eye" is jealous or judgmental of other people's blessings, while one who possesses a "good eye" feels generous and genuine joy at the good fortune of others.

8. The evil eye can only arouse judgment against someone who is undeserving of his or her blessings.

9. One can be protected against the evil eye by acting modestly, looking kindly upon others, engaging in good deeds, and avoiding worry or obsession about such energies.

Additional Readings

Meeting an Angel

by **Theodore Steinberg**

Genesis 28:10 tells of Jacob's hasty departure from his parents' home in Beersheba. He is moving fast to escape the anger of his brother Esau, and is heading north to his mother's family in Haran. He does not know what he is going to find. On his first night out, he came upon a place [*vayifga bamakom*] where he made camp. There he dreamt about a stairway that reaches from earth to heaven, and angels are climbing up and down it. Twenty years later, when Jacob is returning to his parents' home with his wives and children, there is another incident with angels. The word "*vayifga*" occurs again, but this time with the singular form changed to the plural *vayifgu bo malachai Elohim* (32:2).

It must be nice, or at least interesting, to come across an angel now and then. Thus far, Jacob has seen them twice. There is yet an encounter to come, when he wrestles with one at the ford of the Jabbok and receives his new name Israel.

One might wonder, are angels real? Are they visible, even occasionally? Do people ever encounter them? Could that happen to one of us at some time? A midrash focuses on the words quoted above: *vayifga*, and *vayifgu*, forms of the verb "to meet," or "to encounter," or "to come upon." Jacob came upon a *makom* [place]. The midrash tells us that Makom is an ancient rabbinic name for God. God is, so to speak, the space or place of everything, the whole universe!

This interpretation changes the whole verse: Now it says that Jacob came upon no mere place but upon God, the Lord of all space and places.

The American writer Annie Dillard once asked why people read books. Her own answer was that often people read books because they want to be surprised or touched, in some deep and moving way; an experience of love, or wisdom, or courage. Perhaps every reader knows what she means. Just recently, I read a book like that. It was about the American Revolutionary War, with George Washington, Benjamin Franklin, Samuel Adams, and British General Thomas Gage among the characters. I try to read a few pages every night before retiring. It tells of wisdom, courage and other good things that the reader comes across unexpectedly as he reads.

To return to our passages: Jacob came upon God out of the blue, which suggests something to the reader. Is this the way to Jewish faith? Faith here seems to be a chance happenstance if one is lucky that day. Perhaps such an extraordinary encounter does occur now and then, but suppose it never happens. That is the problem with faith-by-surprise. It may never happen. It is not reliable or dependable.

Still, all are invited to partake of the adventure of exploring Judaism. One never knows what sweet surprises may be encountered, something like Judaism in all its grandeur. One may say to oneself: How wasteful it is to go through life hoping to come upon it by chance.

Bright people stay alert—and perhaps an angel or two will show up for you. Good luck in your surprise encounters.

Jewish Bible Quarterly 35, no. 4 (2007):269-270
Reprinted with permission of the Jewish Bible Association, www.jewishbible.org

Not One, Not Two, Not Three

by **Monford Harris**

To see whether a quorum of ten is present for a prayer service it has been customary to count negatively: not one, not two, not three, and so on.

It has always struck moderns as being a quaint practice, the survival of a superstition—fear of the evil eye—resulting from the danger of numbers. To call this custom a superstition, however, does not fully explain the custom. Judaism has no rigorous and functional definition of what constitutes a superstition. It is suggested that negative counting derives from the most exquisite understanding of Jewish faithfulness.

Community prayer in contradistinction to private prayer, requires the presence of ten adult males before prayer commences. The number ten is important; for ten represents the community in miniature. These ten adult males are a small community representing the larger community—a community in prayer. Thus each person is not an isolated individual, rather each is a Jewish person relating to every other Jewish person present. This is the reason that the overwhelming proportion of prayers use the first person plural rather than the first person singular. It is "we," a community, that address the ultimate Person.

A genuine community is not simply a sociological institution made up of objects called individuals. Modern Jews frequently believe that institutions make up a community. Yet it is becoming more and more apparent, by virtue of various problems, that this is not correct. There are those today who believe that when the establishment is destroyed it will be replaced by a genuine community where people have positive feelings for one another. But this, too, is not so; feelings make pure subjectivity. Community depends not on feelings but on relationships. Buber writes: "The true community does not arise through peoples having feelings for one another (though indeed without it), but through, first, their taking their stand in living mutual relation with a living Center, and, second, their being in living mutual relation with one another. The second has its source in the first, but is not given when the first alone is given. Living mutual relation includes feeling but does not originate with them. The community is built up out of living mutual relation, but the builder is the living effective center."[1]

This community presupposes a relationship. Objects can have experiences with, or of, one another; but only persons have mutual relationships. Those who come to a service come as persons living a mutual relationship with a Living Center and living a mutual relationship with one another. Even a stranger passing through town, and therefore attending a service only once, is not really a stranger; for he is a member of the community of Israel, sharing various realities.

Now, to count persons who are in community is to transform them from persons into objects or units; for to count means to objectify. Number reduces the totality ("person") to a fragment—a unit in a series. If the persons who are together for a service are counted, the counting process itself objectifies them [in] others' eyes and each in his own eyes. Each person becomes both to himself and to the other an *It*. They therefore would be not a community in prayer; for a community is made up of persons. They would be simply an institution, and institutions do not pray.

The whole conception of *minyan* is paradoxical. The word *minyan* means "a counting." Yet the men should not be counted. The necessity for counting presupposes an abnormal situation. It would imply an uncertainty as to whether there is a community at prayer. Counting must be resorted to when a small handful of people come together. It is also an indication of a poverty of persons—that less than ten adult males live in the town or area. Counting, therefore, is an indication of the decline of a particular community of believers. It is not only an indication of devotional poverty but indicates the absence of a large community of faithful Jews.

Perhaps in earlier times congregations did not have to be counted; for it is not sentimentality to believe that, historically, most Jews took community prayer seriously.

---

[1] Martin Buber, *I and Thou,* New York, Scribners, 1965, p. 45.

Counting, as we have suggested, is an indication of the community being transformed to institution and the attenuation of a Jewish community. To further guard against corrosion, congregations employ the paradoxical and profound device of negative counting. Negative counting is both an admission of a decline and a guarding against the immediate danger of further transformation.

That counting of persons is a dangerous metaphysical enterprise [that] has evidently a long history in Jewish existence. We read of David's census taking which was punished by a plague. Presumably the negative counting of the *minyan* is rooted in an ancient tradition. The tradition was so deeply rooted that counting must have always been considered a dubious act. Indicative of this is the very use of the term *minyan* for a quorum. The need for counting was a late necessity but which was introduced only by counting negatively; for what must be protected was the reality of the community of persons, protected against being transformed into objects. For if persons should be transformed into objects then community degenerates into an institution. Negative counting is a hedge against deflation—the deflation of persons into statistical units.

Tradition: A Journal of Orthodox Thought 11, no. 1 (1970): 55-57.
Reprinted with permission of the publisher

Worlds, Angels, and Men

by **Rabbi Adin Steinsaltz**

The physical world in which we live, the cosmos which we can observe objectively, is one part in a vast system of worlds. The other worlds are for the most part ethereal, that is, nonmaterial. They can be envisaged as different dimensions of being. They do not exist elsewhere, in different sets of spatial coordinates, but rather in another order or plane of being.

Furthermore, as we shall see, these various worlds interpenetrate and interact with each other. In a certain sense it can be said that each of the worlds is a replication, by means of transformation, change, or even distortion, of that immediately above it. World after world is reflected in that which lies below it, and finally all the worlds—with their complex interrelated influence—are projected in to the world we know and experience.

The terms higher and lower do not indicate a physical relationship of altitude, which does not obtain in the spiritual realm, but rather relative positions on the scale of causality. A higher world is more primary, elemental, concentrated; a lower world is secondary, more remote from the primal source, and thus a replication. However, such a replication is not simply a coarser version, but is in itself a total system with a life and existence of its own, and with its own specific properties and characteristics.

The totality of the world in which we live is known as the World of Action. It is the world of our sensual and nonsensual apprehension. It is not, however, homogenous. The lower part is subdivided into an ethereal realm, and what is known as the material World of Action, which is of a physical nature, and is governed by the laws of nature; the upper part, known as the spiritual World of Action, is the realm of spiritual activity.

Common to both parts of the World of Action is man; situated between them, he partakes of both. Insofar as he exists in the lower part, man is governed by the physical, chemical, and biological laws of nature; from the standpoint of his consciousness, even when it is totally concerned with physical or base matters, he belongs to the spiritual part of the World of Action. The ideas of the World of Action are for the most part bound up with the physical world, indeed, they are functions of it. This obtains both for the most exalted speculations of a philosopher and the cruder thought processes of the ignorant savage or the child.

Human existence is thus dual in nature, partaking of both matter and spirit. Furthermore, in the World of Action, the spiritual is largely subordinate to the material, to the extent that physical objects and the laws of nature are the basis of reality and determine its nature. The spiritual life almost exclusively derives from and acts upon this substrate.

However, the World of Action is but one in a general system consisting of four fundamental worlds, each of which is a complete cosmos in itself, with its own essences and nature. In the literature of the Kabalah, these worlds, form higher to lower, are called Emanation, Creation, Formation, and Action (in Hebrew, Atzilut, Beriah, Yetzirah, and Assiyah.) The world above our own is thus the World of Formation. The differences between those worlds can be understood if we examine the manifestations in each of them or three traditional dimensions of existence known as "world," "year," and "soul."

In modern language these would be termed space, time, and being. For example, in our world, space is a basic system that is necessary for any object to exist; it is the matrix within which, upon which, and from which all living creatures operate. In the higher worlds, this dimension is manifest in what is known as the "mansions" (Heichalot).

It is not space as we know it, but a framework of existence within which all forms and beings are related. A useful comparison to this concept is that of a self-contained system, known in mathematics as a group or a field, in which each unit member is related in a specific and fixed manner to all the other members and to the totality. Such systems may be inhabited, partially or to capacity, or sparsely to empty.

Time, too, is manifest in a totally different fashion in the higher worlds. In our experience, time operates and is measured by the movement of objects in space. More abstractly, it is perceived as the process of change, the transition from state to state, from form to form; it is an essential feature of our concept of causality, which establishes the limitations of transitions within certain laws. In the higher worlds, the system of time becomes increasingly abstract, and its connection with the measurement or perception of change is diminished. It becomes no more than the essence of change, or the potentiality of change.

In the World of Action, the dimension called "soul" is manifest in the totality of living creatures functioning in the time and space. Although they are essentially part of this world, they are distinguished from it by their faculty of consciousness of self and of other. In the higher worlds, too, souls are self-conscious beings acting within the framework of their respective "mansions" and "years."

The World of Formation is a world of sentience. The beings that populate it are pure, abstract manifestations of what we, in our world, would call emotions or feelings. These beings, or creatures, operate in a similar fashion to the way we do in the World of Action. They are called "angels."

There are millions of angels, and each of them possesses its own unique character. No two are alike. The distinctive personality of a particular angel is a function of two features, which can be termed "content" and "degree." The content is the specific feeling or emotion, of which the angel is a pure manifestation, and the degree is its position on the scale of fundamental causality. An angel may thus be an inclination, or impulse, toward love, fear, pity, and so on, at this or that degree. However, each of these contents is subdivided into an almost infinite number of related feelings (no two loves are the same), and angels thus fall into large groups. Such a group is called a "camp of angels."

Another characteristic feature of angels, one that distinguishes them from humans, is the fact that they are unchanging. Circumstance, time, place, and even mood alter the content and the intensity of most human emotions. However, whereas emotion is ultimately secondary to our existence, it is primary and essential to angels. An angel is by definition the constant, unchanging manifestation of a single emotion or feeling.

It would be quite misleading, however, to regard angels as abstractions, as hypothetical conceptualizations of emotions that have no real existence. Each angel is a complete being that possesses consciousness of itself and awareness of its surroundings. It is able to act and create within the framework of its existence, the World of Formation. A characteristic feature of angels is implicit in their Hebrew name, which means "messenger." In fact, the task of angels is mediation, to maintain two-way communications between our world, the World of Action, and the higher worlds. They serve as emissaries of God in bringing divine plenty down into the world, and of men, in raising up certain consequences of our actions.

Men and angels belong to separate categories of existence. Even if we ignore the human body and look only at our apparently more angelic aspect, the soul, the differences are great. The human soul is a heterogeneous, complex entity composed of distinct elements, whereas an angel is homogeneous, a single essence, and thus ultimately unidimensional. Furthermore, the human being, by virtue of the multiplicity of facets in his personality, with the implicit capacity for internal contradictions and conflicts, and by virtue of his soul, which contains a spark of the divine, possesses the power of discrimination, in particular between good and evil. As a consequence, man had the potential to reach great heights, and also to fall to abysmal depths. Not so the angels, which are always the same. Whether an angel is ephemeral or eternal, it is static and remains fixed in the coordinates of content and degree in which it was created.

Some angels have existed since the beginning of time, and are the channels through which divine plenty flows into the world. There is, however, another kind of angel, those that are constantly being created. This process of the creation of new angels takes place as a consequence of actions and phenomena that are performed and occur in all worlds, but especially in our world, the World of Action.

It Is said that with every mitzvah, every good deed that he performs, a man creates an angel. In order to understand this, it is necessary to envisage each such act, or prayer, as being an operation on two levels.

The first level is behavioral; it is the initiating or bringing about or completing of a transformation—no matter how small—in the physical world. The other level is spiritual and involves the thoughts, feelings, emotions, and mystical meditations that should accompany the performance of the external act. These spiritual actions coalesce and form a discrete spiritual entity, which possesses objective reality, and which, in turn, creates an angel in the World of Formation. Thus, by means of the mitzvot he performs, man extends the realm in which his activity is effective from the lower to the upper worlds. He creates angels, which are, in manner of speaking, his messengers in the higher worlds. Whereas a newly created angel retains its essential bond with its human originator in the World of Action, it acquires reality only in the World of Formation. In this way, the spiritual content of the holy deed, by becoming an angel, rises and initiates changes in the upper worlds, and especially in the World of Formation, the world immediately superior to our own. In fact, the nature of the World of Formation is determined by the relationships between the angels and between them and the worlds above them, and they, in turn, influence these higher worlds too.

The angels who serve as emissaries of God and the upper worlds down to our world are apprehended by men in a wide and sometimes strange variety of forms. The reasons for this is that as the angels derive from a totally foreign world of being, they are invisible to man in their "true" forms, for the human sense organs, and faculties of comprehension, are incapable of grasping them. Some kind of "translation" is necessary before they can be seen. A useful analogy is that of a television transmission. The electromagnetic carrier waves are of a frequency that is totally invisible to the human nervous system, which in fact is incapable even of detecting their existence. However, when these waves are processed by the television receiver, the information and signals they bear are translated and become visible on the screen. There is, of course, no resemblance between the electromagnetic waves and the picture, as there is none between the true form of the angel and what is perceived.

The Kabalah describes such a process as "clothing in garments" or "containing in vessels." The garments and the vessels are remote perceptible manifestations of the unknowable essence. This is the form in which angels appear to men.

Such manifestations generally take place in one of two situations: one is the vision of a man who has attained a high level of holiness, such as a prophet; the other is in an isolated incident of enlightenment or revelation from the higher worlds experienced by a more ordinary person. In either case, the person involved experiences the reality of the angel as it is clothed in garments. Even so, frequently the form of this manifestation is of a degree of existence that is not easily processed by the human mind, and especially by that part that involves verbal communication, and the descriptions offered are occasionally strange and fantastic. Given the cultural limitations of our linguistic skills, it is natural that many such images will be, to some degree or another, anthropomorphic. The visionary images one finds in the prophetic works, such as winged animals or eyed chariots, are secondary human translation of indescribable phenomena. When Ezekiel describes the angel that he saw as possessing the face of an ox, it does not mean that the angel had a face at all, let alone a bovine one, but that one aspect of its inner essence, when translated and projected into our physical reality, is expressed in a form that shows a conceptual likeness to the face of an ox.

All articulated prophetic visions are, in fact, depictions in comprehensible human language of abstract, formless, spiritual realities. There are, notwithstanding, cases in which angels are manifest in "ordinary" form, are clothed in familiar material garments, and appear to be natural phenomena; on such occasions, the viewer will encounter difficulties in deciding whether an apparition or a natural object stands before him, whether the pillar of fire or the man he perceives belongs to this world, with its own system of natural causality, or to another. Furthermore, the angel, that is, the force sent from a higher world, may not only be manifest in the physical world, but may also appear to act according to, and be governed by, the laws of nature, either totally or to a limited degree. In such cases, only prophetic insight can determine whether, and to what extent, higher forces are active.

The fact that a man can create an angel, which is instantaneously transposed to another world, is not, in itself, a supernatural event; it is a part of a day-to-day way of life that can on occasion seem ordinary and commonplace—the life of *mitzvot.* When we perform an action that results in the creation of an angel, we are generally aware of no more than that we are acting on, and within, the physical world. Similarly, the appearance of an angel does not necessarily involve a deviation from the normal laws of physical nature. Man is thus in close contact with the upper worlds, and though the actual route, the nature of the link, is hidden, the fact of the relationship is as axiomatic as the duality of his body and soul, of matter and spirit. Man does not pause to wonder every time he moves from the physical to the spiritual part of the World of Action, and takes for granted the occasional penetration of higher worlds into our world. When we use the word "natural" in its widest possible meaning, that is, comprehending everything that we experience and know, the appearance and creation of angels are not "supernatural" phenomena.

The world immediately above the World of Formation is known as the World of Creation, and also as the World of the Chariot, and the Throne. In an image derived from the vision of Ezekiel, it is the Throne above that stands for "the likeness of the Glory of the Lord." This Glory, which is the aspect of divinity revealed to prophets, belongs to the highest world, the World of Emanation. The World of Creation is its Throne, and our world is its footstool. The World of Creation is the matrix through which passes all the divine plenty that descends to the lower worlds, and all things that are raised up to God. It is a sort of crossroads of all modes of existence. A central element of the Jewish esoteric, mystical tradition, called the "Study of the Chariot," deals with this world. It is the highest level to which the mystic can aspire, the limit beyond which even the holiest of visionaries can apprehend only the vaguest impressions. Of course, not even this world can be comprehended in any more than a fragmentary fashion. Deep study of this world places the spiritually developed person at the point of intersection of all worlds, and gives him knowledge of all modes of existence and of change-past, present, and future-and an awareness of God as prime cause and first mover of all forces acting in every direction.

The World of Creation, like the other worlds, is structured according to the manifestations of the dimensions of space, time, and being. The "mansions" of this world are metaphysical realms of existence in which past, present, and future, cause and effect, are related, and time is a genus of rhythm. This world, too, is populated by beings, called "seraphs." Whereas angels are manifestations of feeling or emotion, the beings of the World of Creation are the pure essence of intellect. The word "intellect" has many connotations in modern English, but here its significance is closer to the older philosophical meaning. Seraphs are the potentiality of the ability to grasp the inner content of phenomena, in both creative and perceptive aspects. Like the angels, they are unchanging and characterized only by content and degree. Seraphs of different levels reflect the relative planes of consciousness and comprehension. Like angels, they serve as messengers between the worlds.

The superiority of the World of Creation over the World of Formation is not merely a feature of the relative positions of intellect and emotion on the scale of fundamental causality. It is also a function of another aspect of "highness": the higher worlds are more transparent to the divine light, which is their vitality and being. As one descends in the system of worlds, there is more and more matter. Another way of stating this is that the beings of the lower worlds have a greater awareness of their independent, progressively separate selves, of their private "I." This consciousness of self obscures the divine light, and dims the true, unchanging "I" that exists within each individual being. Nevertheless, this opacity is a prerequisite for existence of any kind. Each of the worlds can only come into and remain in being by virtue of the concealment of divine light. They can only exist when God conceals himself. Were the divine plenty to be manifest in its fullness, there would be no room for anything else. A world can exist only by virtue of the withdrawal of its creator. However, as one descends to the lower worlds, the concealment becomes overwhelming and the divine plenty scant. In our world, the World of Action, this trend has reached such proportions that the inhabitants may, and frequently do, reach a situation in which not only can they no longer perceive the divine plenty, but they deny that it exists.

Whereas the inhabitants of our world must be equipped with prophetic insight, or vision, or faith in order to be able to discern the divine plenty in its various forms, the higher worlds are much more lucid, and there is little impedance to the flow of light. The World of Creation is the highest of the three lower worlds, and so its creatures, the seraphs, possess a very high degree of awareness of the divine light. Nevertheless, it is a separate world, and the seraphs are characterized by individual, separate selves. They are capable of experiencing the divine light, and they accept its sovereignty in everything, but they know that they are separate from it. Consequently, even the seraphs are consumed by a great yearning to approach God.

The highest of the four worlds, the World of Emanation, is of a totally different nature. It is a mode of existence characterized by absolute clarity, no concealment, and no separate beings. There is no individuation, and no "screens" or filters separate God from that which is not God. In fact, the World of Emanation is not a world in the sense that the other three are: in a certain sense, it is the Godhead itself. The gulf between this world and that which lies below it is immeasurably greater than those that separate the other worlds; it is substantial, and not a matter of degree. It marks the border between the realms of differentiated individual beings—each of which is separated from the others and from the source of all by screens of varying degrees of density—and the Godhead, where there are no screens, and unqualified unity prevails.

Before the created, differentiated world could exist, God had to withdraw something of His divine essence and wisdom. This voluntary absence or concealment is depicted as the archetypal screen. It is the critical point of Creation, "the darkness on the face of the deep," on the one side of which is God, and the other, the template, which is the basis for the coming-into-being of the world.

In addition to the physical and spiritual parts just described, the World of Action contains many other ethereal or spiritual realms, which differ widely from each other in both their content and their spiritual significance. On the one hand, there are the realms of the various manifestations of human wisdom and creativity, such as philosophy, mathematics, poetry, and art, which are all ultimately "neutral" as regards their spiritual orientation. On the other hand, there are realms that possess a distinct spiritual charge, which may be either positive or negative. Furthermore, just as man can relate to various physical and spiritual features of the World of Action and thereby raise himself in the direction of holiness, so can he tie himself to the realms of the unholy, and move and act in them. These are the realms of evil, in the most general sense of the word, and are known by their Hebrew name, *Kelippot* (singular, *Kelippah),* which means husks.

The *Kelippot,* like the worlds of holiness, have their own "mansions," and are arranged in an inverted hierarchy, with the evil becoming more intense and distinct as one descends. They are, in their own way, all related to the World of Action. In fact, it can be said that our world, to the extent that it is neutral in its spiritual orientation, belongs to the realm of the *Kelippot,* more specifically to the one known as *Kelippat* Noga. This is a level of existence that contains all things that are not intrinsically directed either to the holy or the evil. Although it is neutral, when a man sinks into it entirely and does not, or cannot, disentangle himself from it, he fails to fulfill his specific human destiny and is wanting at the core of his being.

The relationships between the realms of the *Kelippot* are to a certain degree similar to those obtaining in the higher worlds. Thus, between each successive level, there are translations and replications of the mode of existence, and the manifestations of each are expressed in the same three dimensions: space, time, and being. The *Kelippot* are inhabited by ethereal beings, a species of angels known as destructive, or subversive angels, or alternatively as devils, demons, or evil spirits. Like the holy angels, they all have their own individual personalities, which are defined in terms of their particular unchanging content and their degree. Corresponding to the angels of love-in-holiness and awe-in-holiness are the destructive angels of love-in-wickedness and awe-in-wickedness. Furthermore, some of these destructive angels are ephemeral; that is, they are created by man's actions, whereas others are eternal, or rather, they came into existence with the world and will continue to exist until evil is finally vanquished. Each evil deed that a man performs brings into being a destructive angel, which, in turn, has its effect in the deeper realms of the *Kelippot.* Nevertheless, there is a substantial difference between the two systems. There is obviously no equivalent to the Kelippot in the World of Emanation. Evil has no independent, ontological existence, and its direct source of nourishment is the World of Action; indirectly, it is sustained from the higher worlds. By performing an evil deed, a man not only creates a destructive angel that will accompany him and be bound to him as part of his ambience, but he actually diverts the divine plenty into the upper realms of evil, whence it is dragged down to the deepest *Kelippot.*

The eternal destructive angels are the messengers that mediate between the various realms of evil, just as the holy angels move up and down in the upper worlds. Destructive angels are manifest in our world by means of "clothing in garments," and they appear in ethereal or material forms that are sometimes as bizarre and strange as those of the holy angels. These destructive angels are the tempters who try to incite man to evil by bringing the idea of wickedness to our realm, of existence; in return, they receive the diverted divine plenty. They also serve as the instruments by which a sinner is punished. Just as the reward received by the righteous man or the saint is an extension of his good deeds, so the retribution for shortcomings is part and parcel of the sin itself. In this life, punishment is no more than to be held in close contact with the evil one has created, in a variety of manifestations and translations-bodily and mental torment, despair and anguish, and failure.

One of the most severe forms of punishment is the "mansion" of the *Kelippot* known as Hell. When a man dies, his soul is separated from his body and relates only to the ethereal beings, which he created and with which he was associated in his lifetime. The soul finds its level. In the case of a great sinner, this will be in the company of the destructive angels he created, who will punish him for bringing them into existence, until the full measure of remorse is exhausted. But even this extreme retribution is not extrinsic, for it is an organic continuation of the actual sins committed.

Though the destructive angels are manifestations and the messengers of evil, they are also part of the totality of existence. Like the entire system of *Kelippot,* to which they belong, they are not optimal, but they do fulfill an essential role in maintaining a certain balance in the cosmos, by deterring men from slipping deeper into evil. Were evil to be banished from the world, they would disappear, for ultimately they are parasites on men and cannot exist without his wickedness. But as long as man uses his power of choice to do evil, they feed off, incite, and punish him. In this sense, the existence of destructive angels is conditional, rather like a police force, which is necessary only as long as there is crime.

The fact remains, however, that far from disappearing, the destructive angels are growing stronger and more powerful, as evil waxes in the world. Their ontological status is no longer clear, and far from being mere instruments of deterrence within the total system of existence, they appear to be independent beings acting in their own terms of reference, subjects of a sovereign realm of evil.

The significance of man's role in Creation is thus immense. When the day comes that we free ourselves from the overwhelming temptations to sin, the entire system of evil will fall back into its proper dimensions. Those aspects of it that came into being as a consequence of man's deeds—the ephemeral destructive angels—will disappear, while the eternal structural elements, which now serve as deterrents, will assume a new, entirely different role. That which now appears to be evil will be reintegrated into holiness.

The Strife of the Spirit (Northvale, N.J.: Jason Aronson, 1988), 46-53
Reprinted with permission of the author

The Prayerbook

by **Rabbi Yanki Tauber**

In the years before he went public with his teachings and founded the Chassidic movement, Rabbi Israel Baal Shem Tov would often wander about the countryside where the Jews of Eastern Europe lived in isolated hamlets or managed lonely wayside inns. Rabbi Israel would mingle with these Jews, drawing inspiration from their simple faith and dispensing words of encouragement in turn.

One day, the Baal Shem Tov arrived at a small crossroads inn, many miles distant from the nearest Jewish community. He was warmly invited in, and served a refreshment by the innkeeper's family. "Where is your father?" he asked the children. "He's praying," they replied, and Rabbi Israel settled down to wait for his host.

An hour passed, then two. It was late afternoon by the time the innkeeper emerged from his room. After greeting his guest, he apologized for his long absence. "I am an ignorant Jew," he explained shamefacedly. "I can barely pronounce the words from the prayerbook, and deciphering its instructions, written in vowel-less Hebrew, is beyond me. So I have no choice but to recite the entire prayerbook, from cover to cover, every day.

"Perhaps I can be of assistance to you," said Rabbi Israel. For the next hour, he sat with the innkeeper, patiently instructing him on the proper use of the prayerbook. On small slips of paper, Rabbi Israel wrote out, in simple Yiddish, "morning prayers," "special addition for Mondays and Thursdays," "grace after meals," "afternoon prayers," "evening prayers," "for Shabbat," "for Rosh Chodesh," "for Rosh Hashanah," and so on, and inserted them to mark the proper place in the innkeeper's prayerbook. "Thank you so much," said the innkeeper, when Rabbi Israel took leave to resume his journey. "Now I can begin to pray like a proper Jew."

But the innkeeper's joy was short-lived. Later that day, the prayerbook inexplicably fell from its shelf, and every last slip of paper inserted by the Baal Shem Tov fluttered from its pages. "Woe is me!" cried the innkeeper. "Who knows how many months will pass until a learned Jew will again come this way?" Determined not to let this opportunity to begin praying properly escape him, he grabbed the prayerbook and the notes and ran off in the direction that his guest had gone.

After several miles of brisk walking, he finally sighted the Baal Shem Tov far ahead. From the distance he saw Rabbi Israel reach a river. "How will he cross?" wondered the innkeeper, "This time of year, the water is too deep and swift to ford." He was about to shout a warning, when he saw Rabbi Israel spread his handkerchief on the water, step onto it as if it were the sturdiest of rafts, glide smoothly across, and disappear into the woods on the opposite bank.

In a flash, the innkeeper was at the water's edge. Spreading his handkerchief on the water, he stepped onto it and glided across, and ran down the path Rabbi Israel had taken.

"Wait, Rabbi!" he called. "Wait! You cannot go until you mark my prayerbook again! All your notes have fallen out!"

Hearing the man calling out to him, Rabbi Israel stopped and turned, to see his recent host running toward him, clutching his prayerbook in one hand and the slips of paper in the other. "How did you get here?" asked Rabbi Israel in amazement. "How did you cross the river?"

"With my handkerchief, same as you," replied the simple Jew. "By the way, that's some trick you've got there. I never would've thought it could be done that way."

"I think," said the Baal Shem Tov slowly, "that G-d is extremely satisfied with your prayers as they are. Perhaps you should continue to pray just the way you have up until now."

Reprinted with permission of The Judaism Website, Chabad.org

Lesson 4

Taking a Bite Out of Life

Kosher Food Facts

Introduction

This week you'll learn about food fit for a feast —a kosher feast, that is. How is roasted cow udder like a tofu-cheese burger? Who invented gefilte fish? Why are fried locusts an exclusively Middle-Eastern treat? Finally, which is more likely to be served one day at a bar mitzvah: green eggs and ham or roasted giraffe?

Why We Eat

Figure 4.1

Average Amount of Time Spent on Common Pursuits Over a Lifetime

Pursuit	Men	Women
Cooking	1½ years	3 years
Eating	4 years	4 years
Exercising	2 years	1 year
"Getting ready" (i.e., grooming and dressing)	6 months	2 years
Household chores	1½ years	2½ years
Restroom time	3 years	6 months
Shopping	1 year	2 years
Sleeping	25 years	27 years
Watching TV	10 years	13 years
Work	10½ years	8½ years

Text 1

מאן דבעי לנהמא על פום חרבא ייכול.
זהר ג, קפח,ב

ne who desires bread should eat it with the blade of a sword.

Zohar 3:188b

Text 2

אָדָם לְעָמָל יוּלָּד.
איוב ה,ז

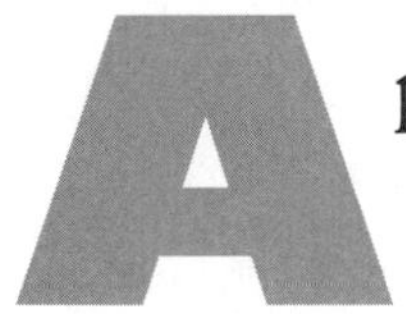

person is born in order to toil.

Job 5:7

Kosher in Outer Space

Colonel Ilan Ramon was the first person to eat kosher meals in space. Although he was not particularly religious, Ramon felt that as Israel's first astronaut, "I'm kind of a representative of all the Jewish community."

You Are What You Eat
Two Signs and the Two-Faced Swine

Text 3a

כֹּל מַפְרֶסֶת פַּרְסָה . . . מַעֲלַת גֵּרָה בַּבְּהֵמָה, אֹתָהּ תֹּאכֵלוּ.

ויקרא יא,ג

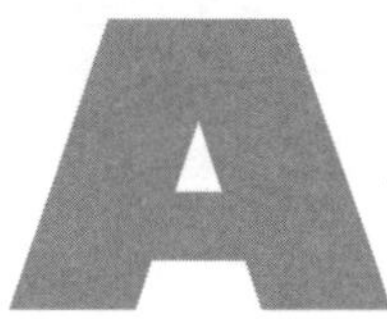

ny animal that has a cloven hoof . . . and which brings up its cud, you may eat.

Leviticus 11:3

Figure 4.2

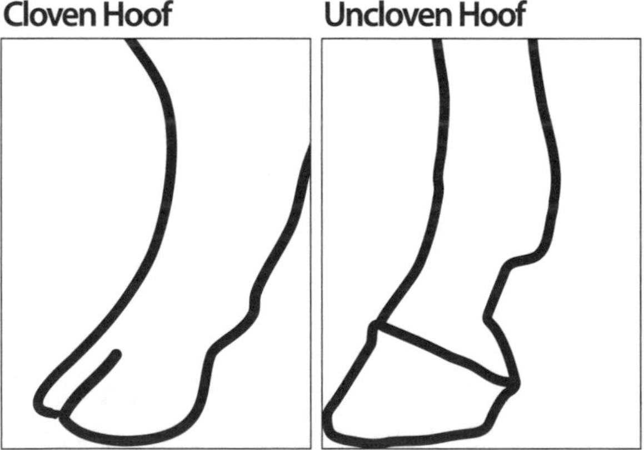

Text 3b

זאת הַבְּהֵמָה אֲשֶׁר תֹּאכֵלוּ: שׁוֹר, שֵׂה כְשָׂבִים, וְשֵׂה עִזִּים. אַיָּל, וּצְבִי, וְיַחְמוּר, וְאַקּוֹ, וְדִישֹׁן, וּתְאוֹ, וָזָמֶר.
דברים יד,ד-ה

These are the animal species that you may eat: ox, goat, and sheep. Gazelle, deer, antelope, ibex, chamois, bison, and giraffe.

Deuteronomy 14:4–5

How About Some Giraffe Stew?

If giraffes are kosher, why are they absent from the kosher supermarket refrigerator? It's commonly believed that giraffes cannot be ritually slaughtered because their necks are so long that it's impossible to know where the knife of the *shochet* (ritual slaughterer) should land. In fact, the opposite is true. The proper location for ritual slaughter on the giraffe's neck is precisely defined by Jewish law and is close to six feet in length. So, it should be *easier* to slaughter a giraffe than any other animal!

Then why don't we eat them? Primarily because it is impractical to commercially raise giraffe for food. They are prohibitively expensive and not particularly tasty. In addition, they are strong and difficult to restrain. Even fierce predators are wary of giraffes—one kick from a giraffe can crush a lion's skull!

Text 4

וְאֶת הַחֲזִיר, כִּי מַפְרִיס פַּרְסָה הוּא וְלֹא גֵרָה, טָמֵא הוּא לָכֶם, מִבְּשָׂרָם לֹא תֹאכֵלוּ.

שם, יד,ח

And the pig, which has a split hoof but does not chew its cud, is unclean to you. You shall not eat their flesh.

Ibid., 14:8

Text 5

Rabbi Shlomo Yitschaki (1040–1105). Better known by the acronym Rashi. Rabbi and famed author of comprehensive commentaries on the Talmud and Bible. Born in Troyes, France, Rashi studied in the famed *yeshivot* of Mainz and Worms. His commentaries, which focus on the simple understanding of the text, are considered the most fundamental of all the commentaries that preceded and followed. Since their initial printings, the commentaries have appeared in virtually every edition of the Talmud and Bible. Many of the famed authors of the *Tosafot* are among Rashi's descendants.

החזיר הזה כשהוא שוכב פושט טלפיו, לומר, "ראו שאני טהור!"

רש"י, בראשית כו,לד

When the pig lies down, it extends its hooves, as if to say, "See, I am kosher!"

Rashi, Genesis 26:34

Kosher = Healthy?

Question for Discussion

Is a kosher diet synonymous with a healthful diet?

Text 6

המשפטים הן המצות שטעמן גלוי וטובת עשייתן בעולם הזה ידועה, כגון איסור גזל, ושפיכות דמים, וכיבוד אב ואם.
והחוקים הן המצות שאין טעמן ידוע. אמרו חכמים, "חוקים חקתי לך ואין לך רשות להרהר בהן" (יומא סז,א), ויצרו של אדם נוקפו בהן, ואומות העולם משיבין עליהן, כגון איסור בשר חזיר ובשר בחלב.
משנה תורה, הלכות מעילה ח,ח

Mishpatim are *mitzvot* whose justifications are revealed, and the practical benefits of their observance are known: for example, the prohibitions against robbery and bloodshed, and the commandment to honor one's father and mother.

Chukim are *mitzvot* whose reasons are not known, as our sages said: "[God says,] 'I order you to observe My *chukim*, and you have no license to question them'" (Talmud, Yoma 67a). A person naturally chafes against their observance, and the nations of the world challenge them. Examples [of *chukim* include] the prohibitions regarding the flesh of a pig, and regarding milk and meat.

Maimonides, *Mishneh Torah*, Laws of Misappropriation of Sacred Property 8:8

Rabbi Moshe ben Maimon (1135–1204). Better known as Maimonides or by the acronym Rambam; born in Cordoba, Spain. After the conquest of Cordoba by the Almohads, he fled Spain and eventually settled in Cairo, Egypt. There, he became the leader of the Jewish community and served as court physician to the vizier of Egypt. His rulings on Jewish law are considered integral to the formation of halachic consensus. He is most noted for authoring the *Mishneh Torah*, an encyclopedic arrangement of Jewish law, and for his philosophical work, *Guide for the Perplexed.*

Text 7

Rabbi Shlomo Ephraim ben Aharon of Luntshits (1550–1619). Rabbi and renowned preacher of Luntshits. In his youth, Ephraim studied in the yeshivah of the Maharshal. He gained a reputation as a distinguished preacher and traveled widely to deliver his fiery sermons, which were collected and published. He is mostly known today for his work *Keli Yakar*, his commentary on the Pentateuch, which was subsequently printed in many editions of the Bible. In 1604, he arrived in Prague where he served as president of the rabbinical court and head of the yeshivah. He composed three penitential poems in response to the devastation wrought by the invasion of Prague in 1611 by the army of the bishop of Passau.

כתבו רבים מן המפרשים ענין איסורי המאכלות, שיש שחשבו שהמה בריאות הגופות . . . ואינו כן, שהרי כל האומות אוכלי בשר השקץ והעכבר וכל הטמאים, וכולם חזקים אף בריאים אין כושל בהם ואוכליהם לא חלי ולא מרגיש. אלא ודאי שכל אלו אין הכוונה בהם כי אם אל רפואות הנשמה.

כלי יקר, ויקרא יא,א

Many of the commentators explain that there are physical health benefits to be gained from abstaining from non-kosher foods. . . . This is not so, for the nations eat the flesh of mice and [those creatures that the Torah describes as] abominable and unclean. And they all are healthy and strong; none are adversely affected by the foods. It is therefore certain that all these laws are intended only to maintain the health of the soul.

Rabbi Shlomo Ephraim Luntshits, *Keli Yakar*, Leviticus 11:1

Text 8

Christians, Muslims, Jews and Atheists alike are helping fuel the robust market for kosher foods, according to a new report by market research firm Mintel. In a consumer survey of adults who purchase kosher food, Mintel found that the number one reason people buy kosher is for food quality (62%).

The second most common reason people say they purchase kosher food is "general healthfulness" (51%) and the third is food safety (34%). This contrasts sharply to the just 14% of respondents who say they purchase kosher food because they follow kosher religious rules. Another 10% buy kosher because they follow some other religious rules with eating restrictions similar to kosher.

Mintel Press Release, February 2009

How the OU Began

The first national company to be certified kosher by an established rabbinical institution was H. J. Heinz, in 1923, for their vegetarian version of canned pork-and-beans. They were, however, concerned about having the word "kosher" on their label, for fear that it would alienate their non-Jewish customers. After much negotiation, the Orthodox Union agreed to drop the word "kosher" from the original design proposal, and instead came up with the "circle U" logo that is still in use.

Text 9

כל מה שאסרתו התורה עלינו מן המאכלים, מזונם מגונה. ואין בכל מה שנאסר עלינו מה שיסופק שאין היזק בו רק החזיר והחלב.

מורה נבוכים ג,מח

All the foods that are forbidden by the Torah are nutritionally unwholesome. There is none among the forbidden [foods] whose injurious character is in doubt besides pork and fats.

Maimonides, *Guide for the Perplexed* 3:48

Kosher Film?

In the 1980s, rabbis noticed an OU symbol on Fuji film! When Fuji headquarters in Japan was contacted, they apologized for using the trademark symbol. It turned out that they had been advised that products with kosher symbols "sell better in the United States," so the company figured it would be worth giving it a try.

Kosher Pig!

Rabbi Yeshayah HaLevi Horowitz (1565–1630). Preeminent kabbalistic authority, also known as the "Shelah," the acronym of the title of his work, *Shenei Luchot Haberit*. Born in Prague, he studied under Rabbi Meir of Lublin and Rabbi Yehoshua Falk. He served as rabbi in several prominent Jewish communities, including Frankfurt am Main and his native Prague. After the passing of his wife in 1620, he moved to Israel. In Tiberias, he finished the *Shenei Luchot Haberit*, an encyclopedic compilation of kabbalistic ideas. He is buried in Tiberias, next to Maimonides.

Text 10

עתיד חזיר ליטהר.

שני לוחות הברית, פרשת חיי שרה

In the future, the pig will become kosher.

Rabbi Yeshayah HaLevi Horowitz, *Shenei Luchot Haberit, Parashat Chayei Sarah*

Question for Discussion

In your estimation, does eating kosher imitations of non-kosher foods violate the spirit of Judaism?

Text 11

אמרה ליה ילתא לרב נחמן, "מכדי כל דאסר לן רחמנא שרא לן כוותיה.
אסר לן דמא, שרא לן כבדא . . .
חלב בהמה, חלב חיה; חזיר, מוחא דשיבוטא . . .
בעינן למיכל בשרא בחלבא".
אמר להו רב נחמן לטבחי, "זויקו לה כחלי".
תלמוד בבלי, חולין קט,ב

Yalta said to [her husband] Rabbi Nachman: "It has been established that for every food that God forbade us to eat, He has permitted another food that has a similar taste.

"He forbade blood, but He permitted liver. . . .

"[He forbade certain] fats of domesticated animals, [but He permitted those same] fats of undomesticated animals.

"[He forbade] swine, [but He permitted] the brain of the *shibuta* fish. . . .

"Now I would like to eat [something that tastes like] milk and meat!"

Rabbi Nachman instructed his chefs, "Prepare for her an udder on a spit."

Talmud, Chulin 109b

Question for Discussion

Why would God intentionally create a kosher substitute to match the taste of every non-kosher food?

What's on the Menu?

Glatt Kosher

Learning Activity 1

A "glatt kosher" product is:

a. a food that is produced under constant rabbinical supervision.

b. a food that is produced by an Orthodox Jewish company.

c. a food that meets a stricter set of kosher rules.

d. both kosher and organic.

e. none of the above.

Text 12a

וְאַנְשֵׁי קֹדֶשׁ תִּהְיוּן לִי, וּבָשָׂר בַּשָּׂדֶה טְרֵפָה לֹא תֹאכֵלוּ.
שמות כב,ל

ou shall be holy people unto Me; an animal that was mortally wounded in the field you shall not eat.

Exodus 22:30

Text 12b

כל מקום שאסרו סרוכת הריאה, אין הפרש בין שתהא הסרכא דקה כחוט השערה בין שתהא עבה וחזקה ורחבה כגודל, ולא כאותם שממעכים ביד ואם נתמעכה תולין להקל.
שולחן ערוך, יורה דעה לט,י

In all instances where an animal is rendered non-kosher due to an adhesion on the lung, it does not matter whether the adhesion is fragile and slight like a hair, or thick, sturdy, and wide like a thumb. [While some] massage the adhesion with their hands and permit the animal for consumption if it can be gently removed, [this is not proper].

Rabbi Yosef Caro, Shulchan Aruch, *Yoreh De'ah*, 39:10

Rabbi Yosef Caro (1488–1575). Born in Spain, fled the country with his family during the expulsion in 1492, and eventually settled in Safed, Israel. Also known as "the Beit Yosef," after the title of his commentary on the *Arba'ah Turim*, and Maran ("our master") for his status as a preeminent authority on Jewish law. Author of 10 works on Jewish law and the Torah, including the *Beit Yosef*, *Kesef Mishneh*, and a mystical work, *Magid Meisharim*. Rabbi Caro's magnum opus, the *Shulchan Aruch* (Code of Jewish Law), has been universally accepted as the basis for modern Jewish law.

Text 12c

ויש מתירין למשמש בסרכות ולמעך בהם, ואומרים שסרכא אם ימעך אדם בה כל היום לא תנתק ולכן כל מקום שיתמעך תולין להקל, ואומרים שאינו סרכא אלא ריר בעלמא. ואף על פי שהוא קולא גדולה, כבר נהגו כל בני מדינות אלו, ואין למחות בידם מאחר שיש להם על מה שיסמוכו.
רמ״א שם, לט,יג

There are those who permit the massaging and rubbing of the adhesions, for they maintain that a real adhesion [which would render an animal *tereifah*] would not dislodge even if massaged all day. Therefore, they are lenient with regard to any adhesion that can be rubbed off, saying that it is only a *rir* [a lower class of adhesion]. Even though this is a great leniency, those who do so should not be reprimanded, for this is

Rabbi Moshe Isserles (1525–1572). Known by the acronym *Rema*; renowned Polish authority on Jewish law. He is considered the definitive authority on Jewish Law among Ashkenazic Jewry. Author of the *Mapah*, halachic glosses on the Shulchan Aruch, and *Darchei Moshe*, a commentary on the halachic compendium *Arba'ah Turim*. As a youth, he studied in Lublin under Rabbi Shalom Shachna, who became his father-in-law. He returned to Cracow, where he was appointed rabbi. He is buried in the old Jewish cemetery in Cracow.

the common practice in our entire region, and there is basis for their practice.

Rabbi Moshe Isserles, ibid., 39:13

Kosher Salt

Text 13

וָאֹמַר לִבְנֵי יִשְׂרָאֵל, "דַּם כָּל בָּשָׂר לֹא תֹאכֵלוּ".
ויקרא יז,יד

nd I say to the children of Israel, "You shall not eat the blood of any flesh."

Leviticus 17:14

Text 14

לא ימלח במלח דקה כקמח, ולא במלח גסה ביותר שנופלת מעל הבשר.
שולחן ערוך, יורה דעה סט,ג

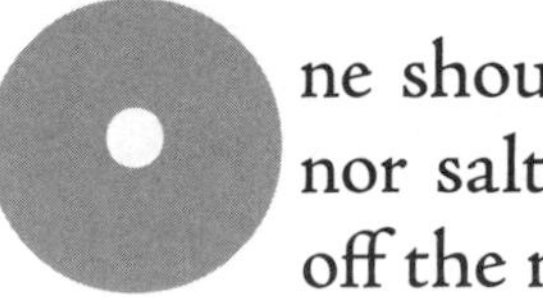

ne should not use salt that is fine like flour, nor salt that is exceedingly coarse that rolls off the meat.

Rabbi Yosef Caro, Shulchan Aruch, *Yoreh De'ah* 69:3

Birds

Text 15

למה נקרא שמה חסידה? שעושה חסידות עם חברותיה.
תלמוד בבלי, חולין סג,א

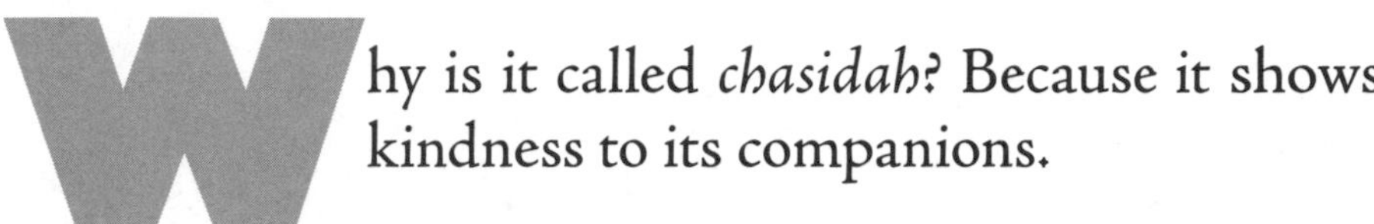

Why is it called *chasidah*? Because it shows kindness to its companions.

Talmud, Chulin 63a

Insects

Text 16

כֹּל שֶׁרֶץ הָעוֹף הַהֹלֵךְ עַל אַרְבַּע שֶׁקֶץ הוּא לָכֶם. אַךְ אֶת זֶה תֹּאכְלוּ מִכֹּל שֶׁרֶץ הָעוֹף הַהֹלֵךְ עַל אַרְבַּע, אֲשֶׁר לוֹ כְרָעַיִם מִמַּעַל לְרַגְלָיו לְנַתֵּר בָּהֵן עַל הָאָרֶץ. אֶת אֵלֶּה מֵהֶם תֹּאכֵלוּ: אֶת הָאַרְבֶּה לְמִינוֹ, וְאֶת הַסָּלְעָם לְמִינֵהוּ . . .
ויקרא יא,כ-כב

Any flying insect that walks on four is an abomination for you. Among all the flying insects that walk on four, you may eat [only] one that has jointed [leg-like] extensions above its [regular] legs with which it hops on the ground. From this [locust] category, you may eat the following: the red locust after its species, the yellow locust after its species. . . .

Leviticus 11:20–22

Fish

Text 17

אֶת זֶה תֹּאכְלוּ מִכֹּל אֲשֶׁר בַּמָּיִם: כֹּל אֲשֶׁר לוֹ סְנַפִּיר וְקַשְׂקֶשֶׂת בַּמַּיִם בַּיַּמִּים וּבַנְּחָלִים.
ויקרא יא,ט

Among all [the creatures] that are in the water, you may eat these: any that has fins and scales, whether [it lives] in the waters, in the seas, or in the rivers.

Leviticus 11:9

Meat and Milk

Text 18

לֹא תְבַשֵּׁל גְּדִי בַּחֲלֵב אִמּוֹ.
שמות כג,יט

You shall not cook a kid in its mother's milk.

Exodus 23:19

Text 19a

מצות לא תעשה שלש מאות וששים וחמש, סימן להם מנין ימי שנת החמה.
הקדמה למשנה תורה

The number of days in a solar year serves as a mnemonic for the 365 negative commandments (prohibitions).

Maimonides, Introduction to *Mishneh Torah*

Text 19b

הלאו של "לא תבשל גדי בחלב אמו" הוא כנגד חג השבועות . . . וזהו טעם למנהג שאנו אוכלים בחג השבועות מאכלי חלב . . . ושוהין קצת ואחר כך אנו אוכלין בשר, כדי שיהיה ניכר קיום המצוה לא תעשה של איסור בשר בחלב.
שיח שרפי קודש א, ע' 237-238

The prohibition against consuming meat and milk corresponds to the holiday of Shavuot. . . .This is one reason for our custom to eat dairy foods on Shavuot. . . . We then wait a bit and eat meat to demonstrate our observance of the prohibition against consuming meat and dairy together.

Rabbi Yitschak Meir Alter, cited in *Si'ach Sarfei Kodesh*, 1:237–238

Rabbi Yitschak Meir Alter (1789–1866). Founder of the chasidic dynasty of Gur. A disciple of Rabbi Menachem Mendel of Kotsk, Yitschak Meir was acknowledged as his successor by the majority of the chasidim of Kotsk. His work, the *Chidushei HaRim*, consists of commentary and expositions on the Talmud and Shulchan Aruch. During the Polish uprising of 1830, he was suspected of sympathizing with the Polish loyalists. To avoid detection, he changed his name from Rothenberg to Alter. In his private life he experienced considerable suffering, losing his 13 children during his lifetime. He followed the Kotsk approach of rigorously seeking unadulterated truth and continuously striving for self-perfection.

Text 19c

רֵאשִׁית בִּכּוּרֵי אַדְמָתְךָ תָּבִיא בֵּית ה׳ אֱלֹקֶיךָ, לֹא תְבַשֵּׁל גְּדִי בַּחֲלֵב אִמּוֹ.
שמות כג,יט

The choicest of the first fruits of your land you shall bring to the house of God, your God. You shall not cook a kid in its mother's milk.

Exodus 23:19

How to Eat
Proper Intentions

Text 20a

שהיה כח זה של עץ החיים ועץ הדעת טוב ורע בכל עצי הגן.
פרי צדיק, פרשת בראשית ח

All the trees in the garden possessed the potential of both the Tree of Life and the Tree of Knowledge of Good and Evil.

Rabbi Tsadok Hakohen Rabinowitz, *Peri Tsadik, Parashat Bereishit* 8

Rabbi Tsadok Hakohen Rabinowitz of Lublin (1823-1900). Chasidic rebbe and prolific author of works on Chasidism. Born into a Lithuanian rabbinic family, he became a follower of Rabbi Mordechai Yosef Leiner of Izhbitsa as a young man. After the passing of his colleague Rabbi Leibel Eiger, he became rebbe in Lublin. He authored many works on Jewish law, Chasidism, Kabbalah, and ethics, as well as scholarly essays on astronomy, geometry, and algebra. He is buried in Lublin.

Text 20b

ואם היה טועם מעץ החיים, היינו שלא בהנאת הגוף, אז היה מרגיש בכל אכילתו מכל העץ שהיה אוכל קדושת עץ החיים, והיינו אכילה בקדושה . . . אבל כיון שאכל מעץ הדעת, היינו שהרגיש הנאת הגוף באכילה, על ידי זה נעשה ערבוב וכל אכילות שאכל הרגיש מעץ הדעת טוב ורע, הנאת הגוף.
פרי צדיק, שם

Had Adam eaten from "the Tree of Life"—that is, had he eaten properly, and not merely to indulge his body—he would have experienced the holiness of the Tree of Life in his eating. . . . But because he ate from the Tree of Knowledge, that is, with the awareness of his sensory pleasure, all subsequent eating was tainted with the desire for bodily gratification.

Rabbi Tsadok Hakohen Rabinowitz, ibid.

Text 21

Rabbi Shlomo Yosef Zevin (1890–1978). Born in Kazimirov, Belarus; considered one of the eminent rabbis of the 20th century. A student of both the Lithuanian and chasidic traditions, he was ordained by numerous prominent rabbis, including Rabbi Yosef Rosen of Rogatchov and Rabbi Yechiel Michel Epstein, author of *Aruch Hashulchan*. His activities to aid Soviet Jewry led to a correspondence with other dissidents, especially the previous Lubavitcher Rebbe, Rabbi Yosef Yitschak Schneersohn. In 1934, he immigrated to Israel, where he resumed his life of scholarship. He was the chief editor of the *Talmudic Encyclopedia*.

"ואנשי קודש תהיון לי", ואמר הרבי מקוצק: "כך אמר ה': 'מלאכים ושרפים וחיות הקודש יש לי די מבלעדיכם, איני זקוק שתהיו לי מלאכים, אלא "ואנשי קודש תהיון לי", שתהיו בני אדם ותחיו כבני אדם, וכבני אדם תהיו לי קדושים ואנשי קודש'".

לתורה ולמועדים, שמות כה,ב

"You shall be holy people unto Me." The Rebbe of Kotsk said, "This is what God is saying: I have enough angels without you, I have no need for you to be angelic. Instead, 'you shall be holy *people* unto Me.' Be human, live as humans do—but be holy humans, a holy people."

Rabbi Shlomo Yosef Zevin, *LeTorah Ulemo'adim*, Exodus 25:2

Kosher Dining at 1600 Pennsylvania Avenue

In December 2005, the White House kitchen was made kosher for the first time in history for President George W. Bush's annual Chanukah party. Since then, the White House kitchen has been koshered annually in honor of the traditional Chanukah reception.

Blessing

Text 22

כִּי לֹא עַל הַלֶּחֶם לְבַדּוֹ יִחְיֶה הָאָדָם כִּי עַל כָּל מוֹצָא פִּי ה׳ יִחְיֶה הָאָדָם.
דברים ח,ג

For not by bread alone does man live, but by all that emanates from God's mouth.

Deuteronomy 8:3

Text 23

אסור לו לאדם שיהנה מן העולם הזה בלא ברכה . . . כל הנהנה מן העולם הזה בלא ברכה, כאילו נהנה מקדשי שמים, וכתיב (תהלים כד,א), ״לה׳ הארץ ומלואה״.
תלמוד בבלי, ברכות לה,א

It is forbidden to enjoy anything of this world without reciting a blessing. . . . To enjoy anything of this world without a blessing is like making personal use of things consecrated to heaven, because it says, "The earth and all that is in it belongs to God" (Psalms 24:1).

Talmud, Berachot 35a

Blessings Recited Before Eating Food

All food blessings begin with the same words:

Blessed are You, Lord our God, King of the Universe . . .

בָּרוּךְ אַתָּה ה׳ אֱלֹקֵינוּ מֶלֶךְ הָעוֹלָם . . .

The concluding words depend on the food you are eating:

For fruit of a tree	"... Who creates the fruit of the tree."	. . . בּוֹרֵא פְּרִי הָעֵץ
For a vegetable or fruit of a plant	"... Who creates the fruit of the earth."	. . . בּוֹרֵא פְּרִי הָאֲדָמָה
For food made from wheat, barley, oat, spelt, or rye flour (besides bread)	"... Who creates various kinds of foods."	. . . בּוֹרֵא מִינֵי מְזוֹנוֹת
For bread or matzah	" ... Who brings forth bread from the earth."	. . . הַמּוֹצִיא לֶחֶם מִן הָאָרֶץ
For wine or grape juice	"... Who creates the fruit of the vine."	. . . בּוֹרֵא פְּרִי הַגָּפֶן
For everything else, e.g., dairy, meat, beverages	"... by Whose word all things came to be."	. . . שֶׁהַכֹּל נִהְיָה בִּדְבָרוֹ

Note: If you've said the blessing over bread, all other foods and drinks (other than wine) in that meal are included. There are also blessings recited when we finish eating to thank God for the food we ate. Refer to a prayer book for the texts of those blessings.

Key Points

1. Eating properly is a struggle. The Jew struggles with eating only those foods allowed by the laws of *kashrut*.

2. When we eat an animal, we ingest all of its properties, including its nature and characteristics. Kosher animals do not possess certain negative traits. For example, they are not carnivorous.

3. For an animal to be kosher, it must have cloven hoofs and chew the cud. For a fish to be kosher, it needs to have fins and scales. There are no signs to identify which birds are kosher, but there is a tradition transmitted from teacher to student regard-ingt regarding regarding the *kashrut* of certain birds.

4. The pig is the quintessential non-kosher animal because it hides its lack of holiness behind a false façade and pretends to be kosher.

5. Although there may be physical health benefits to eating kosher food, the reason for the laws of *kashrut* is to maintain the health of the soul of a Jew.

6. The challenge of eating with holy consciousness is rooted in Adam and Eve's eating from the Tree of Knowledge in the Garden of Eden.

7. Saying a blessing before eating helps us to eat with mindfulness. The blessing reminds us that everything was created by God and that we were created to fulfill His will.

Additional Readings

A Set of Dishes

by **Dr. Velvl Greene**

Even before we met Rabbi Moshe Feller in 1962 we would have been considered active and even committed Jews. Most of our friends were Jewish, our families were Jewish, our interests included Jewish "things," and our outlook was certainly Jewish. We read books published by the JPS, we listened to Jewish records, we treasured the Chagall prints in our home, and were dues-paying members of a Conservative synagogue. Gail was a leading soprano in the synagogue choir and I was one of the very few members who attended on most Friday nights, regardless of whose bar mitzvah was being celebrated that weekend. We were probably Zionists, too. We regularly contributed to the UJA, attended our city's Farband picnics, and were officers on the board of Herzl Camp.

Before we met Rabbi Feller, however, I don't remember doing anything deliberately, or for that matter, abstaining from anything deliberately, because and only because it was a Torah Commandment. Such thoughts never really entered my mind. One went to synagogue and lit candles and ate gefilte fish and wore a *tallit* (prayer shawl) because it was a traditional thing to do, and a pleasant tradition at that. Not to do so would be making a statement of denial, or of disinterest, or of apathy. I didn't care to deny or to be disinterested. It wasn't part of my self-image. On the other hand, we didn't keep kosher or refrain from driving on Shabbat, or any of those other things. They were simply not relevant. They played no role in my value system. Note that we were not consciously protesting or transgressing, as one hears about the early Jewish socialists or freethinkers having done. Those would be statements that we didn't care to make. We were, quite simply, "good American Jews" who didn't want to make waves. Of course, we knew that some Jews avoided non-kosher food and didn't drive on Shabbat. (There were remarkably few of them in our town, then.) And those were *their* traditions and *their* choices. We didn't think they were wrong—only slightly behind on the social evolution scale.

Looking back at those simpler days, I think that our lives reflected the characteristic paradox of the modern secular Jew: interested in Jewish things but basically ignorant; active in Jewish circles but limited in choice; committed to community, family, profession and the "Jewish People" but quite unaware of the foundation that informs this commitment. And above all, quite devoid of the learning and experience which permit discrimination between significance and triviality, reality and fraud. There must have been thousands like me. There still are. You see them arriving in Israel by the busload in "young leadership groups" or "fact finding missions" or "synagogue tours". They are too busy raising funds to spend much time thinking; they are too involved with the present to research the past; they are too committed to the global picture to worry about the Jewish survival of their own children, or even themselves.

Actually, if we hadn't been in this kind of pattern ourselves, we probably wouldn't have met Rabbi Feller. He sought me out because I was a potentially rising star of the Jewish community. He was trying to organize his first banquet and wanted my name as well as others like me on his sponsors' committee.

The story of our first meeting has been told often enough (it was even mentioned in *Time* magazine) to obviate the need for retelling. On the surface it looked like a comedy. A strange, bearded, black-hatted young man remembers, just before sunset, that he has not yet said his afternoon prayers. Disregarding the fact that he is in my office, that he had asked for the appointment, that he is requesting a favor—he stands up, walks to the wall, ties a black cord around his waist and proceeds to mumble and shake. I will never forget my bewilderment and embarrassment. I didn't know what he was doing or why. I didn't know Jews prayed outside a synagogue. I didn't know they prayed in the afternoon. I didn't know they prayed on weekdays. And I didn't know how anyone could pray without someone announcing the page!

There were a lot of things I didn't know, then. But I did develop a definite interest and a special affection for this young man who was so pleasant and so different. He had a completely different set of rules to guide him—at once so radical and so archaic. He not only marched to the beat of a different drum—he seemed to enjoy the music more than we did ours. Above all, he was committed and consistent. I related to that. It is a beautiful trait in a world of laissez-faire religion and situation ethics.

In a short time we became friends—his family and ours. We discussed, we debated, we visited, we socialized. Gail and I were impressed with their sincerity and genuine warmth, but we still thought of them as anachronisms—as remnants of a past, as out of tune with the realities and needs of the modern American world. We didn't change our lifestyle because of them. Instead we kept waiting for them to change theirs. After all, nearly everyone else who had started out with a beard and hat ultimately did.

If he tried to influence us, during those early months, it must have been a very subtle effort. There was certainly no overt pressure or demand. Of course, they wouldn't eat at our house. But that wasn't a signal that something was wrong. They were so far out that their dietary idiosyncrasies were the least things one noticed. We started studying together, but our progress was infinitesimal. I asked too many questions, challenged too many axioms. I was definitely not a compliant student.

It could have gone on like this for a long time, if it weren't for our trip to Warsaw.

In the summer of 1963 I was invited to participate as a member of the American delegation in an international conference on space research in Poland. My balloon-borne samplers had discovered viable microorganisms in the stratosphere at a time when the field of exobiology was too full of speculation and embarrassingly lacking in real biological data. Whatever the real reasons for the invitation, it was an opportunity to be grabbed. In 1963, visits to Warsaw and Eastern Europe were very rare. Few of my professional colleagues had been to Warsaw since the war. None of my Jewish friends, certainly.

Gail and I left the three children with my parents in Canada and we flew to Warsaw. It was a dismal visit. In those years the city had not yet recovered from the destruction of World War Two. Physical destruction was evident in the piles of rubble that covered huge sections of the city. The emotional destruction was worse. The indigenous Polish anti-Semitism which had been fueled generously by the German occupation was now being nurtured by the Jew-hatred of the new Russian masters. We were told that there were a few thousand lonely Jews left in Warsaw: a handful of Jewish Communists, some of whom we met in the office of the Yiddish newspaper; less than a handful of old men who attended services in the only synagogue left standing; several in the performing arts; and the rest who had returned from the camps after the war and didn't want to leave their dead and/or their memories. They had survived the war and now they were surviving the peace.

One evening we attended a performance in the Jewish Theater. It was an edited version of *Tevyeh the Milkman* in Yiddish. The only part of the script written by Sholem Aleichem that remained described the misery and pogroms of the Tzarist times. The rest of the play dealt with the promise of the coming Soviet revolution. The hero of the play was not even Tevyeh. As one can imagine, it was Tevyeh's son-in-law Feferl, the revolutionary who was exiled to Siberia. It made no difference. We were the only ones in the theater who listened to the performance. The rest of the audience was a tour group from Sweden who were listening to a simultaneous translation with earphones.

Even twenty years later, I still remember the chill (it was the middle of June) as we walked through the area where the ghetto had once stood. The walls and all the buildings had been leveled. Piles of stone and burned timbers still lay there. But one could see where the streetcar tracks had ended because a wall had once been built across them. And it was possible, with the aid of maps we had copied from Holocaust literature, to recognize the original street lines, and even their identities. We could find our way to the Umschlagge Platz, to Mila Street and to the old Jewish cemetery.

I remember crying at the tomb of I.L. Peretz, the great Jewish writer after whom the day school I attended in Winnipeg was named. I remember crying at the large mounds of earth that covered unmarked mass graves. I remember walking a lot and crying a lot. This, after all, was the Jewish heritage that I knew. There, but for the luck of somebody emigrating in time, was my home or my grave. This was the end of the Yiddishist, Socialist, Zionist, European Judaism I knew. I was affected more by Warsaw than I would be ten years later by the Yad Vashem Holocaust Memorial in Jerusalem. The latter is a more beautiful monument, tastefully done. It is a museum, a history lesson, a shrine, an antiseptic display. Warsaw was death and cultural annihilation.

Through it all, I wondered how Gail was being affected. After all, I was a product of the "Old Country" culture of Winnipeg. She came from the sterile culture of Southern California's Reform temples. Peretz and Sholem Asch and Warsaw were part of my upbringing. How was all of this moving her?

I found out on Saturday afternoon. We had visitors—a Polish Jew and his two children whom we had met at the cemetery and whom we invited for tea. We had heard that there was a Jewish school and wanted to hear more about it. He, it developed, was looking for a handout. The seven-year-old child knew nothing. The eleven-year-old proudly recited the sum total of his Jewish knowledge: the four questions from the Passover Haggadah. We drank tea. I gave them a gift and my business card, and they left. Then we both cried. The end of Warsaw's centuries of Jewish creativity was a little boy who could barely stammer out *"Mah Nishtanah."*

Then Gail reacted. She sat up on her bed where she had been crying and spoke the most firm words I had heard in our seven years of marriage:

"I don't know what you think and I don't really care, but I've made up my mind. As soon as we get back I'm going to ask Moishe to make our house kosher. We're the only ones left. There's no one else. If we lose it, if we don't do it, if our children don't know about it, there won't be any Jews anymore. You can do what you want. But our house is going to be Jewish."

It was a defiant proclamation and she meant it. The pictures, the books and the music were not enough. She intended to transform the house organically, its very essence. Moreover, she was as good as her word. When we arrived in Minneapolis, the first person she called was Rabbi Feller, and he was only too willing to comply.

I don't remember all of the details. But I do remember the shocked look on his face when he first looked into our refrigerator. To this sweet young man, fresh out of the *yeshiva,* non-kosher meant a scar on the pleura of the animal who supplied the meat; or one drop of milk in fifty drops of chicken soup. The sight of real pork and shellfish must have been shattering. But bit by bit he "put our house in order." He introduced us to a kosher butcher; he taught us to look for the *kashrut* emblem on packaged food; he spent hours boiling silverware and metal utensils; he supervised the blowtorching of our oven; Mrs. Feller helped Gail buy new dishes.

One item gave him trouble: an expensive set of English bone china which we had received as a wedding gift from my sisters in Canada. It was a beautiful set and without doubt, one of our more precious possessions. Gail was quite eager to "kasher" the dishes by soaking and heating. She wanted to use them for Shabbat. I'm sure the whole project would have ended if she had been told then that the only way to kasher china, even English bone china, is to break it. He didn't have the heart to destroy our china. Or maybe he was a better psychologist than we took him for. When he discovered these dishes and what foods they had been used to serve, he suggested that we put them away. "Don't use them until I ask about such things in New York. Someone in New York must have more experience with things like this than I do."

They were put away. Every time he returned from a New York trip, Gail would ask what he had learned. And each time he had "forgotten." But he would be sure to remember next time. In the meantime, "Make sure they are put away in a safe place. You haven't used them, have you?"

This went on for months; then for years. The china was on display but it was never used. We kept waiting for expert advice that never came. Somehow, life went on without Minton Twilight in Grey.

We became closer to the Fellers during those years. Slowly the transformation which started in the kitchen moved into other areas of our life. Rabbi Feller introduced us to the Lubavitcher Rebbe, and we started growing in observance. Gail stopped singing in the synagogue choir; I started to put on *tefillin* sporadically at first, a little more regularly later on. I stopped driving on Shabbat. A few months later, so did Gail. We stopped eating at McDonalds. One Shabbat, we didn't switch on the television altogether. We bought a pair of *tzitzit* for the little boy. We switched membership to a synagogue with a *mechitzah* separating the men from the women. Gail started going to immerse in the *mikvah* (ritual bath). A few steps forward; a little backsliding; more steps forward. Years.

But the English bone china remained in the cabinet. Until one day, I came home from the university, and it was gone . . .

It was after a series of traumatic and melancholy miscarriages. Before observing *taharat ha'mishpacha* (the laws of family purity), it seems we had no difficulty having healthy and normal children. But when the *mikvah* became a feature of our family life, we started having trouble—three miscarriages in four years. Gail was sad; I was sad. Our friends comforted us. The Rebbe wrote letters of encouragement to Gail—private letters which I still have not read. But when I came home that singular day, she was smiling again:

"I took the china next door and sold it to Dorothy (our Gentile neighbor). Then I took the money and bought this *shaitel* (wig). What do you think of it?"

All this happened about 15 years ago. In 15 years you buy and discard a lot of *shaitlach*. Our two older daughters grew up and got married. They live with their husbands and their own children in Jerusalem. The little boy recently completed his rabbinic studies in the Lubavitch yeshiva in Montreal. We had two more children since then—the delights of our middle age. We have grown, both of us, both personally and professionally.

And we have another set of English bone china, from which we eat every Shabbat.

B'Or Ha'Torah Journal: Science, Art and Modern Life in the Light of Torah, 6 (1987): 167-171
www.borhatorah.org, info@borhatorah.org
Reprinted with permission of the publisher

The Human Biosphere

by **Rabbi Yanki Tauber**

Land animals, which were created from the soil, are rendered fit to eat by the severing of both vital passages (the windpipe and the gullet). Fish, which were created from the water, do not require any shechitah *to render them fit to eat. Birds, which were created from a mixture of soil and water, are rendered fit to eat with the severing of either one of the two vital passages* (Talmud, Chulin 27b).

In the terminology of Kabbalah and Chassidism, "soil" and "water" are analogs for materiality and spirituality. Aside from the usual association of soil with earthiness and mundanity, and of water with purity and sublimity, soil and water express one of the basic distinguishing characteristics between matter and spirit. Soil is comprised of distinct granules, while water forms a cohesive expanse. When two types of soil (or any two solids[1] are combined, they remain separate entities, however thoroughly mixed; liquids, on the other hand, blend to the point of indistinguishability.[2] Indeed, the way to fuse solid particles to an integral whole is either to introduce a liquid element (as in the kneading of dough), or to heat them to the point of liquidity (as in welding).

1 The four basic elements, soil, water, air and fire, also represent the four states of matter—solid, liquid, gas and energy.

2 This mechanical fact also has halachic implications—see Shulchan Aruch and commentaries, Yoreh Deah, 109.

By the same token, materiality tends to plurality and divisiveness, while the hallmark of the spiritual, is unity and oneness. The material world presents us with a great diversity of creatures, elements and forces, each bent on the preservation and enhancement of its individual existence. The material being is egocentric in essence, striving to consume whatever it needs (or merely desires) for itself, and resisting all attempts to consume it. While there are instances of cooperation and symbiosis in the material world, these are always toward the aim of mutual benefit rather than altruistic unity; furthermore, even this usually represents a triumph of mind over matter, and must be enforced upon a resisting egocentric instinct (witness the clash of egos in a marriage or the race and class-related tensions in a society).

On the other hand, spirituality, like water, is characterized by unity and cohesiveness, and, like water, is an agent of unity when introduced into the soil of the material. The soul amalgamates a diversity of cells and limbs into a "life"; the idea connects a myriad of disjointed facts into a cogent whole; love (that is, spiritual, altruistic love) supplants the instinctive "me" with a common "we." And when man shifts the focus of his life from the pursuit of material gratification to the service of his Creator, the diverse and belligerent granules of material life coalesce to a singular flow, as his every act and endeavor becomes an exercise in bringing harmony to the world and uniting it with its supernal source.

Beast, Fowl and Fish

The laws of *kashrut*, commanded by the Torah (primarily in Leviticus 11 and Deuteronomy 14) and interpreted and expounded upon in the Talmud (particularly in the tractate Chulin), establish which foods are permitted to the Jew, and which are forbidden. In regard to the consumption of animals, the laws of *kashrut* distinguish between three categories of animal: a) land animals, b) birds, and c) fish.[3]

One of the halachic distinctions among these three groups regards the requirement of *shechitah*, "slaughtering." Once an animal is determined to be kosher,[4] an array of laws govern how it may be slaughtered—the smallest nick in the knife, or the slightest deviation from the prescribed manner of slaughtering, renders the animal *tereif* and unfit for consumption. However, these laws differ from category to category. The most stringent *shechitah* requirements pertain to the "land animal": the slaughtering knife must cut through a majority of both of two vital passages, the windpipe and the gullet. At the other end of the spectrum are fish, which require no *shechitah* at all. Birds occupy the middle ground between land animals and fish: they do require *shechitah*, but the severing of (a majority of) only one of the vital passages—either the windpipe or the gullet—is sufficient.

The Talmud explains these differences as related to the primordial origins of these three categories of animals. Land animals were created from the earth (Genesis 1:24), and thus require a full-fledged *shechitah*; fish were created out of water (ibid., verse 20), and therefore do not require any *shechitah*; birds, which were created from a mixture of earth and water (ibid., and 2:19[5]), require the "lesser" *shechitah* prescribed for them.

What is the connection? Why is it that the "earthier" a creature is, the greater the need for *shechitah*? To understand this, we must first examine how all of the above applies to the inner world of the human soul. "Man is a universe in miniature,"[6] our sages have said, echoing King Solomon's adage, "Also the world He placed in their hearts"[7]; if there are three categories of animal life on the macrocosmic level, the same is true of man—our interior biosphere also includes the land beast, the water creature, and the earth/water composite that rides the winds. Here, too, the laws of *kashrut* and *shechitah* apply, instructing us how to distin-

[3] These three groups each have a different set of criteria for distinction between kosher and non-kosher animals. For a land animal to be kosher, it must chew its cud and have split hooves; in practice, this means that only ten species of land animal are permitted for consumption. With birds, the situation is reversed: the Torah lists twenty species of non-kosher birds and permits all others. Finally, kosher fish are distinguished by two "signs"—fins and scales.

[4] See previous note.

[5] See Talmud, Chulin 27b.

[6] Midrash Tanchuma, Pikudei 3.

[7] Ecclesiastes 3:11.

guish the desirable from the undesirable in our psyche, and how to make its "kosher" elements fit for consumption and metabolization in the daily process of life.

The Three Souls of Man

In the opening chapters of Tanya, the "bible" of Chabad Chassidism, Rabbi Schneur Zalman of Liadi establishes that we each possess two distinct souls: the "animal soul" (*nefesh habehamit*)[8] and the "G-dly soul" (*nefesh ha'elokit*).[9] The animal soul is the essence of physical life. Its focus is entirely self-oriented, its every act and desire motivated by the quest for self-fulfillment and self-enhancement; in this, the animal soul shares the nature of every physical being, whose most basic tendency is the preservation and betterment of its own existence. In contradistinction, the essence of the "G-dly soul" is the striving to unite with its source, to be nullified within the all-pervading reality of G-d. Were this striving to be fully realized, the G-dly soul would cease to exist as a distinct entity[10]; nevertheless, such is its nature and desire. This makes for the perpetual struggle of life: the struggle between matter and spirit, between self-assertion and self-transcendence. Any thought, desire, or act of man stems from either of his two souls, depending upon which has gained mastery over the other and is asserting itself in the person's mind, heart and behavior.

Chassidic teaching also speaks of a third, intermediary soul in every man—a soul less subjective than his animal soul, though not quite as transcendent as his G-dly soul. This is the *nefesh hasichlit*, the "intellectual soul." The intellect of man is the most transcendent element of his natural self, capable of objective thought and self-examination. This is not to say that the intellect is entirely free of the inhibitions of ego and self-interest; but it at least possesses the capacity to conceive of greater realities, and thus perceive the insignificance of the self before a higher truth. The intellectual self is thus the bridge between the G-dly soul, which strives toward a self-obliterating union with G-d, and the animal self, which is blind to everything save the gratification of its egocentric instincts. It is via the intellectual soul that the G-dly soul can influence the animal soul: when a person gains a recognition of the divine truth and an appreciation of the purpose to which he was created, this very knowledge and understanding serves to refine his character and behavior.[11]

These are the beast, bird, and water-creature within man. The animal soul of man is the "land animal" in man[12]—a wholly material being, individualistic and self-engrossed as the soil from which it is fashioned. At the other end of the spectrum is the wholly spiritual G-dly soul, characterized by the unity and adhesiveness of the water from which it derives. The G-dly soul of man also resembles the water creature in that it lives wholly immersed in its source—just as a fish cannot survive outside of the water that spawned it, so, too, the G-dly soul cannot conceive of an existence apart from its divine source.[13] In the words of Rabbi Schneur Zalman of Liadi, the G-dly essence of man, "never desires, nor is it ever capable of distancing itself from G-d," so that "even at the very moment a person sins,

8 The word *beheimah* actually means "beast" or "land animal" (see Rashi on Deuteronomy 14:5); thus, a more precise translation of *nefesh habehamit* would be the "beastly soul" or the "land-animal soul."

9 The concept of a "good inclination" (*yetzer tov*) and "evil inclination" (*yetzer hara*) in the heart of man abounds in the Talmud and the Midrashim (cf. Talmud, Berachot 61a). What is unique about the Tanya's thesis (which is based on the teachings of Rabbi Chaim Vital, a disciple of master Kabbalist Rabbi Isaac Luria) is that it speaks of two *souls*—two entire personas, each with a full set of traits and faculties. The two "inclinations" are actually the drives and desires of their respective souls.

10 This is the deeper significance of what happened to Nadav and Avihu, who "came close to G-d, and died" (Leviticus 16:1; see ibid., 10:1-7). In the words of Rabbi Chaim ibn Atar, theirs was "a death by divine 'kiss' like that experienced by the perfectly righteous—it is only that the righteous die when the divine kiss approaches them, while they died by their approaching it.... Although they sensed their own demise, this did not prevent them from drawing near [to G-d] in attachment, delight, delectability, fellowship, love, kiss and sweetness, to the point that their souls ceased from them." (Ohr Hachaim commentary on verse).

11 Likkutei Torah, Bechukotai 47c-48a; Sefer Hamaamarim 5702, pp. 106-109.

12 See note 8 above.

13 See Talmud, Berachot 61b.

his quintessential self remains loyal to G-d,"[14] taking no part in the deed—it has merely been suppressed and overwhelmed by his animal self.

Then there is the "bird" in man: a creature fashioned from soil and water, an admixture of matter and spirit. A creature that is capable of soaring to the most sublime heights, though it repeatedly returns to earth to rest and feed between flights. This is the intellect of man, capable, on the one hand, of raising itself above the materiality of earth and attaining a higher vantage point on life and self, yet nevertheless bound, in many ways, to the physical reality of which it is part.

Drawing Forth

Before an animal can be eaten, to become the stuff of our bodies and the motor of our lives, two conditions must be met: it must be determined to be kosher, and it must undergo *shechitah* as dictated by Torah law.

"*Shechitah* is only to draw forth,"[15] states the Talmud. The most basic meaning of this rule is that the slaughtering knife must be *drawn across* the "vital passages"—pressing downward, or other deviations from the required back-and-forth movement, disqualify the *shechitah*. Chassidic teaching, however, uncovers the deeper significance of this law: that the function of *shechitah* is to "draw forth"—to draw the animal out from its beastly state and into the domain of a life consecrated to the service of the Creator. This is achieved by "slaughtering" the beast—i.e., taking its life. The material world is not, in itself, a negative thing; what is negative is material *life*—the passion and zeal for things material. The Jew knows that while "the entire world was created to serve me," "I was created to serve my Creator"[16]—the reason why man has been granted mastery over the physical world is that he utilize it in his fulfillment of the divine will. Man was created to live a spiritual life that is sustained by the material, not a material life which his spiritual prowess has been harnessed to serve; to crave the physical for its own sake, is to become part of it rather than to make it part of you and a partner to your transcendent goals. So even after man has separated the "kosher" aspects of life from non-kosher ones, rejecting all that is irredeemable and corrupting,[17] he must still "slaughter" the material beast before it can be consumed. Only after its "life" has been taken out of it can it be sublimated as an accessory to the life of the spirit.

Hence the differing *shechitah* requirements for the three components of inner life of man. The "animal soul" requires a full-fledged *shechitah*: comprised solely of the soil of materialism, it must be drained of all vitality and passion so that its substance might be "drawn forth" into the realm of holiness. The "intellectual soul," comprised of both "soil" and "water," requires a partial *shechitah*—its material and egotistic elements must be subdued, but there remains much about the intellect that is desirable also in its "animated" form. [18]Finally, the wholly selfless, wholly transcendent "G-dly soul" requires no *shechitah* at all, for both its substance and spirit are desirable and "digestible" elements in the life of man.

Based on the Rebbe's writings, including a letter dated, Tishrei 25, 5703 (October 6, 1942) and a journal entry marked "Shechitah. Vichy. 5700" (1940-41)[19]

www.meaningfullife.com
Reprinted with permission

14 Tanya, ch. 24. See Mishneh Torah, Laws of Divorce, 2:20.

15 *Ein v'shachat ela umashach*—Talmud, Chulin 30b. Thus, *shechitah* is equated with the halachic concept of *meshicah*, which effects the transfer of an object from on domain to another.

16 Talmud, Kiddushin 82a.

17 Indeed, there are non-kosher elements in all three categories, including the utterly selfless "fish." For while the G-dly soul's self-abnegation before G-d is its highest virtue, there also exists a negative type of self-abnegation, as in the case of one who lacks the pride and self-assurance necessary to resist those persons and forces that seek to prevent his doing what is right. In chassidic terminology such a tendency is called *askufah hanidresses*, or a "doormat personality."

18 This is also why there are more non-kosher land animals than kosher ones, while the reverse is true of birds (see note 3 above).

19 Igrot Kodesh, vol. I, pp. 46-48; Reshimot #23, pp. 5-10

Is Kosher Food Safer?

by **Deborah Kotz**

Not only Jews look for the kosher symbol on food these days. In a surprising turn of events, "kosher" has become the most popular claim on new food products, trouncing "organic" and "no additives or preservatives," according to a recent report. A noteworthy 4,719 new kosher items were launched in the United States last year—nearly double the number of new "all natural" products, which placed second in the report, issued last month by Mintel, a Chicago-based market research firm.

In fact, sales of kosher foods have risen an estimated 15 percent a year for the past decade. Yet Jews, whose religious doctrine mandates the observance of kosher dietary laws, make up only 20 percent of those buying kosher products. What gives? "It's the belief among all consumers that kosher food is safer, a critical thing right now with worries about the integrity of the food supply," says Marcia Mogelonsky, a senior research analyst at Mintel.

Whether kosher foods are actually less likely to be contaminated with, say, *E. coli* bacteria remains up for debate. While research is scant in this area, experts say it makes sense that kosher food could be safer because it's more closely monitored. "Jews aren't allowed to ingest bugs, so produce must go through a thorough washing and checking to ensure that no bugs are found within the leaves or on the surface of the fruit or vegetable," says Moshe Elefant, a rabbi and chief operating officer of the Orthodox Union, a kosher certification organization based in New York. But bacteria can remain even after this type of washing, so consumers can't assume they're less likely to get food poisoning with bagged spinach marked kosher than with a conventional bag.

The same caveat applies to poultry and beef. A salting process that removes blood from the meat has antibacterial effects, but salmonella and *E. coli* can still survive, says Joe Regenstein, a professor of food science who teaches a course on Jewish and Muslim food laws at Cornell University. Kosher beef, though, is much less likely to contain the misshapen proteins that cause mad cow disease, rare as that is, probably because the animals are slaughtered young, before the disease sets in.

Another selling point of kosher foods is that they're easily decoded by those looking to avoid dairy or meat. "One of the fundamental rules of kosher certification is that you can't mix meat and milk," says Elefant. So each product is labeled either dairy or meat—or "pareve" (also spelled parve) if it contains neither. Pareve foods can't even be manufactured on equipment previously used for dairy or meat products. "People with severe dairy allergies are looking for that pareve designation," Elefant says. They might also turn to kosher salami and hot dogs, since nonkosher cured meats often contain a preservative made from milk sugar, though [they] may simply buy kosher because they prefer the stricter supervision that goes into certifying kosher foods. "Food companies agree to allow a third-party inspector to come in unannounced, at essentially any time," says Regenstein. These inspectors check, among other things, that products are being manufactured only with those ingredients listed on the label. Companies, he says, must carefully keep records of where ingredients come from—not always the case for small nonkosher food manufacturers—which allows for quick recall if a product gets contaminated with a nonkosher ingredient or food-borne pathogen. "That alone is worth the price of kosher," Regenstein opines. Contrary to what some folks think, however, a rabbi doesn't bless the food. "Kosher dietary laws are actually just a simple set of rules," explains Elefant, "and the kosher certification helps those who make a commitment to live under those rules."

U.S. News and World Report, January 11, 2008
Reprinted with permission of the publisher

Spiritual Molecules

by **Dr. Velvl Greene**

Most of us "believe" in molecules.

Hardly any one of us has ever seen a molecule, and unless we have studied a lot of chemistry and physics and physical chemistry, we probably don't understand the tests and criteria used by scientists to detect molecules, analyze them, identify them or describe their structure. Still, we believe they exist, have definable structures, weights and shapes and possess predictable properties. We have been taught that all molecules are made up of a hundred or so elemental atoms—just as all words are made up of the same basic letters. The countless and varied molecules that make up our physical world differ from each other only with respect to the type of atoms they contain, the numbers of atoms present, their pattern of organization and their location in the molecular structure—just as all of the words in our language differ from each other only with respect to the letters they contain and their sequence. And the same words can be used to write a psalm or a political pamphlet—just as the same molecules can be found in an ant or an elephant.

There is nothing mystical about this anymore. It isn't imaginary or hypothetical. The concept of molecules and atoms and their reactions is as accepted as are things we can see and judge with our own senses.

If a chemist tells us that a given molecule has three carbon atoms and another molecule has six, we believe him. If the chemist tells us that the six carbon atoms of one molecule are in a ring, while in another molecule they are forked, we believe him. Sometimes we believe because it makes sense. More often, we believe because we have no reason to disbelieve. Most of the time we believe because we have a basic confidence in the chemist's honesty and competence.

Chemists and their colleagues have more credibility in our eyes than merchants, lawyers and most of the public servants we choose to run our country. And much of the confidence is justified. Molecular theory and manipulation are the very basis of the exciting discoveries being made almost daily in physiology, genetics, microbiology and pharmacology. The chemist has used his molecular models quite effectively to make predictions and products that have changed our lives.

For example, people long ago discovered, by empirical trial and error, that certain foods were nutritious while others were poisonous; certain beverages were intoxicating while others were innocuous; certain diets were fattening while others, which also satisfied hunger, were less so. In the early years of this century nutritionists learned that the absence of certain foodstuffs from normal diets resulted in pathological consequences. About the same time, allergists learned that adding certain ingredients to normal diets also resulted in pathological consequences. It wasn't until the chemists provided us with "metabolic maps" that we started to sort out the mass of confusing empirical data. These metabolic maps described the molecular pathways involved in food digestion and cell synthesis. They showed how the complex minerals, proteins carbohydrates and lipids present in our dietary foodstuffs could be broken down into simpler and simpler molecules; concurrently, these simple molecules could be utilized by our own bodies for putting together the proteins, minerals, carbohydrates and lipids that constitute our tissues. The maps showed how the whole process was regulated by other molecules (vitamins). The molecular models explained how and why certain foods generated toxic responses and other foods generated allergic responses; the bases of some classical deficiency diseases like rickets, pellagra, goiter and beriberi; the rationale of weight-reducing diets; and dozens of other physiological and pharmacological phenomena.

It can be fairly said that molecular chemistry and molecular biology established nutrition, physiology and nutritional pathology as sciences and took them out of the grasp of alchemists and quacks.

Kashrut and Chemistry

Thoughts of this nature kept intruding as I was reviewing the Torah portion *Shemini* (Leviticus 9-10), wherein the Jewish people were commanded, eternally, to avoid certain foods while being permitted to consume others.

The Torah itself gives no reason for these laws. But anyone familiar with the modern molecular theories of nutrition and nutritional pathology can hardly avoid the temptation of creating molecular models and maps to explain everything in this field.

But it is futile speculation . . .

In his classic volume on biblical and talmudic medicine, written 73 years ago. Dr. Julius Preuss introduced his discussion on *kashrut* (dietary laws) with the following statement:

> The biblical dietary laws are included in the chapter on "Hygiene" solely because we can conceive of no reason other than sanitary for their ordination. It must be emphasized, however, that the Torah gives us no reason at all for these laws and the later sources do so only rarely. Thus, nearly everything which one alleges to be the reason for the dietary laws is only a hypothesis and is read into the sources . . .

This statement establishes precisely the frustrating paradox confronting anyone who would like to explain the laws of kashrut using modern knowledge of nutrition and public health as a model. We don't know why certain animals, birds and fish are permitted for food while others are banned; we don't know why the permitted quadrupeds and birds must be slaughtered in a given fashion; we don't know why blood, certain fatty tissues and the sciatic nerve are forbidden; we don't know the hazards associated with cooking and/or consuming meat and milk; and we don't know why certain specific anatomical imperfections render an animal or fowl *traifa* (not kosher) and thus prohibited. We are provided with remarkably detailed guides and instructions about the criteria that distinguish between prohibited and acceptable, but nothing about why. Though we very much want to know why, any rational explanation is simply an exercise in human imagination.

The greatest minds ever produced by the human race have struggled for thousands of years to explain these laws. Dozens, if not hundreds of hypotheses have been proposed to elucidate these mysteries. Why is the ox kosher and the camel not? Why cannot a Jew eat pork and benefit from the well-known nutritional quality of swine flesh? Why is carp acceptable while eels are not? The rational mind yearns to understand and unfortunately, because it cannot understand, sometimes decides to ignore the laws altogether!

In the last hundred years or so, it has become fashionable to explain kashrut with analogies from public health. The basic argument is that Moses was really a primitive health commissioner, and the Parshah of *Shemini* was an early model of current Pure Food and Drug laws. It is an intriguing concept, but its adherents today are mainly Jews who do not want to observe the dietary restrictions in the first place. Very little support for this point of view will be found in authentic public health research. Rabbits are as nutritious as chickens; gefilte fish can be made as well from sturgeon as from trout; there isn't that much difference—microbiologically or chemically—between lamb and pork.

It would be easier to understand (and adhere to?) the dietary restrictions if we would find a chemical reason. It would be easier particularly if we could isolate some kind of substance or harmful chemical from a forbidden food that is not present in a permitted food. Or if we could show that the processes described in the *Shulchan Aruch* (Code of Jewish Law) inhibit some obscure molecular reaction which produces a toxin. That would make sense. We have a lot of empirical experience with food poisoning and allergies. Undoubtedly our ancestors did also. There are certain foodstuffs in nature that are intrinsically poisonous—certain mushrooms, for example, some fish and some mollusks. It would be quite reasonable for a primitive lawmaker to ban them as food for his tribe. We also know that foods, if improperly stored or processed, can become vehicles for transmission of infectious agents or their toxins. Thus a primitive lawgiver, concerned with the physical health of his tribe, would also ordain laws about processing and storing the materials which have been permitted as food.

If non-kosher foods or improper processing resulted in food poisoning or infection or skin eruptions, we could understand.

But they really don't. From a nutritional and toxicological perspective, there is no difference between a kosher and non- kosher diet. The answer certainly is not chemical. It isn't the physical atoms and molecules of pork that render it inedible for Jews. Otherwise, why is it not forbidden to non-Jews? Is it possible that there are chemical receptors or Jewish cells that are sensitive to molecules of *traifa* foods? It is not beyond medical experience. Some humans are allergic to strawberries while others are not. Indeed, the only difference between the allergic and the retractile is a subtle molecular reaction that occurs in the former and not in the latter. A better example might be the genetic (some say racial) inability of some humans to digest bovine milk while others literally thrive on it. Thus there are molecular reactions, in the realm of nutritional pathology and which are hereditary that can serve as a justification for dietary taboos.

Unfortunately, it doesn't wash clean. Jewish racial qualities are more a Nazi myth than a chemical reality today. When the dietary prohibitions were announced, the 12 tribes encamped around Sinai several thousand years ago certainly shared a similar genetic make up. But in the thousands of years since then and particularly in the thousands of years of diaspora, the genetic homogeneity became significantly diluted. Jews today differ greatly in blood types and immunological make up and physiological response to nutrients. Today a chemical explanation of kashrut—which remains extremely binding despite the gradual genetic diversification is—simply an inadequate hypothesis. A convert to Judaism is obligated to observe the kashrut laws as soon as she or he becomes a Jew, even if he or she has thrived physiologically on the now-forbidden foods until that very moment.

Spiritual Molecules

Many of the rabbinic commentators make reference, while humbly denying that they know the true answer, to the "spiritual damage" that derives from non-kosher foods. For example. Rabbi Shimshon Raphael Hirsch comments on the Torah portion *Kedoshim* (Leviticus 19-20) as follows:

> You must . . . conscientiously keep . . . the choice of nourishment . . . as the very first preliminary . . . for spiritual, mental and moral clarity, purity and holiness . . . right from the beginning, at the actual forming of the tissues of your body, the physical formation of the fibers of your brain, nerves and muscles . . .

The forbidden foods are thus not materially poisonous, but they are harmful to our soul. The dangerous components of pork cannot be detected by chemists, and the toxicological effects of its consumption cannot be diagnosed by physicians, but the damage does certainly occur. If we want to think in terms of molecules, we must think about "spiritual molecules."

In this respect, I once read that there are spiritual poisons in certain proscribed foods that dull the spiritual senses or, as is put so well in Yiddish, "stuff up the nose and ears of the soul" to the extent that the individual can no longer receive spiritual messages. I also heard that the animals forbidden as food by Torah possess certain spiritual characteristics which the consumer is in danger of acquiring. Whatever the rationale, spiritual molecules make more sense than chemical ones.

But they make sense only to one who already believes in the authority of Torah and that person is already willing to obey the rules without any rationalizations. To the rest of the world, spiritual molecules are too much the subject of mystery and superstition. In the spiritual realm, according to those who consider themselves modern and scientific there are no rules and no logic—just a lot of fairy stories, visions, magic, witchcraft and gurus.

Of course, real molecules are also invisible and intangible to most of us. Real molecules are also the subjects of speculation by the gurus (of science) who wear their priestly garments and who officiate in their esoteric temples (called laboratories) after years of apprenticeship. But spiritual molecules are too much for the twentieth century.

(Parenthetically, I wonder if our rabbis would be more successful in getting their message across if they exchanged their black frocks for white lab coats? I wonder if the observance of kashrut would be enhanced by impressive lab equipment and periodic tables and diagrams of covalent electron bonds or their spiritual equivalent? Probably not. The contemporary Jewish non-observer is too sophisticated for that; he wouldn't fall for such gimmicks. If he doesn't obey the rules when G-d Himself issues them, why would he change because a rabbi put on a white coat?

Then why does he believe in molecules made up of carbon atoms? But that's another story . . .)

I submit that the real barrier to accepting the role of spiritual molecules derives from two handicaps in conceptualization:

1) The lack of immediate empirical proof of spiritual harm when the laws are disregarded;

2) The matter of particularism, i.e., the selective nature of the dietary laws which permit the majority of humans to eat and benefit from a given food while denying the same opportunity to a very small group of people who are indistinguishable in any detectable way from the majority and who also seem to benefit from the food.

PKU—a Medical Model of Kashrut?

We are taught in Chassidism that the spiritual world and the material world are parallels of each other. Thus phenomena experienced in the flesh and blood universe are modeled on spiritual phenomena. Similarly, the spiritual universe is reflected in things and events which are detected by our mortal senses.

This permits us to postulate the existence of spiritual molecules based on our knowledge of chemical structures. Indeed, there are those who would say that the material molecules we study and teach about in chemistry courses are really the reflection of the intangible spiritual molecules the Creator used as a blueprint!

With this in mind I present the natural history of a rare genetic disease that might provide some kind of answer to those who reject kashrut because they lack empirical proof of harm and feel uncomfortable with strict particularism.

Medicine is familiar with a condition called phenylketonuria or PKU. First described fifty years ago, this hereditary metabolic disorder affects about one out of 15,000 children born in the northern hemisphere and leads, among other things, to an irreversible and severe retardation.

The newborn child appears healthy and normal. He cannot really be distinguished during a routine physical examination, from his 14,999 unaffected peers. He has a normal appetite and an apparently unremarkable metabolism. He eats, sleeps, cries and does all of the other things babies are expected to do. But gradually—over the course of several years—he develops a characteristic appearance and brain damage.

Many years after the disease was first described, physiologists determined that the brain damage was a result of the accumulation in the body of a certain amino acid—phenylalanine—which is a common molecule in many proteins. Normal people have the ability to metabolize phenylalanine and to convert it to other, non-harmful (and essential) nutrients. But one child in 15,000 lacks the necessary enzyme and the phenylalanine accumulates and accumulates until it harms the developing brain.

About 35 years ago, a chemist named Guthrie described a blood test which permits the early diagnosis of PKU, within a few days after birth, long before the neurological damage has occurred. This test is now compulsory in most Western countries (including Israel). Every baby born in a hospital is tested for PKU. If the results suggest that the condition is present, the mother is provided with nutritional advice and counseling. If the diet is modified early enough, if the phenylalanine-containing protein is replaced with a synthetic substitute and fed for the first four or five years, the retardation can usually be avoided. The solution isn't simple; it is also inconvenient, unappetizing and expensive. But, it is effective.

Now consider the following scenario: a public health nurse visits a young mother who has just come home from the hospital with her precious newborn baby. The nurse conveys the frightening news that according to the lab tests the baby has PKU. She also provides the mother with a list of prescribed foods and instructions for preparing a suitable preventive diet.

Neither the nurse nor the mother is a chemist. The mother knows nothing about molecules or physiology or metabolism. She knows what she sees—a healthy, normal baby, like any other baby in the world, who enjoys eating and is apparently thriving on the diet being provided. The nurse knows a little more. She has studied a little chemistry and understands the best physiology of metabolism. Or at least, she believes the teachers who taught her. The nurse doesn't really know the basis of the diagnostic tests; nor could she prescribe a diet out of her own experience. All she is doing is her job of transmitting the information she was taught. She believes she is acting in the best interests of the child and the community. But she is mostly acting out of duty and acceptance of higher authorities—such as doctors, chemist and nutritionists—who have studied more and know more and have better sources of knowledge.

The mother refuses to accept the diagnosis or the diet. She doesn't believe in the mysteries of chemistry or accept the authority of the doctors. Doesn't her baby look normal? Isn't the baby happy? Besides, the recommended diet is too expensive and inconvenient and unappetizing. What is all this nonsense about molecules anyway?

I end with the following question:

If you were the nurse, what would you do when the mother demands, "Show me the danger now! Show me the difference between my baby and all the others!"

B'Or Ha'Torah Journal: Science, Art and Modern Life in the Light of Torah 6 (1987): 159-164
www.borhatorah.org, info@borhatorah.org
Reprinted with permission of the publisher

Holy Shibuta
A Fishy Tale for Rosh Hashana

by **Rabbi Dr. Ari Z. Zivotofsky** and **Dr. Ari Greenspan**

Imagine the great talmudic scholar Rava, his mouth watering, thinking about the next bite of his Shabbat meal and knowing that it will taste like ham. That image is what brought us to a most unusual meal, sitting in a forest overlooking the Euphrates River in Turkey. We dined with the provincial governor and a fish expert from the University of Harran with the apt name of Zafer Dogu, while we munched on a fish that in Arabic is called *shabut*.

Our main quest on this journey that had brought us to south central Turkey was for lesser-known Jewish customs and traditions, and while trawling for Jewish lore just 60 km. north of the Syrian border, we hit the mother lode. To understand this fish's tale, a bit of seining of the traditional sources is needed.

As we sit down to our Rosh Hashana meal, Jews all around the world begin their first course with foods that symbolize hopefulness and dreams of happiness and peace for the coming year. The most common custom is the dipping of an apple into honey, symbolizing that the impending year should be sweet. A less well known custom, but one with venerable and ancient roots, is dipping a ram's head in honey as a reminder of the binding of Isaac and the anticipation of a pleasant year.

Another common custom is to eat the head of a fish or ram, upon which we pronounce our desire that "we should be as a head and not as a tail." Many people also eat fish and recite "may it be Your will, our God Who is the God of our fathers, that we increase and multiply like fish."

The fish in Judaism is seen as a particularly common and positive symbol. Fish bear many offspring and are a symbol of fertility. The protective shield used by *mohelim*, ritual circumcisers, is often made in the shape of a fish because it represents fertility. The body of water where we say *tashlich*, the symbolic "casting of our sins into the sea," during this High Holy Day season, ideally should contain fish because fish are considered immune to the "evil eye." Because of this, fish is also the symbol of the month of Adar.

As opposed to animals, birds and grasshoppers, no fish are named in the entire Bible. Talmudic literature does mention several species by their common names, with the fish mentioned most often being the *shibuta*. Whatever this shibuta was, it was well known by the Diaspora community of Babylonia of old.

The Talmud discusses shibuta in several contexts. We are told that the great sages of the Talmud rolled up their sleeves and involved themselves directly in preparations for the Shabbat. The amora Rava would personally salt the shibuta fish for the Shabbat meal. We surmise from this that the fish was well known and considered enough of a delicacy to be served for the Sabbath repast.

It is described as both having medicinal value or posing a health risk, depending on the season of the year and the medical condition involved. A salted head of shibuta boiled in beer is a cure for a disease called *yarkona* (jaundice?). On the other hand, according to the Gemara, eating the shibuta during the spring month of Nisan could cause leprosy.

One of the more interesting references has to do with the unique taste of the creature. The Talmud relates that for everything that God prohibited in this world, He also created a counterpart that was permitted. For example, blood is prohibited, but the liver, which contains an abundance of the vital fluid, was permitted. Even though milk and meat may not be eaten together, the udder of a lactating cow is permissible.

Now here's the kicker. The pig, the most detestable of animals to the Jewish people, is of course forbidden as food. However, should one have a penchant to taste the forbidden swine, we are informed that the flavor of pork is identical to (part of) the shibuta.

For the last few centuries the identity of the talmudic shibuta has puzzled European scholars and at least a half dozen possible species have been proposed. But it is no longer a mystery for us. Having an interest in Jewish culinary traditions, several years ago I asked an Iraqi-born Tel Aviv cab driver which kosher birds they used to eat in his native land. When the nostalgia of his youth warmed his soul, he smiled and said that by far the tastiest item in their cuisine was neither fowl nor meat, but a fish called the shabut. His response electrified me. Could his shabut in Arabic be the shibuta of the Talmud?

As I later discovered, the great rabbinic leader of Baghdadi Jewry from the early 20th century, Rabbi Yosef Haim (known as the Ben Ish Hai) had no doubt. He listed the five most common kosher fish eaten in Baghdad and after mentioning the shabut he says "that is the shibuta of the Talmud." So here was the shibuta—it is a type of carp known in Arabic as shabut and by the scientific name *Barbus grypus*, from the family *Cyprinidae* (carps and minnows). The Europeans were stymied because they were looking in Europe, while the shibuta of the Babylonian Talmud is obviously found in Babylonia, modern-day Iraq.

That taxi ride ignited a passion to behold and maybe even taste this talmudic delicacy. We turned to the largest collection of preserved fish in the country, a true national treasure located at Hebrew University in Jerusalem, but alas, it was lacking *shibuta* .

The next step would be more difficult and was our conundrum: The fish lives in the Tigris and Euphrates rivers, which flow through Iraq, Iran and Syria and are not readily accessible to Israelis. But with the help of several parties outside of Israel, we managed to get our first few shibuta shipped from its natural territory via a third country. The trouble was that they were preserved in formaldehyde, so we could not get a taste. A side benefit was that we were able to donate a *Barbus grypus* to the Hebrew University collection.

Our desire for a frozen sample to eat on Rosh Hashana was not quelled. Travel to Iraq, Iran and Syria may be difficult for us, but there are many US military and civilian personnel in Iraq and US army chaplain Lt.-Col. Jeremy Steinberg is among them. He had already served a tour of duty in Afghanistan and was serving his second tour in Iraq. Having known him for many years and knowing that he is good at detective work (he has a forthcoming book on Hebrew etymology), I e-mailed him about my search and finally convinced him that I was really serious about wanting him to find a shabut.

He agreed to look, though doubted that he would be successful. But succeed he did. He approached an Iraqi who was employed on the US Army base and asked him to find out about the possibility of getting a shabut for him. The base, being near the Euphrates and the shabut being popular, the Iraqi returned the next morning not with information but with a box containing two big and two small specimens. Chaplain Steinberg promptly purchased the fish, recorded the event with many pictures that quickly clogged my inbox, but alas the fish are still in Iraq because we have not found a legal means to ship them from there to Israel.

Our search was not over and took a positive turn when we "discovered" that the Tigris and Euphrates have their sources in a friendly country, Turkey. Quite fortuitously, I found not just a fish expert but a *Barbus grypus* expert, Dr. Zafer Dogu, from the Department of Fisheries, Bozova Vocational School, Harran University. He was more than glad to cooperate and find a few fish for us. But things improved even more when we contacted the Turkish embassy, which graciously assisted us with arrangements for our trip to study the shibuta in the Euphrates, just a stone's throw from Harran, the city of our forefather Abraham.

We flew to Istanbul and from there to Sanliurfa, landing on the longest runway in Turkey in a deserted, brand new airport that was opened only the previous week. One's initial impression upon arriving in this area near the Euphrates is that of the lush green patches irrigated by the majestic river among the otherwise moon-like landscape of the harsh arid region of south-central Turkey. We stepped out of the airport into 44-degree heat and proceeded to the office of Governor Mehmet Özel, who warmly welcomed us and assisted us with all of our needs.

After an initial meeting with the governor, the fish expert and his boss, we were taken to a lake that was formed when the Atatürk Dam on the Euphrates was completed in 1993. The dam, one of the largest in the world, is part of the massive $32 billion public project known as the Great Southeastern Anatolia Project (GAP) that has greatly improved the standard of living in the region. The lake covers 815 sq. km., and when it was filled for the first time it submerged 25 villages, displacing 55,000 inhabitants, and several important unexplored archeological sites.

Waiting for us on the lake were two boats that took us to the middle of this placid body of water, where we observed local fishermen pulling in nets full of fish. Unfortunately, none of the fish caught while we were there were shibuta. So as not to disappoint us, Dogu, took out and prepared (very cooperatively according to our instructions so that it remained kosher) one of the shibuta he had caught for us in advance, and a lovely lakeside "state dinner" with the governor was held. From there, we were taken to see the fish research facility where work is being done on raising, among other fish, the shibuta by, among others, Dogu who is a leading researcher on *Barbus grypus* sperm.

Perhaps the most interesting aspect of the story came to light when we reached our hotel, an old stone structure built right near an early Arab holy site called the Mosque of Abraham in the ancient part of Sanliurfa. According to Muslim tradition, King Nimrod was angered by Abraham having smashed his father's idols, and had him catapulted into a fiery furnace. God in His benevolence miraculously caused the fire to turn into water and the logs into fish. And not just any fish, but shabut. On the site of the furnace-turned-pond an ancient church existed and then a mosque was built.

In 1896 this pool was visited by a Christian traveler who described the experience (See http://armenianhouse.org/harris/armenia/letter11.html):

> I was visiting, under guard of a Turkish soldier, the most beautiful part of Edessa, the fish-pond on the borders of which stands the Mosque of Abraham the friend of God, and a Moslem college. This college is the successor of the famous Christian school of Edessa, and the mosque, no doubt, marks the site of an ancient Christian church. The pool is full of fish, which it is prohibited under severe penalty to kill, and which every one feeds with bread and pennyworths of parched corn. Such a rush when you throw it in! They tumble over one another, and jump half out

of the water. Obviously the protection and support which the fish enjoy comes from a time when they were considered sacred. So I asked my soldier what was the name of the fish, and his answer was, "In Arabic they are called shabut."

This was not the end of the story. It was time to take a fish to Los Angeles for an OU "halachic dinner" to share with the rest of the Jewish world (see http://www.greenspandental.com/JewishJournal.com.html). But how could we get the fish into the US legally and with it staying fresh? This turned out to not be a concern. We were informed in an e-mail by the deputy chief of Trade Operations, Customs and Border Protection of the Port Authority of New York and New Jersey that "non living fish [from Turkey] that are for personal consumption and free from live pests/insects are not regulated and permitted entry."

Dogu's boss, Asst. Prof. Erdinç Sahinöz confirmed the health status of our fish. Going through security is often a tense experience. In the isolated, new empty Sanliurfa airport, the security people sat up straight in their chairs and their eyes popped when they saw a large fish on the X-ray scanner. A lot of explaining and laughing went on in security offices that day, and we gave a new meaning to flying fish. They found it so amusing (and we were the only passengers in sight) that they even permitted us to photograph the X ray of the shibuta.

Had our Turkish been better, we might have found dry ice in Istanbul, but given its current state our precious cargo was wrapped in regular ice, hand carried and stored in the overhead bins, and off we went. The dripping water we explained to fellow passengers must be faulty air-conditioning units on the planes, and we headed to LA hoping for the best. It arrived still frozen, was masterfully prepared by the chef at the Prime Grill with applesauce, instead of an apple in its mouth, and was willingly consumed at the Baron Herzog winery in Oxnard by a group of OU rabbis.

The question we are often asked is "does it taste like pig?" Having never tasted pork, we cannot personally answer that question. But the final verdict of the chef at the Prime Grill, after finding commonality between their textures and consistency, was a definite "no."

What is interesting is that three different texts exist regarding the exact description of the shibuta's taste. One source says the fish tastes like pig. Another says its brain does, and a third states the tongue is the tasty morsel. Could the rabbis have been talking tongue in cheek? As any angler will tell you, the tongue or brain of a small freshwater fish is so tiny as to be almost nonexistent.

Might the lesson be more along the lines of being satisfied with what we have and transmitting to us that we should not feel as if we are missing anything in this world? Basically, the lesson might be that if you feel like you are lacking, search far and hard enough and you might even find what you thought you never could.

As of now, the shibuta does not live in Israel. However, it has the potential to, and indeed some of its close relatives do. Two such species are *Barbus longiceps*, a species that exists nowhere else except the Kinneret and its tributaries, and *Barbus canis*, a fish found in the Jordan River. This brings us to a beautiful midrash.

As we start a new year and dream of peace and prosperity and of the days to come, let us contemplate the eschatological message that the rabbis tell us the shibuta has the potential to share with us. The midrash allegorically tells us that when the Jews went into exile at the hands of the Babylonians, "700 types of kosher fish, 800 types of kosher locusts and an unlimited number of kosher birds were exiled with them to Babylonia, and when they returned all of them returned with them except for the fish called the shibuta . . . and in the days to come, all are destined to return."

Shana Tova to all, and a year of great fishing, wherever your pond may be.

The Jerusalem Post, Septermber 17, 2007
Reprinted with permission of the publisher

Lesson 5

It's All Hebrew to Me

An Exploration of the Holy Tongue

Introduction

In this lesson, we'll explore the Hebrew language from *alef* through *tav*. Good thinking will be rewarded with buttons and flowers, and you'll find out why a prayer book is like a Passover seder. You'll learn how to make your own mazal, and we will all say, "Amen."

Jewish Linguistics

Learning Activity 1

Many popular English idioms and expressions come from the Bible. Some popular ones include "a drop in the bucket" (Isaiah 40:15); "holier than thou" (Isaiah 65:5); "from the mouths of babes" (Psalms 8:2); and "pouring out your heart" (Psalms 62:9). Can you identify the biblical context of each of the following phrases?

My brother's keeper

Fire and brimstone

Coming out of one's nose (expression of disgust)

Escaping by the skin of one's teeth

How the mighty have fallen!

Putting your house in order (preparing for death)

Figure 5.1

Hebrew Idiom	Literal Translation	Meaning
kaftor vaferach	a button and a flower	an elegant argument in which the pieces are arranged clearly and logically
otiyot kidush levanah	letters of the blessing of the moon	very large print
bechiyah ledorot	crying for generations	an act that results in a great amount of heartache
berachel bitecha haketanah	for your youngest daughter, Rachel	something that is carefully stipulated down to the last and minutest detail
keli rishon	a vessel containing food or liquid that has been directly heated by fire	a firsthand observer
kire'ach mikan umikan	bald from here and from there	losing out either way

Shades of Meaning
Lost in Translation

Figure 5.2

Genesis 25:28

וַיֶּאֱהַב יִצְחָק אֶת עֵשָׂו כִּי צַיִד בְּפִיו. (בראשית כה,כח)

First Translation
Isaac loved Esau because [Esau's] trapped [game] was in [Isaac's] mouth.

Meaning
Isaac loved Esau because Isaac ate from Esau's hunting.

Second Translation
And Isaac loved Esau because [Esau] trapped [Isaac] with [Esau's] mouth.

Meaning
Isaac loved Esau because Esau deceived him.

Figure 5.3

Genesis 48:22

וַאֲנִי נָתַתִּי לְךָ שְׁכֶם אַחַד עַל אַחֶיךָ. (בראשית מח,כב)

First Translation

I have given you one [city of] Shechem over your brothers.

Meaning

Jacob gave the city of Shechem to Joseph's descendants.

Second Translation

I have given you one portion over your brothers.

Meaning

Jacob arranged for two tribes to descend from Joseph: the tribe of Ephraim and the tribe of Manasseh.

Figure 5.4

Exodus 34:9

וַיֹּאמֶר אִם נָא מָצָאתִי חֵן בְּעֵינֶיךָ ה׳ יֵלֶךְ נָא ה׳ בְּקִרְבֵּנוּ, כִּי עַם
קְשֵׁה עֹרֶף הוּא, וְסָלַחְתָּ לַעֲוֹנֵנוּ וּלְחַטָּאתֵנוּ. (שמות לד,ט)

First Translation

And [Moses] said, "If I have now found favor in Your eyes, my Lord, let my Lord now go in our midst; *despite* their being a stiff-necked people, You shall forgive our iniquity and our sin."

Meaning

Despite their stiff-necked nature, forgive them.

Second Translation

And [Moses] said, "If I have now found favor in Your eyes, my Lord, let my Lord now go in our midst; *because* they are a stiff-necked people, You shall forgive our iniquity and our sin."

Meaning

Their stiff-necked nature is also a wonderful quality; because of their stubbornness, they will loyally cling to You through thick and thin—and, therefore, You should forgive them.

Synonyms

Learning **Activity 2**

Below are five synonyms for "looking." Insert the one that fits best into each sentence. (You may need to conjugate the verb to make the sentence grammatically correct.)

gaze glance glare peer stare

The young teen____________adorningly at the famous musician on the stage.

She____________ into the dark room, trying to find her misplaced glasses.

The child____________at the woman with pink hair and her arm in a cast.

The old lady____________at the boy who answered his cell phone during the concert.

Because the salesman was late for a meeting, he only had time to quickly____________at his mail before dashing out the door.

Learning Activity 3

There are several Hebrew words that are usually translated as "to want" or "desire," but each has a particular connotation.

Hebrew Root	Transliteration of Root	Connotation
אבה	A-B-H	to acquiesce to another's wishes
אוה	A-V-H	a bodily craving
חפץ	CH-F-TS	a deep soulful desire
רצה	R-TS-H	a rational, mindful desire

Each of these verses can be translated using the English word "desire," but uses a different root word in Hebrew. Based on the above table, can you figure out which Hebrew root is used in each verse?

1. "He does not maintain His anger forever, for He *desires* loving-kindness." (Micah 7:18) __________

2. "You shall slaughter, as I have commanded you, of your cattle and of your sheep that God has given you, and you may eat [meat] in your cities as per your hearts' *desire*." (Deuteronomy 12:20) __________

3. "But Sihon, king of Heshbon, did not *desire* to let us pass through [his land]." (Deuteronomy 2:30) __________

4. "You open Your hand and satisfy every living thing [by giving it that which] it *desires*." (Psalms 145:16) __________

Text 1a

וַיֹּאמֶר אֵלָיו, ״אֲנִי ה׳ אֲשֶׁר הוֹצֵאתִיךָ מֵאוּר כַּשְׂדִּים״.

בראשית טו,ז

nd [God] said to [Abraham], *"Ani* (I am) God, Who took you out of Ur Kasdim."

Genesis 15:7

Text 1b

אָנֹכִי ה׳ אֱלֹקֶיךָ אֲשֶׁר הוֹצֵאתִיךָ מֵאֶרֶץ מִצְרַיִם.

שמות כ,ב

nochi (I am) God, your God, Who took you out of the land of Egypt.

Exodus 20:2

Text 1c

וַיַּעַן שְׁמוּאֵל אֶת שָׁאוּל וַיֹּאמֶר, ״אָנֹכִי הָרֹאֶה״.

שמואל א, ט,יט

amuel responded to Saul and said, *"Anochi* (I am) the seer."

I Samuel 9:19

Text 1d

ההפרש בין אני ובין אנכי, דשניהם ענין אחד, הודעת עצמותו ומהותו, רק כשמודיע דרך שפלות אומר, "אני פלוני", וכשמודיע דרך הגבהה והתנשאות אומר, "אנכי", כמו, "אנכי הרואה".

אור התורה, דברים ב, ע' תתרעא

There is a distinction between *ani* and *anochi*, though both words are used to introduce oneself. When one introduces himself in a humble fashion, he says, "*Ani* so-and-so." When one introduces himself in a proud and grand manner, he says "*Anochi* [so-and-so]," as in, "*Anochi* the seer."

Rabbi Menachem Mendel of Lubavitch, *Or HaTorah*, Deuteronomy 2:1071

Rabbi Menachem Mendel Schneersohn of Lubavitch (1789–1866). Also known as "the Tsemach Tsedek," after the title of his compendium of responsa literature. Third leader of the Chabad chasidic movement, and noted authority on Jewish law and Kabbalah. Raised by his grandfather, Rabbi Shne'ur Zalman of Liadi, after his mother's passing. Active in the plight of Russian Jewry, he worked to free the Cantonists, Jewish children kidnapped and forcibly conscripted to the Czar's army. He is buried in the village of Lubavitch.

More on Mazal

Mazal is an acronym for three Hebrew words:

Makom—Place—מקום
Zeman—Time—זמן
Limud—Study—לימוד

In addition to our fortune (*mazal*) being determined by that which flows down from above, it is also man's responsibility and privilege to learn from every experience at every time and place.

Getting Down to the Root
Word Families

Figure 5.5

The Root S-D-R

Word in Hebrew	Transliteration	Meaning
סֵדֶר	*seder*	order
סִידּוּר	*sidur*	ordered prayers
סֵדֶר	*seder*	order of Passover rituals
בְּסֵדֶר	*beseder*	all is in order

Kipah

The popular Hebrew word for the skullcap worn by men is *kipah*, which literally means a "dome." In Yiddish, the more common word is *yarmulke*. The head covering is a constant reminder of the One "above" Who watches over us and pays attention to our every deed.

Interestingly, it has been suggested that the word *"yarmulke"* contains an allusion to the aforementioned symbolism: *yarmulke* can be said to be a contraction of a Hebrew word, *yarei*, to fear, and the Aramaic word *malka,* the king.

Figure 5.6

The Root A-M-N

Word in Hebrew	Transliteration	Meaning
אָמֵן	*amen*	may this prayer come true
אָמְנָם	*amenam*	truly
נֶאֱמָן	*ne'eman*	faithful, loyal
אֱמוּנָה	*emunah*	faith
אוֹמֵן\אוֹמֶנֶת	*omen/omenet*	foster parent; one who supports, nourishes, trains
אוּמָן	*uman*	artist or trained craftsman
יָמִין	*yamin*	right side
תֵּימָן	*teiman*	south

Text 2

העיקר הוא ההרגל, להרגיל דעתו ומחשבתו תמיד להיות קבוע בלבו ומוחו תמיד אשר כל מה שרואה בעיניו, השמים והארץ ומלואה, הכל הם לבושים החיצונים של המלך הקדוש ברוך הוא . . . וזה נכלל גם כן בלשון "אמונה", שהוא לשון רגילות, שמרגיל האדם את עצמו, כמו אומן המאמן ידיו.

תניא, פרק מב

The most important thing is practice. [If one wants to attain faith and awareness of God,] one needs to engage in a habit of thought and mind, constantly imprinting on one's thought and mind that all that one sees—the heaven and earth and all they contain—are only God's outer "garments" [but their essence is Godly energy]. . . .

This idea is implicit in the word *emunah,* which implies training, for a person trains himself [to have faith], like a craftsman who practices his skill.

Rabbi Shne'ur Zalman of Liadi, *Tanya,* ch. 42

Rabbi Shne'ur Zalman of Liadi (1745–1812). Chasidic rebbe and founder of the Chabad movement, also known as "the Alter Rebbe" and "the Rav." Born in Liozna, Belarus, he was among the principal students of the Magid of Mezeritch. His numerous works include the *Tanya*, an early classic containing the fundamentals of Chasidism; *Torah Or; Likutei Torah*; and *Shulchan Aruch HaRav*, a reworked and expanded code of Jewish law. He is interred in Hadiach, Ukraine, and was succeeded by his son, Rabbi Dovber of Lubavitch.

Ears and Scales

The Hebrew word *ozen* means an "ear"; *oznayim* is the plural form, and means "ears." A very similar word is *moznayim* (see Leviticus 19:36; Psalms 62:10), which means a "balance scale." Both words share the exact same root: *aleph-zayin-nun*.

Though the two words have seemingly no connection, today we know that the ear—specifically, the inner ear—is responsible not only for hearing, but also for balance. Thus, vertigo, a condition that causes an abnormal sensation wherein a person feels as though he is spinning or that the world is spinning around him, is most often associated with an inner-ear problem.

Learning Activity 4

In previous lessons, we examined underlying roots of words and their associations. Can you recall some examples and the teachings that were gleaned from them?

Text 3a

קְדֹשִׁים תִּהְיוּ כִּי קָדוֹשׁ אֲנִי ה׳ אֱלֹקֵיכֶם.
ויקרא יט,ב

You shall be *kedoshim* (holy ones), for I, God your God, am *kadosh* (holy).

Leviticus 19:2

Text 3b

ברוך אתה ה׳ אלוקינו מלך העולם אשר קדשנו במצותיו וצונו . . .
נוסח ברכת המצוות

Blessed are You, God our God, King of the Universe, who has made us holy with His commandments and commanded us to . . .

Opening of blessings recited upon performing a mitzvah

Text 3c

לֹא תִהְיֶה קְדֵשָׁה מִבְּנוֹת יִשְׂרָאֵל וְלֹא יִהְיֶה קָדֵשׁ מִבְּנֵי יִשְׂרָאֵל.
דברים כג,יח

There shall not be a *kedeshah* (female prostitute) among the daughters of Israel, nor shall there be a *kadesh* (male prostitute) among the sons of Israel.

Deuteronomy 23:18

Unholiness and Worldliness

Text 4

ולהבדיל בין הקודש ובין החול.

ויקרא י׳, י׳

o distinguish between the *kodesh* (holy) and the *chol* (mundane).

Leviticus 10:10

Figure 5.7

The Root CH-L(-L)

Word in Hebrew	Transliteration	Meaning
חוֹל	*chol*	mundane, everyday, common, secular
חִילּוּל	*chilul*	profaning
חָלָל	*chalal*	vacuum, hollow
חָלָל	*chalal*	corpse
חוֹלֶה	*choleh*	ill person
חָלִיל	*chalil*	recorder (flute-like musical instrument)

Text 5

כל אחד ואחד חייב לומר, ״בשבילי נברא העולם״.
משנה, סנהדרין ד,ה

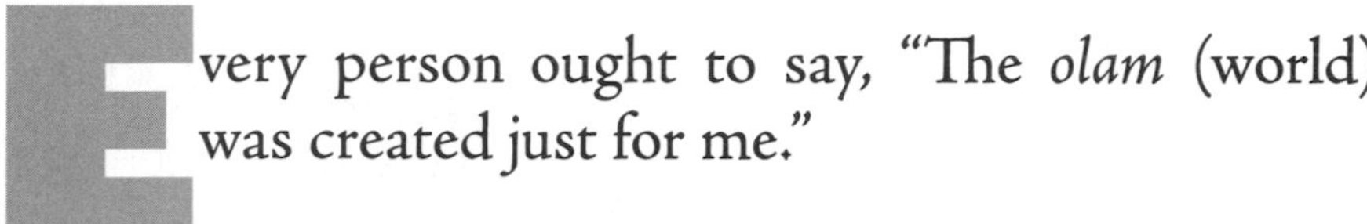

Every person ought to say, "The *olam* (world) was created just for me."

Mishnah, Sanhedrin 4:5

Repentance

Text 6

Teshuvah means "returning" to the old, to one's original nature. Underlying the concept of *teshuvah* is the fact that the Jew is, in essence, good. Desires or temptations may deflect him temporarily from being himself, being true to his essence. But the bad that he does is not part of, nor does it affect, his real nature. *Teshuvah* is a return to the self. While repentance involves dismissing the past and starting anew, *teshuvah* means going back to one's roots in God and exposing them as one's true character.

Rabbi Dr. Jonathan Sacks, *Torah Studies* [Brooklyn N.Y.: Kehot Publication Society, 1996], p. 335 (adapted from discourses of the Lubavitcher Rebbe)

Rabbi Dr. Jonathan Sacks (1948–). Born in London, chief rabbi of the United Hebrew Congregations of the Commonwealth. Attended Cambridge University and received his doctorate from King's College, London. A prolific and influential author, his books include *Will We Have Jewish Grandchildren?* and *The Dignity of Difference.* Recipient of the Jerusalem Prize in 1995 for his contributions to enhancing Jewish life in the Diaspora. Knighted in 2005.

A Language unto Itself

A Holy Language

Abracadabra

Many believe that "abracadabra" has its origin in the Aramaic language, in which *abra* means "I will create" and *cadabra* means "as I speak."

This theory is intriguing, especially considering that Judaism believes that creation is a result of God's speech, and that every person creates realities every time he or she speaks (as explained in Lesson 3).

Also, interestingly, "Avada Kedavra," is the dreaded killing spell in the Harry Potter series. Author J.K. Rowling claims that "it is an ancient spell in Aramaic, and it is the original of 'abracadabra,' which means 'let the thing be destroyed.' Originally, it was used to cure illness—the 'thing' was the illness—but I decided to make the 'thing' the person standing in front of me." Rowling does not provide a source for her assertion.

Nevertheless, there is no Jewish source—nor is there consensus among linguists—that "abracadabra" is indeed rooted in Aramaic.

Text 7a

Rabbi Moshe ben Maimon (1135–1204). Better known as Maimonides or by the acronym Rambam; born in Cordoba, Spain. After the conquest of Cordoba by the Almohads, he fled Spain and eventually settled in Cairo, Egypt. There, he became the leader of the Jewish community and served as court physician to the vizier of Egypt. His rulings on Jewish law are considered integral to the formation of halachic consensus. He is most noted for authoring the *Mishneh Torah,* an encyclopedic arrangement of Jewish law, and for his philosophical work, *Guide for the Perplexed.*

וסיבה בקריאת לשוננו זה לשון הקודש . . . מפני שזה הלשון הקודש לא הונח בו שם כלל לכלי המשגל, לא מן האנשים ולא מן הנשים, ולא לגוף המעשה המביא להולדה, ולא לזרע, ולא ליציאה. אלו הדברים כולם לא הונח להם שם ראשון כלל בלשון העברי, אלא ידברו בהם בשמות מושאלים וברמיזות.

מורה הנבוכים ג,ח

e call our language the "holy language"... because this holy language has no designated name for the procreative organs of males or females, nor for the procreative act itself, nor for semen or bodily excretions. . . . Rather, it describes these things in figurative language and by way of hints.

Maimonides, *Guide for the Perplexed* 3:8

Text 7b

לעולם אל יוציא אדם דבר מגונה מפיו, שהרי עקם הכתוב שמונה אותיות ולא הוציא דבר מגונה מפיו, שנאמר (בראשית ז,ח), "מן הבהמה הטהורה ומן הבהמה אשר איננה טהורה".

תלמוד בבלי, פסחים ג,א

A person should never emit a course expression from his mouth, for the Torah deviated [by adding] eight letters in order not to emit a coarse expression from its mouth, as it is stated (Genesis 7:8), "From the animals that are pure and from the animals that are not pure."

Talmud, Pesachim 3a

Text 8

מה שרבותינו קוראין לשון התורה "לשון הקודש", שהוא מפני שדברי התורה והנבואות וכל דברי קדושה כולם בלשון ההוא נאמרו. והנה הוא הלשון שהקדוש ברוך הוא יתעלה שמו מדבר בו עם נביאיו ועם עדתו . . . ובו נקרא בשמותיו הקדושים . . . ובו ברא עולמו, וקרא שמות שמים וארץ וכל אשר בם, ומלאכיו וכל צבאיו לכולם בשם יקרא—מיכאל וגבריאל—בלשון ההוא, ובו קרא שמות לקדושים אשר בארץ: אברהם, יצחק, ויעקב, ושלמה, וזולתם.

רמב"ן שמות ל,יג

Rabbi Moshe ben Nachman (1194–1270). Also known as Nachmanides, or by the acronym Ramban. Nachmanides authored a classic commentary on the Pentateuch that includes everything from critical examination of the text to kabbalistic insights. He also authored numerous other works, including a commentary on the Talmud. Born in Spain, he served as leader of Iberian Jewry. In 1263, he was summoned by King James of Aragon to a public disputation with Pablo Cristiani, a Jewish apostate. Though he was the clear victor of the debate, resulting persecution led to his expulsion from Spain. Settling in Israel, Nachmanides helped reestablish communal life in Jerusalem

Our sages call the language of the Torah the "holy tongue," because the Torah and its prophecies and all the holy matters were said in that language. Indeed, it is the holy language that God uses to speak with His devoted prophets and His people. . . . Also, God's holy names are in [Hebrew]. . . . With this [language] God created His world, and gave names to the heaven and earth and all they contain. In this language, God gave names to His angels, [such as] Michael and Gabriel. In this language, God gave names to the holy ones here on earth: Abraham, Isaac, Jacob, Solomon, and others.

Nachmanides, Exodus 30:13

The Code

Text 9

אף על פי שבכל לשון ולשון מע׳ לשונות יש גם כן קריית שם לכל הנבראים והנוצרים והנעשים, וקורים לכל דבר בשמו, עם כל זה אינו שם העצם לדבר ההוא, רק שם הדבר בעלמא כדי להכיר בין דבר לחבירו, אבל לא שמו האמיתי הוא . . . מה שאין כן בלשון הקודש, כל מה שנקרא שמו כך הוא שמו האמיתי, שם העצם משורשו.

אור תורה יד

Rabbi Dovber "the Magid" of Mezeritch (d. 1772). Was the primary disciple and eventual successor of the Ba'al Shem Tov. Amongst his disciples were the founders of various chasidic dynasties, including Rabbi Nachum of Chernobyl, Rabbi Levi Yitschak of Berditchev, and Rabbi Shne'ur Zalman of Liadi. His teachings, recorded by his students, appear in various volumes including the *Magid Devarav LeYa'akov.*

In all 70 languages, although each creation is given a name and defining term, the name is not connected to the essence of that matter but is merely an arbitrary name that distinguishes one thing from another. [On the other hand,] in the holy tongue, each name is the true name, the essential name that is connected to its source.

Rabbi Dov Ber of Mezeritch, *Or Torah* 14

Text 10

ידוע בספרי המקובלים כי ראשית הכל נאצלו האותיות, ואחר כך באותיות ברא הקדוש ברוך הוא כל העולמות. וזה סוד "בראשית ברא אלקים א"ת" (בראשית א,א), פי' האותיות מא' עד ת'. נמצא כי הבריאה ראשונה . . . היינו האותיות.

שם, ג

It is known in kabbalistic literature that the letters [of the *alef-beit*] were the first entities to be created. Thereafter, by use of the letters, God created all the worlds. This is the secret [meaning of the first phrase in the Torah], "In the beginning God created את (*et*)* . . ." (Genesis 1:1); that is, God's first act was to create the letters from *alef* to *tav*.

Rabbi Dov Ber of Mezeritch, ibid., 3

* Hebrew contains a preposition (את/et) that precedes definite direct objects.

Text 11

יודע היה בצלאל לצרף אותיות שנבראו בהן שמים וארץ.

תלמוד בבלי, ברכות נה,א

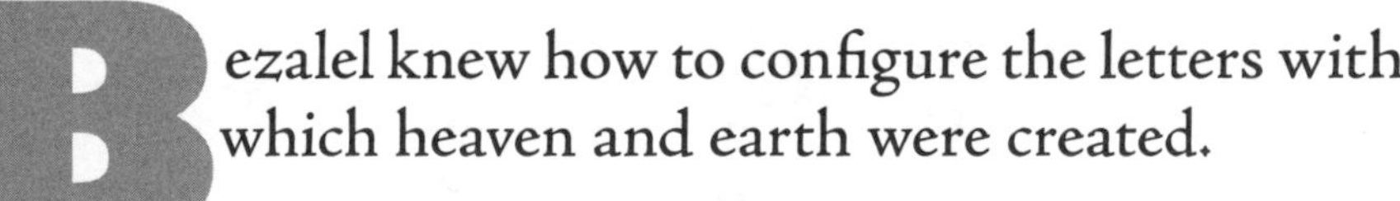

Bezalel knew how to configure the letters with which heaven and earth were created.

Talmud, Berachot 55a

Telling Letters

Text 12a

אלף בית, אלף בינה.
גימל דלת, גמול דלים. מאי טעמא פשוטה כרעיה דגימל לגבי דלת? שכן דרכו של גומל חסדים לרוץ אחר דלים. ומאי טעמא פשוטה כרעיה דדלת לגבי גימל? דלימציה ליה נפשיה. ומאי טעמא מהדר אפיה דדלת מגימל? דליתן ליה בצינעה, כי היכי דלא ליכסיף מיניה.

תלמוד בבלי, שבת קד,א

Alef bet, "learn wisdom."

Gimel dalet, show kindness to the poor. Why is the foot of the *gimel* stretched toward the *dalet?* Because it is fitting for the benefactor to run after the poor. Why is the roof of the *dalet* stretched out toward the *gimel?* Because [the pauper] must make himself available to [the benefactor]. Why is the face of the *dalet* turned away from the *gimel?* Because [the benefactor] must give [the pauper] in secret, lest [the pauper] be ashamed of [the benefactor].

Talmud, Shabbat 104a

Figure 5.8

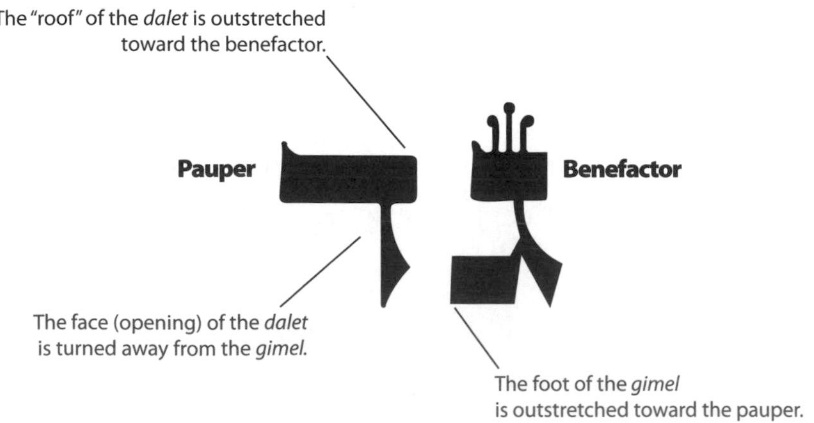

Text 12b

קוף, קדוש. ריש, רשע. מאי טעמא מהדר אפיה דקוף מריש? אמר הקדוש ברוך הוא, "אין אני יכול להסתכל ברשע". ומאי טעמא מהדרה תגיה דקוף לגבי ריש? אמר הקדוש ברוך הוא, "אם חוזר בו, אני קושר לו כתר כמותי". ומאי טעמא כרעיה דקוף תלויה? דאי הדר ביה, ליעייל וליעול בהך.

תלמוד בבלי, שם

Kuf [stands for] *kadosh* (holy); *reish* [for] *rasha* (wicked). Why is the face of the *kuf* averted from the *reish*? Because God said: "I cannot look at the wicked." Why is the crown of the *kuf* turned toward the *reish*? Because God says, "If he repents, I will bind a crown on him like Mine." Why is the foot of the *kuf* suspended? [To show] that if [the wicked one] repents, he can enter and be brought in [to God's favor] through this [opening].

Talmud, ibid.

Figure 5.9

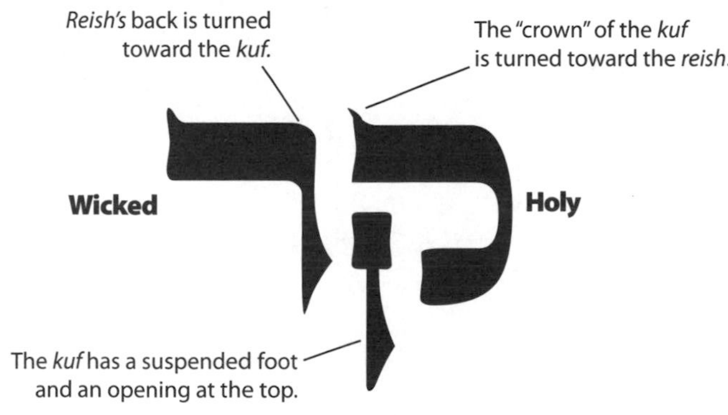

Text 12c

שין, שקר. תיו, אמת. מאי טעמא שקר מקרבן מיליה, אמת מרחקא מיליה? שיקרא שכיח, קושטא לא שכיח. ומאי טעמא שיקרא אחדא כרעיה קאי, ואמת מלבן לבוניה? קושטא קאי, שיקרא לא קאי.

תלמוד בבלי, שם

Shin [stands for] *sheker* (falsehood); *tav* [for] *emet* (truth). Why are the letters of *sheker* close together, whilst those of *emet* are far apart? Falsehood is frequent, truth is rare. And why does falsehood stand on one foot, while truth has a brick-like foundation? Truth can stand, falsehood cannot stand.

Talmud, ibid.

Figure 5.10

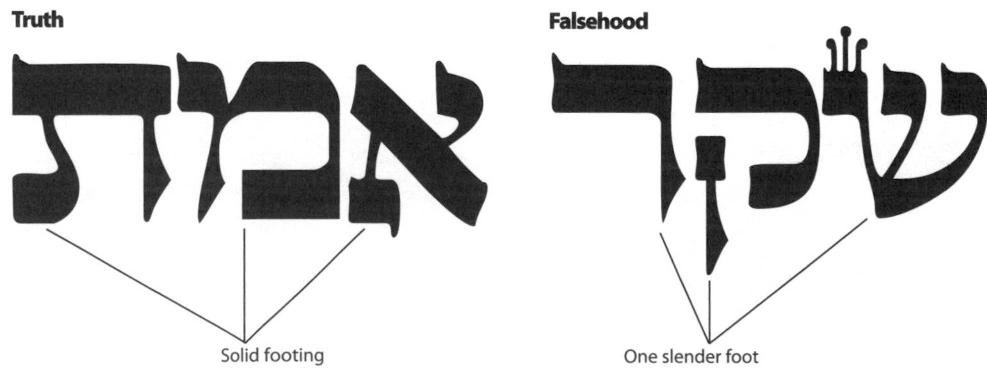

Figure 5.11

ו וָו vav	ה הֵא hei	ד דָּלֶת dalet	ג גִּימֶל gimel	ב בֵּית beit	א אַלֶף alef
ל לָמֶד lamed	כ כַּף kaf	י יוּד yud	ט טֵית tet	ח חֵית chet	ז זַיִן zayin
צ צָדִי tsadi	פ פֵּה pei	ע עַיִן ayin	ס סָמֶךְ samech	נ נוּן nun	מ מֵם mem
		ת תָּו tav	ש שִׂין sin	ר רֵישׁ reish	ק קוּף kuf

Sukkah Blueprint

The Hebrew letters of the word sukkah (the foliage covered hut in which we dwell during the autumn holiday of Sukkot) give us the blueprint for the structure of its walls.

ס–A sukkah can be constructed with four walls.

כ–A sukkah is also kosher if it has only three walls.

ה–The minimum a sukkah requires in order to be kosher is two and a half walls.

Key Points

1. The field of language has been strongly influenced by religion. Indeed, the Torah is the source for many well-known idioms and aphorisms.

2. Shared points of reference by members of a particular nationality allow for a unique "insider" dialogue that creates a sense of community.

3. Many Hebrew words contain dual meanings, and a translation is compelled to make a choice between the two. As a result, a translation cannot convey the multi-layered meaning of a text.

4. The nuances that different synonyms suggest are also often lost in translation.

5. Hebrew words that share a common root are usually related in meaning. Understanding this offers us a deeper insight that is unattainable through reading a translation.

6. The root of the word *kodesh,* "holy," means "separate" and "designated." To be holy means to be separated from the mundane (*"chol"*) aspects of this world and designated to God. The root of *chol* means "gap" and connotes a disconnect from God.

7. Hebrew is called the "holy tongue." Maimonides suggests that this is because it is a refined and dignified language. Nachmanides explains that it is because it is the language in which God converses.

8. The mystics explain that the Hebrew name of every object is the conduit for the divine energy that creates it and gives it its form and function.

Additional Readings

What's the Truth about ... the Meaning of "Pesach"?

by **Rabbi Dr. Ari Zivotofsky**

Misconception: The only meaning of "Pesach," the Hebrew name for the holiday of Passover, is "to pass over."

Fact: While that is a correct translation, an equally valid, and possibly older, translation is "to have compassion for."[1]

Background: The name of the spring holiday, and its associated temple animal offering, is based on a description first found in Exodus 12:12-13, where God declares, "And I shall pass through the land of Egypt on that night [of Passover], and I shall smite every firstborn in the land of Egypt from human to animal . . . and I will see the blood [on the doorposts], *ufasachti* you. . . . " The root *peh-samach-chet* is commonly translated as "and I will pass over." In this verse, the word *fasachti* indicates that God will "pass over" the Jewish houses in Egypt. However, it is a rare word in the Bible, and its translation is uncertain.

In his Aramaic translation of that verse, Onkelos (circa first century CE) uses the word *"ve'eychos,"* which means "I will have compassion." Another early translator, Targum (pseudo-)Yonatan, also translates the word in a number of places as "having mercy" (Exodus 12:13; 12:17). But in 12:23 he translates *ufasach* as *veyagin*—to protect.

The Septuagint offers both definitions. In Exodus 12:23 it uses the classical translation of "to pass over," while in Exodus 12:13 and 12:27, it uses the word for shelter/protection.

The Mechilta records a dispute between Rebbi Yoshiya and Rebbi Yonatan over the word *pasachti*. Rebbi Yoshiya links it to *"pasaiti,"*[2] I stepped over, and explains that it means that God "skipped or passed over" the Jewish homes.[3] (This notion of God "skipping along" to expedite redemption,[4] he tells us, is found in a verse in Song of Songs (2:8): "The voice of my beloved, it comes suddenly to redeem me, as if skipping over the hills.") Rebbi Yonatan disagrees and explains that *pasachti* means that God had mercy on the Jews. Mechilta d'Rebbi Yishmael expresses this thought as well that *"Ein pischa ela chayis"*—"There is no [translation of] pesach other than mercy."

Rav Saadya Gaon[5] explains *"pasach"* (Exodus 12:23) as *veyerachem*, to have mercy, and *"zevach pesach"* (Exodus 12:27) as *"zevach chamlah,"* the sacrifice of mercy. Similarly, the Hebrew grammarian Ibn Janach,[6] in his *Sefer HaShorashim*, understands the word *pasach* as "to derive from mercy or grace."

Rashi quotes both opinions. Commenting on Exodus 12:13, he first compares *ufasachti* to a word with the same root[7] in Isaiah 31:5 and defines it as "to have com-

---

[1] Two sources that discuss some of this material are Raphael Weiss, "Pesachchamal, Chos" [Hebrew], *L'shonainu* (5723-5724): 27-28, 127-130 and S.P. Brock, "An Early Interpretation of Pasah: 'Aggen in the Palestinian Targum," *Interpreting the Hebrew Bible: Essays in Honour of EIJ Rosenthal*, ed. JA Emerton and Stefan C. Reif (Cambridge,1982), 27-34.

[2] Interchanging a *chet* and an *ayin* is not uncommon, as noted by Ramban to Deuteronomy 2:23, where he posits that *"eivim"* and *"cheivim"* are the same.

[3] Both Josephus (Antiquities 2:313) and Philo also understood it to mean "pass over." See Louis H. Feldman, *Translation of Josephus, Antiquities*, Book 2, p. 222, note 823.

[4] See also *Oznayim LaTorah* to Exodus 12:11.

[5] Lived 882-942. See *Encyclopaedia Judaica* 14:543-555.

[6] Lived in the first half of the eleventh century. See *EJ* 8:1181-1186.

[7] It is worth noting that the root *peh-samach-chet* has another meaning in Arabic, and possibly did in Aramaic as well. It means,

passion." He then compares it to I Kings 18:21 and says that it means "to skip over."[8] Rashi prefers the second alternative, and on Exodus 12:11 cites only that translation. Interestingly, Rashi's biological and spiritual descendant, Rashbam, drops the other definition and offers only to "skip over" and to "pass by."

Those who reject "pass over" as the translation may be motivated by an aversion to ascribing physical characteristics to God, and, in particular, what Rambam calls *"po'alei tenu'ah,"* action verbs. Onkelos consistently reinterprets anything that even resembles anthropomorphizing God. He would rather ascribe an emotion, such as mercy, to God than suggest that God physically skipped over houses.

There is, however, an intriguing suggestion[9] concerning this enigmatic word. If, as stated emphatically in the Haggadah and in Exodus 12:13, God himself killed all the Egyptian firstborn sons, then *pasachti* refers to God, so to speak, skipping over the Jewish houses. However, according to another verse in Exodus (12:23), it appears that the Angel of Death, not God, carried out the killing of the firstborns. In 12:23, the Bible states that God *"ufasach* the entrance and He will not permit the destroyer to enter your homes. . . ."[10] Based on the literal reading of this verse, *ufasach* cannot mean God "passed over" the houses, since He wasn't doing the destroying; it must mean that God had mercy and protected the Jews from the Angel of Death.

The common notion that pesach means "pass over" is probably because the commentator par excellence, Rashi, inclined towards that approach. It is also possible that our conception of the word was influenced by non-Jewish society. St. Jerome, in his fourth-century Vulgate, translated Exodus 12:13 as, "I will see the blood and I will pass over (*ac transibo*) you," and this passed into the overwhelming majority of Christian translations, including the English King James Bible.

There are a number of ramifications to the debate over the translation of the root *peh-samach-chet*. The discussion in the Mechilta, as explained by Malbim, is more than just a debate over translation; it is a debate over who was killed during the Plague of the Firstborn. Rav Yoshiya maintained that God, as the destroyer, "passed" or "skipped" over the Jewish homes and did not enter them at all. If an Egyptian was resourceful enough to hide out with a Jew, Rav Yoshiya believes that he was spared. Rav Yonatan, however, believes that God had mercy on the Jews, wherever they were, and only on the Jews. Thus, an Egyptian in a Jewish house was killed, and a Jew in an Egyptian house was spared.

This debate also has ramifications for every Jew at the Seder table. The Haggadah cites a Talmudic statement of Rabban Gamliel (Pesachim 116a-b) that whoever neglects to mention [*Korban*] *Pesach*, matzah and marror and fails to explain[11] the reason for their appearance at the Seder has not fulfilled his obligation.[12] He also

"to clear an area." Thus, the statement in *Ha Lachma Anya: kol ditzrich yaitay v'yifsach*—is usually understood to mean that all should partake of the *Korban Pesach*. This presents a problem because the *Korban* is supposed to be eaten only *limnuyav*—to those pre-registered. With the alternate meaning the phrase can be understood as, "Come, clear a space, sit and eat," with no mention of the *Korban Pesach*.

8 On this verse Radak and Metzudat Tzion say it means alternating or skipping between possibilities, as a cripple hobbles from side to side. Commenting on I Kings 18:26 (the verse that Chizkuni to Exodus 12:13 uses as his proof text that it means to step over), Metzudat Tzion, Metzudat David and Rashi all offer only one possibility, that it means to skip or to step over.

9 Offered by my friend Shimon Gesundheit in his Ph.D. dissertation (Hebrew University).

10 Note the use of the word *pesach* ("pass over" or "had mercy") in conjunction with *pesach* (entrance way). The words, of course, sound the same, assuming one uses the Ashkenazic pronunciation. A humorous example where Ashkenazic pronunciation has led to a comic error occurs in *Zevachim* 115a, Rashi s.v. *yachol she'ani*, where the word *pesach* in the verse "to the entrance (*petach/pesach*) of the *Ohel Moed* " is written with a *samach* instead of a *taf*.

11 See for example Rashbam, *Pesachim* 116b; Meiri, *Pesachim* 116a; Tosafot Yom Tov on the *mishnah*; the Abudraham on the Haggadah and *Chayei Adam* 129:11 that it is not sufficient to merely mention the three items. The explanation of their appearance must also be provided.

12 Whether Rabban Gamliel was referring to the obligation to recite the Haggadah or to eat the requisite items is hotly debated by the commentators on the Talmud and the Haggadah. This statement is cited as the *halachah* (Rambam, *Chametz Umatzah* 7:5).

states that one is required to explain to the assembled that the [*Korban*] *Pesach* is because God *pasach* over our ancestors' homes in Egypt as the verse (Exodus 12:27) states: "And you shall say, 'It is a Pesach sacrifice to Hashem who *pasach* the houses of the Israelites.'" It thus seems that in order to fulfill one's obligation, one is required to properly translate the word "*pasach*." (In this vein, some of the Haggadah commentators try to help out. For example, the *Perush Kadmon*, an anonymous, early commentary, written around the twelfth century, explains, based on I Kings 18:21 and Isaiah 31:5, that it means to pass over and not dwell on a spot.[13] The Shibbolei Haleket[14] similarly endorses the "skip over" translation based on the verse in I Kings. Rashbatz,[15] while also explaining it to mean "pass over," rejects the notion that *pasach* means "to rest," an explanation that must have been current in his time but is not readily found in other sources.)

Irrespective of what the root *peh-samach-chet* means, that night in Egypt revealed both God's mercy and the bypassing of Jews from destruction. How to precisely translate the Biblical term "*pasach*" is unclear and was already subject to debate more than 2,000 years ago. It seems that towards the medieval period the translation of "pass over" gained in prominence. That, however, does not negate the alternative possibility; and an opinion found in the Mechilta, Onkelos, Rav Saadya Gaon and other important sources should be accorded appropriate respect. At the Seder, both options should be raised, and Biblical verses with this root should be explored.

Jewish Action 64, no. 3 (2004)
Reprinted with permission of *Jewish Action*, the magazine of the Orthodox Union

13 Similar to Rebbi Yoshiya in the Mechilta.

14 Born approximately 1220 (4980).

15 Rav Shimon ben Tzemach Duran 1361-1444.

The Kabbalah of the Dreidel

By **Rabbi Yisrael Rice**

Do you know the rules of Dreidel? You spin a top with four Hebrew letters on it. A *Gimmel* wins the whole kitty, a *Hei* gets you half, *Nun* gets nothing and for a *Shin* you must pay in. Aside from the inherent Kabbalistic meaning behind this method, there is the practical Yiddishe origin. *Gimmel* stands for *Gantz*, meaning the whole thing. *Hei* is for *Halb*, meaning half. *Nun* stands for *Nisht* or nothing. And *Shin* is for *Shtell arein* or put in.

These are four basic modes of being, depending upon the person, his or her period in life, or the particular day. We all have our *Gimmel* days. This is when we feel that everything is going great and turning out in a sensational way. (It's been a while, eh?) We have our *Hei* days, when things are going quite well. The *Nun* and *Shin* need no explanation.

But each of these letters represents only one face of the Dreidel -- only a single angle or perspective of the whole. What do the letters spell out? What is the "whole" of the Dreidel? *Ness Gadol Hayah Sham*, "a great miracle happened there." This refers to the great miracle of Chanukah that occurred in the Holy Land. The situation there seemed dire and beyond hope. They were definitely having a *Shin* day. The commitment of a few people turned the situation around (like a Dreidel) and brought out the miracle and G-d's salvation.

The Macabees did not dwell on the fact that they were being oppressed and persecuted. They focused on the *Gimmel* that was on the other side of the *Shin*. And then they acted to create a vehicle for a Divine miracle.

It is vital to remember that whatever letter we seem to be getting at a particular point in life, it's all part of one Dreidel. And that Dreidel is telling us that miracles happen. We can transform the dark situations of life into the bright light of the Chanukah Menorah. This depends upon our faith in G-d's plan, and our commitment to create a vehicle for the miracle.

The Dreidel in the Bible?

Based on this theme we find a phenomenal "coincidence" with these four letters of the Dreidel. The first place where these letters occur as a word in the Torah is in the Parshah (Torah Reading) of *Vayigash* (Genesis 44-47, always in proximity to Chanukah), where they spell the word *Goshnah*, meaning "to Goshen."

The Patriarch Jacob was sending his son, Judah, to the Egyptian city of Goshen to set up a house of study, in advance of Jacob's, and his entire family's relocation to that land. Our patriarch was aware that this was a dreadful descent into exile. But he looked at all of the letters of the Dreidel, and realized that hidden in the exile are the seeds of redemption. Study must continue, especially in exile. As long as we are able to retain the vital Divine information, the exile cannot hold sway over us. And our study and performance become the vehicle for the ultimate redemption.

This is similar to the origin of the Dreidel. According to tradition, during the times of Greek oppression Torah study was forbidden. When the children were studying, they would keep a Dreidel nearby to pull out and play in case they were discovered. (A bit opposite from our Hebrew school experience, perhaps.) At the time, the students may have thought that the game was a distraction from their true purpose in life.

But in truth, G-d conceals His countenance to draw out our commitment and connection to Him. It's all about revealing the Divine in the least likely places. That's what a miracle is.

The Dreidel was the formula to elicit the underlying truth of the Jewish soul.

The Dreidel and Moshiach

And one more idea. If you add up the *Gimatria* (the Hebrew numerical value) of the letters of the Dreidel, you get 358 (*Nun* (50) + *Gimmel* (3) + *Hei* (5) + *Shin* (300) = 358). This is the same value as *Moshiach* (*Mem* (40) + *Shin* (300) + *Yud* (10) + *Chet* (8) = 358), the Messiah. When the Moshiach comes, he will teach each individual how to see the Divine purpose in every facet of life. Even the time of exile and darkness will be illuminated.

We may have been focusing on one particular letter. Moshiach will teach us to see that all of life is a tapestry of Divine wonder

The Letters of the Ten Utterances

by **Rabbi Adin Steinsaltz**

The Baal Shem Tov explains the Divine Word, not as a metaphor, but as possessing specific actuality. This speech of God, which created the heavens, is actually present in the heavens; the very syllables and the letters of "Let there be a firmament" uphold the heavens and make it possible for the heavens to exist. It is not only something that occurred in the past, but is something that is taking place all the time; God speaks always. When a man speaks, his words, as definite substances, fade into nothingness. The Words of God remain forever. We comprehend this metaphorically, as though to illustrate that Divine speech makes things happen. But it is not only that which is manifested that endures, but also the very words and letters continue to exist.

Let us endeavor to imagine that Divine speech is not a transient phenomenon, but a continuous one, repeating itself over and over. As though—and one must realize that this is only an illustration—one were to switch on an electric light. In alternating currents, such as we use here for ordinary purposes, the electric current goes back and forth all the time. One may thus see the Creation of the world as such a switching on of a current. What is done by throwing a switch is not a completed action; it only releases a continuous and repeated movement of energy that remains dependent on the source. Divine speech is thus eternal in manifestation and is continually renewed. It is the formation of a pattern that endures as a dynamic interaction. The Baal Shem Tov once explained, in another context, how this was true of the Revelation of the Torah on

Mount Sinai. It was a speaking of the Eternal Word in the sense, too, that it is being eternally spoken. There has not been any ceasing of this Divine speech; it is we who have ceased to listen. At the confrontation of Sinai, not only was that said which was said, but it was granted us that our ears be opened to hear what was being said. And the Baal Shem Tov concludes by saying that anyone can be privileged to stand on Mount Sinai and hear the Torah at any moment in his life. The confrontation at Mount Sinai is unique and single, not because the word of God has ceased to be spoken, but because we do not let our ears remain open to hear it.

Therefore, we read, "If the letters of the ten utterances by which the earth was created during the six days of creation were to depart from it (but) for an instant, God forbid, it would revert to naught and absolute nothingness, exactly as before the six days of creation." By which it is reiterated that the departing of the letters is not only a matter of loss of life force or of some other deprivation. If the Divine speech ceases, the result is a reverting to nonbeing. The letters of this Divine utterance did not create the things of the world; they are the very substance of things.

Here it would be helpful perhaps to bring another example and again it has to be understood only as an illustration and not as any sort of description. When in our modern view of the world we speak of matter, it is only in very general and relative terms that we recognize it as solid and inert. An object like a table is composed of constantly moving particles whose physical solidity is rather questionable. Electrons may actually be apprehended as concentrated points of energy waves. In short, even within the realm of the physical world we are caught in a net of unreality; that which seems solid is not really so. It is not a matter of our senses deceiving us; the senses give a straightforward enough projection of things as they appear to be and as they are meant to be. What is being said by the teacher is that all matter, even that which appears to us real and solid, derives its existence from the Divine word.

Thus, even in earth or water there is spiritual essence. The stone has more of a soul, in a way, than the human body because it is more completely dominated by the soul-of-the-stone, while man has more soul than the stone, because he has more independent essence. The soul-of-the-stone is the Divine, form-giving force that substantiates the stone; if this Divine force should depart from the stone, there is no stone at all. When the soul of man departs from his body, the body continues to exist for a short while. To remove the soul of the stone is like switching off the electric current; there is no more light and all is extinct.

We are confronted with the very human problem based on the fact that the soul and the body are not identical. Were the soul to so dominate the human being that life would express only the soul, then the human being would disappear as soon as the soul left. Which, incidentally, is connected with the matter of sin and repentance. For if a person sinned in such a way that his punishment is to be cut off, then his soul would be consumed and the person would cease to exist. The whole point of repentance is that a human being does, somehow, continue to exist, at least certain remnants do, in order to be able to make amends. In other words, human beings have, in this sense, a double life; there is the life of the body and the life of the soul. And it is this that makes for problems in the spiritual life, because the body has its own desires; it does not merely express the desires of the soul. For instance: I decide to put my hand into the fire and I can observe how the body protests.

This is what happens in the relations between body and soul in man. But inert matter has no such soul; there is no conflict of desires. The soul of an object is the essence of its physicality. That which we know as the physical stone is a physical projection of the letters of the Divine speech that gives the stone its being. Just as the spatial dimensions characteristic of matter are projections of the movement and arrangements of molecules, so is all that we know as the world a result of Divine utterance, which appears as stone, flower, or anything.

We read that "although the name 'stone' is not mentioned in the Ten Utterances recorded in the Torah, nevertheless life-force flows to the stone through combinations and substitutions of the letters that are transposed in the 231 gates." This endeavors to explain the relation between that which is divinely spoken and the infinite detail that is created thereby. When, for instance, it is written, "God said 'Let there be a firmament,'" the words we read are some human version of that which God said. The inconceivable that is spoken by the Divine is translated in two ways. First it is translated by the firmament itself (in all its details). Second it is translated into that which is written in the Torah.

To use an example, we may conceive sound waves as being received and registered either by a magnetic tape or by a phonograph record. The magnetic tape will convert them into some sort of electromagnetic signals; the record will convert them into grooves on the plastic material. These are two different translations of the sound waves that, when the sound is projected, are translated back into the same thing. Now—sound waves, in themselves, are neither a magnetic signal on tape nor grooves in a record. When I wish to show them to anyone, I have to resort to one or another of the conversions or translations. In this sense, the letters of the Divine speech as manifested by the firmament are a different version, or another translation, of the same thing that is written in the Torah. Although one realizes that they are identical, one has to be aware of the fact that they are both humanized projections, that is, capable of being received and understood by man through his limited faculties. Thus, too, there are gifted persons who can look at a page of musical notes and not only sing them, but read them with pleasure as another reads a book and sometimes with even greater enjoyment than if they were to hear a concert rendering of the piece. This is more or less similar to what one may say of a great soul who reads the Torah—he hears the word of God in it, and it is for him a very different thing than for the one who reads logical sentences. Indeed, it may be said that the same thing holds true for any kind of reacting to the world; reception depends on one's capacities. There is the famous story of the Baal HaTanya who, a short time before his death, called his grandson, later known as the Tzemach Tzedek, and asked him, "What do you see?" The boy replied that he saw the ordinary things of a house. "And I," said the old man, "see only the word of God." There is a level, then, at which a person ceases to see—when he becomes aware of the thing itself rather than what is apparent from its modes of projections.

The letters, and the words of Torah we make of them, are translations into a specific mode of communication, a contrivance called writing. On the other hand, every letter is a Divine force, and therefore these letters cannot appear to us directly as they are; moreover, there are also different combinations of letters. The same letters combine, not only in the form of words, but also in various other ways, circles within circles, from one level of meaning to higher levels, from essence to essence; and within these circles there are various revelations of the same thing.

The letters thus combine in various permutations until we get the word "stone." Which is only partly to explain that the Ten Utterances contain all the letters—for the combination is not an accidental one resulting from chance groupings of the letters: it is a very definite union of three specific letters that belong to the earth. The word "stone" does not have any of the "letters" of "heaven" in it, but rather the three earthly letters it needs to undergo its various transmutations. Examples from modern chemistry may help us grasp the point. When working with chemical formulas, it makes a considerable difference if I replace any one letter by another. In modern organic chemistry, it is important even to designate direction, whether it is left or right—just as there are certain words, in Hebrew, composed of three letters, the third the same as the first, which have two distinct meanings depending on which "direction" they are read.

Hence, every created object has its own form, its own special essence, which is connected with the letters that formed it; and these letters are a certain expression of the Ten Utterances. When the Ten Utterances express themselves in another realm, and on another level, it does not manifest in the form of a stone. In a higher world, these Ten Utterances have another meaning; only as they are transmuted and descend to this world do they assume the meaning they have for us. It might be in place here to observe that in almost every domain these divisions are necessary and useful. For in the complex jumble of almost all compounded things in the world, an individual thing is defined by "number," i.e., by size and the level occupied by the formula of its composition, and so on. In integral calculus there is a similar problem, of taking a formula and raising it to a certain power, the fourth or fifth or whatever, by which it undergoes a certain transmutation that gives the result another meaning. All of which is only a reflection of a part of the problem we are dealing with here, in which the levels are not raised to the fourth or fifth power or even to the hundredth power, but to the millionth, in which the levels expand and grow in all directions. So that the basic formula of the Ten Utterances is broken up into a vast number of worlds in each of which there are different instructions given, the Divine forces manifest differently so that every object and detail, not only the stone as rock fragment, but every particle of substance in the universe no matter where, derives its special being from a particular life-force. And this Divine speech, the special combination of letters that supports the being of this particle, is single and unique, and the particle next to it is another, with another history and another essence and another name.

Indeed, It Is afterward mentioned that every single thing has its own name, even the smallest and most inconspicuous item. So that, incidentally, it is said that when parents give their child a name, thinking that they know exactly why they are doing so, the truth is that they don't know why they are choosing it. And if they make a mistake and give a wrong name, the child will afterward change it because the name is not his correct one. This attempt to define who one is spills over into the identity of every soul, which also has an appropriate name, a specific formula. It is so for every star in the sky, too, each one with its name: "He counts the number of the stars; He calls them all by their names . . ." (Psalm 147:4). On the other hand, there are things that, like points on a topographical map, can be sufficiently defined by their coordinates, the intersection of latitude and longitude. And if there are three dimensions, the appropriate numbers of each provide sufficient information to define it. Now, let us imagine something with thousands of dimensions, or even millions, each one requiring its own number or name, in order to express the formula of its being that is its animating power, its life-force. It is from this that the thing draws sustenance and that explains the essence of its soul, even if it is a stone, which does not mean, of course, that if I speak to a stone the stone will understand me, but rather that everything created out of Divine speech necessarily has a sort of soul of its own.

Interestingly, the great sage, the Maharal, also speaks of this, in his own terms, without Kabbalistic overtones, saying that miracle is based on the fact that the human being who performs a miracle sees the Divine speech in the world more clearly than he sees the material substance of the world, and Divine speech is, to a degree, given to manipulation by the one who comprehends it. That is to say, the one who realizes that there is no table here has gone beyond the table, while for the one who does not see this, the table remains a table. It seems to be a question then: Where am I in terms of things? What is my relation to the objects of the world? Such as, for instance, the miracle that everyone can perform—walking on what is called the waters of the lake, when it is frozen over. The problem, then, is how I can relate to things in their changing state, and to what extent I am able to expand my relations to a static, immobile condition. From this point of view, the miracle is a matter of shifting things about a little in the world.

Incidentally, the matter of repentance is also a similar problem. By repentance, I reach a certain level, by virtue of which I change something—and the whole point of repentance is that it alters some genuine reality in the world. Only when a person reaches such a level can he be said to atone. The world and its objects seem to be fixed only because we are all suspended within the same dimension. The man who is able to act on things in a different dimension, such as that of the microscopic world or of nuclear physics, does not feel that there is any difference between solid matter and any other kind of matter. As far as electrons are concerned, it is all the same, whether they go through gases or through solid metal. We may add that also in our ordinary existence we live on a number of levels, and when I am on a certain level, then for something to have a distinguishable form on another level, it is sufficient for it to appear to be so. So that what is spiritual and what is physical depends on the relation I have, from my vantage point, to the things concerned.

The Sustaining Utterance (Lanham, MD: Rowman & Littlefield, 1989), 16-23
Reprinted with permission of the author

Lesson 6

Beyond the Nose Job

Judaism's Answers to Life's Biggest Questions

Introduction

In life, you have to learn not to sweat the small stuff. In this lesson, we will discuss what to live for and what do die for, and when a will is a won't. You'll find out what's engraved upon your heart—as well as the difference between a nose job and a tattoo.

The Uniquely Jewish Path

Satan

Learning Activity 1

Circle the answer you find most accurate. Be prepared to defend your choice.

Satan is:

a. the archenemy of God.

b. a fallen angel who sinned and was punished.

c. a devoted angel who is doing exactly what he is meant to do.

d. nonexistent in the Jewish tradition.

Is God in the Bedroom?

Learning Activity 2

Which of these best represents the Jewish attitude toward sexual intimacy?

a. It is reluctantly allowed in the context of marriage as a necessary concession to human frailties.

b. It is justified because it enables the noble goal of procreation.

c. It is the ultimate vehicle for God's expression.

d. For reasons of modesty, Jewish literature avoids the topic entirely.

Text 1a

כתיב (איוב כג,יג), "והוא באחד . . ."
לא שארי קודשא בריך הוא ולא אשתכח אלא באחד. "באחד"? "אחד" מבעי ליה! אלא במאן דאתתקן בקדושה עלאה למהוי חד, כדין הוא שריא באחד ולא באתר אחרא. ואימתי אקרי בר נש אחד . . . בזמנא דאשתכח בר נש בזווגא . . . וכד מתחברן דכר ונוקבא כדין אתעבידו חד גופא, אשתכח דאינהו חד נפשא וחד גופא ואקרי בר נש אחד, כדין קודשא בריך הוא שארי באחד.

זוהר ג, פ,א-ב

t is written (Job 23:13): "He is *in* one. . . ."

"[He is] *in* one"? Should it not read, "[He] *is* one"? [The meaning of this verse is that] God only abides and dwells "in one," in the person who achieves a holy oneness—nowhere else.

When is a person called "one"? . . . When a person is in the union of intimacy. . . . When male and female join, they become one. They are one in body and one in soul; they are one person. And God dwells in the oneness.

Zohar 3:80a-b

Text 1b

וַיִּבְרָא אֱלֹקִים אֶת הָאָדָם בְּצַלְמוֹ, בְּצֶלֶם אֱלֹקִים בָּרָא אֹתוֹ, זָכָר וּנְקֵבָה בָּרָא אֹתָם.
בראשית א,כז

And God created man in His image; in the image of God He created him; male and female He created them.

Genesis 1:27

Rabbi Yeshayah HaLevi Horowitz (1565–1630). Preeminent kabbalistic authority, also known as the "Shelah," the acronym of the title of his work, *Shenei Luchot Haberit*. Born in Prague, he studied under Rabbi Meir of Lublin and Rabbi Yehoshua Falk. He served as rabbi in several prominent Jewish communities, including Frankfurt am Main and his native Prague. After the passing of his wife in 1620, he moved to Israel. In Tiberias, he finished the *Shenei Luchot Haberit*, an encyclopedic compilation of kabbalistic ideas. He is buried in Tiberias, next to Maimonides.

Text 1c

דעו בניי כי אין קדושה בכל הקדושות כקדושת הזיווג, אם הוא בקדושה ומקדש עצמו בתשמיש כאשר הזהירו רבותינו זכרונם לברכה, כי אז הוא כדמות וצלם העליון.
שני לוחות הברית, שער האותיות, עמק ברכה עה

Know my children that of all that is holy, there is none as holy as the holiness of the marital union—if it is performed with holiness and sanctity as our sages, of blessed memory, have instructed us—for then one is in the form and image of the One Above.

Rabbi Yeshayah HaLevi Horowitz, *Shenei Luchot Haberit, Emek Berachah* 75

Text 2

שְׁאֵרָהּ, כְּסוּתָהּ, וְעֹנָתָהּ לֹא יִגְרָע.

שמות כא,י

He must fully provide for [his wife's] food, clothing, and conjugal needs.

Exodus 21:10

Text 3

לא ינהג בה מנהג פרסיים, שמשמשין מטותיהן בלבושיהן . . . האומר, "אי אפשי אלא אני בבגדי והיא בבגדה"—יוציא.

תלמוד בבלי, כתובות מח,א

A husband may not treat [his wife] in the manner of the Persians, who have marital intercourse while clothed. . . . Saying, "I can only [perform my marital duties] while I wear my clothes and my wife wears hers," is grounds for divorce.

Talmud, Ketubot 48a

Value of Life
When Life Is on the Line

Learning Activity 3a

Based on your impression and/or knowledge of Jewish beliefs, which is the greater value: God's word (the *mitzvot*) or human life?

a. God's word is the greater value.

b. Human life is the greater value.

c. The two are of equal standing.

d. I don't know.

Text 4a

כשיעמוד גוי ויאנוס את ישראל לעבור על אחת מכל מצות האמורות בתורה או יהרגנו, יעבור ואל יהרג, שנאמר במצות (ויקרא יח,ה), "אשר יעשה אותם האדם וחי בהם"—וחי בהם, ולא שימות בהם.
משנה תורה, הלכות יסודי התורה ה,א

If a Gentile attempts to force a Jew to violate one of the Torah's commandments on pain of death, the Jew should violate the commandment rather than be killed, because it is stated concerning the *mitzvot* (Leviticus 18:5): "A person shall perform them and live by them." One should live by them and not die because of them.

Maimonides, *Mishneh Torah*, Laws of the Fundamentals of the Torah 5:1

Rabbi Moshe ben Maimon (1135–1204). Better known as Maimonides or by the acronym Rambam; born in Cordoba, Spain. After the conquest of Cordoba by the Almohads, he fled Spain and eventually settled in Cairo, Egypt. There, he became the leader of the Jewish community and served as court physician to the vizier of Egypt. His rulings on Jewish law are considered integral to the formation of halachic consensus. He is most noted for authoring the *Mishneh Torah,* an encyclopedic arrangement of Jewish law, and for his philosophical work, *Guide for the Perplexed.*

Learning Activity 3b

Based on this passage by Maimonides, which is the greater value: God's word (the *mitzvot*) or human life?

a. God's word is the greater value.

b. Human life is the greater value.

c. The two are of equal standing.

d. I still don't know.

Text 4b

חלל עליו שבת אחת כדי שישמור שבתות הרבה.
תלמוד בבלי, שבת קנא,ב

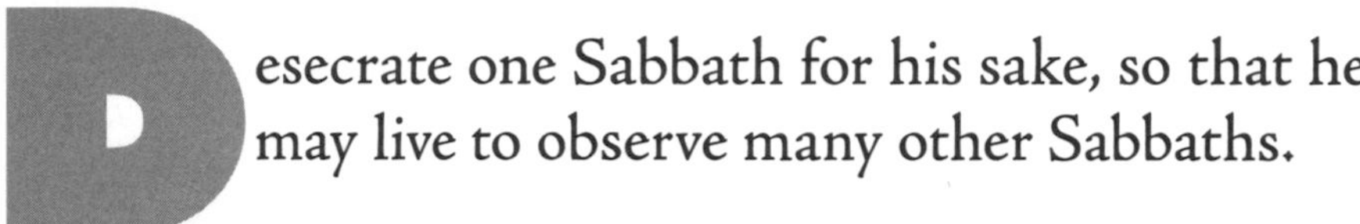

Desecrate one Sabbath for his sake, so that he may live to observe many other Sabbaths.

Talmud, Shabbat 151b

Learning Activity 3c

Based on this passage from the Talmud, which is the greater value: God's word (the *mitzvot*) or human life?

a. God's word is the greater value.

b. Human life is the greater value.

c. The two are of equal standing.

d. I still don't know.

Text 4c

חביבה נפשן של ישראל לפני המקום יותר מן המצוות. אמר הקדוש ברוך הוא, "תבטל המצוה ויחיה זה".

רש"י, יומא פב,ב

The lives of Israel are more precious before God than the *mitzvot*. God says, "Let the commandment remain unfulfilled, so that this person should live."

Rashi, Yoma 82b

Rabbi Shlomo Yitschaki (1040–1105). Better known by the acronym Rashi. Rabbi and famed author of comprehensive commentaries on the Talmud and Bible. Born in Troyes, France, Rashi studied in the famed *yeshivot* of Mainz and Worms. His commentaries, which focus on the simple understanding of the text, are considered the most fundamental of all the commentaries that preceded and followed. Since their initial printings, the commentaries have appeared in virtually every edition of the Talmud and Bible. Many of the famed authors of the *Tosafot* are among Rashi's descendants.

Learning Activity 3d

Based on this passage from Rashi's commentary on the Talmud, which is the greater value: God's word (the *mitzvot*) or human life?

a. God's word is the greater value.
b. Human life is the greater value.
c. The two are of equal standing.
d. I thought I had the answer, but now I'm just plain confused . . .

Text 4d

Rabbi Menachem Mendel Schneerson (1902–1994). Known as "the Lubavitcher Rebbe," or simply as "the Rebbe." Born in southern Ukraine. Rabbi Schneerson escaped from the Nazis, arriving in the U.S. in June 1941. The towering Jewish leader of the 20th century, the Rebbe inspired and guided the revival of traditional Judaism after the European devastation and often emphasized that the performance of just one additional good deed could usher in the era of Mashiach.

פקוח נפש דוחה כל התורה כולה, ויש לומר שגם כאן הכוונה שאין זו דחיה, אלא אדרבה שמירת התורה . . . מצד מעלתם של ישראל על התורה, שכל התורה היא בשבילם.

ספר השיחות תשמ"ט א, ע' 129 הערה 61

All the laws of the Torah are suspended in an instance of mortal danger. It would seem that the intention in this case is not to override the laws of the Torah, but to preserve them. . . . This reflects the exaltedness of the Jewish people, for all of Torah exists for their sake.

Rabbi Menachem Mendel Schneerson, *Sefer Hasichot* 5749, 1:129, fn. 61

Text 5

כשעושים דברים האלו אין עושין אותן . . . אלא על ידי גדולי ישראל וחכמיהם.

משנה תורה, הלכות שבת ב,ג

When [life-saving] treatment is administered, it . . . should be administered by the leaders and sages of Israel.

Maimonides, *Mishneh Torah*, Laws of Shabbat 2:3

Your Integrity or Your Life!

Text 6

A man who won't die for something is not fit to live. . . . I submit to you that if a man hasn't discovered something that he will die for, he isn't fit to live.

Dr. Martin Luther King, Jr., June 23, 1963

Martin Luther King, Jr. (1929–1968), clergyman and prominent leader in the African-American Civil Rights Movement. Between 1957 and 1968, King traveled over six million miles and spoke over twenty-five hundred times. King was awarded five honorary degrees and was named Man of the Year by *Time* magazine in 1963. At the age of 35, King was the youngest man to have received the Nobel Peace Prize. King was assassinated on April 4, 1968, while standing on the balcony of his motel room in Memphis, Tennessee, where he was to lead a protest march in sympathy with striking garbage workers.

Learning Activity 4

Patrick Henry famously proclaimed, "Give me Liberty, or Give me Death!" He undoubtedly felt that life devoid of basic liberties was not worth living. Are there any ideals about which you feel just as strongly? Are there any lines in the sand that, if crossed, would render your life meaningless?

a. ______________________________

b. ______________________________

c. ______________________________

Text 7

במה דברים אמורים בשאר מצות חוץ מעבודת כוכבים וגלוי עריות ושפיכת דמים.
אבל שלש עבירות אלו אם יאמר לו, "עבור על אחת מהן או תהרג"—יהרג ואל יעבור.
משנה תורה, הלכות יסודי התורה ה,ב

The above rule applies to all *mitzvot* with the exceptions of idolatry, forbidden sexual relations, and murder. With regard to these three sins, if one is ordered: "Transgress one of them or be killed," one should allow one's life to be taken rather than transgress.

Maimonides, *Mishneh Torah*, Laws of the Fundamentals of the Torah 5:2

Rabbi Samson Raphael Hirsch (1808–1888). Born in Hamburg, Germany; rabbi and educator; intellectual founder of the *Torah Im Derech Eretz* school of Orthodox Judaism, which advocates combining Torah with secular education. Beginning in 1830, Hirsch served as chief rabbi in several prominent German cities. During this period he wrote his *Nineteen Letters on Judaism*, under the pseudonym of Ben Uziel. His work helped preserve traditional Judaism during the era of the German Enlightenment. He is buried in Frankfurt am Main.

Text 8

The only exceptions to the rule [that preserving life trumps mitzvah observance] are the prohibitions against idolatry, murder, and forbidden sexual relations. These are never preempted, even at the risk of death, for they represent the epitome of *mitzvot* between man and God, *mitzvot* between man and his fellow man, and personal sanctity.

Rabbi Samson Raphael Hirsch, Leviticus 18:5

Bodily Affairs

Body on Loan

Text 9

לפי שאין נפשו של אדם קניינו, אלא קנין הקדוש ברוך הוא, שנאמר (יחזקאל יח,ד), "הנפשות לי הנה".
הילכך לא תועיל הודאתו בדבר שאינו שלו.
רדב"ז, הלכות סנהדרין יח,ו

A person's life is not his own possession, but God's possession, for it is stated, "The souls are mine" (Ezekiel 18:4).

[Just as a person has no right to give up someone else's property,] a person's testimony about his own guilt [in a capital crime] is not accepted, for [his life] is not his own.

Rabbi David ben Shlomo ibn Zimra, Laws of Sanhedrin 18:6

Rabbi David ben Shlomo ibn Zimra (1479–1573). Born in Spain; emigrated to Safed, Israel, upon the expulsion of the Jews from Spain in 1492. In 1513, he moved to Egypt and served as rabbi, judge and head of the yeshivah in Cairo. He also ran many successful business ventures and was independently wealthy. In 1553, he returned to Safed where he would later be buried. He authored what would become a classic commentary to Maimonides' code of law, and wrote many halachic responsa, of which more than ten thousand are still extant.

Tattoos

Text 10a

וּכְתֹבֶת קַעֲקַע לֹא תִתְּנוּ בָּכֶם.
ויקרא יט,כח

You shall not place a tattoo on yourselves.

Leviticus 19:28

Text 10b

Sefer Hachinuch is a work on the 613 commandments, arranged in the order of the *mitzvot's* appearance in the Torah. Four aspects of every mitzvah are discussed in this work: the definition of the mitzvah and its sources in the Written and Oral Torah; ethical lessons which can be deduced from the mitzvah; basic laws pertaining to the observance of the mitzvah; and who is obligated to perform the mitzvah and when. The work was composed in the thirteenth century by an anonymous author who refers to himself in the introduction as "the Levite of Barcelona." It has been widely thought that this referred to Rabbi Aharon HaLevi of Barcelona (Re'ah); however, this view has been contested.

שהיה מנהג הגוים שרושמים עצמם לעבודה זרה שלהם, כלומר שהוא עבד נמכר לה ומורשם לעבודתה.
ספר החינוך מצוה רנג

It was the custom of the heathens to brand themselves for their deity, thereby demonstrating that they are servants branded for its service.

Sefer Hachinuch, Mitzvah 253

Elective Plastic Surgery

Text 11

אסור לאדם לחבול בין בעצמו בין בחבירו, ולא החובל בלבד אלא כל המכה . . . דרך נציון הרי זה עובר בלא תעשה.

משנה תורה, הלכות חובל ומזיק ה,א

It is forbidden for a person to injure himself or another. Not only a person who causes an injury, but anyone who strikes . . . with malice violates a biblical prohibition.

Maimonides, *Mishneh Torah*, Laws of Injury and Damages 5:1

Question for Discussion

How is this passage from Maimonides' code instructive with regard to the issue of plastic surgery?

Text 12

כיון דכבר דשו בו רבים לילך להרופאים, אף שנתוח בחזקת סכנה, "שומר פתאים ה'" (תהלים קטז,ו), ועינינו רואין, ברוך ה', שרובא דרובא מהחולאים שעושין להם נתוח (השם יצילנו) מתרפאים.

חלקת יעקב, חושן משפט לא

Rabbi Mordechai Ya'akov Breish (1895–1976). Born in Poland, he served as rabbi in various communities in Poland and Germany. After the rise of Nazism, he fled to Switzerland where he served as chief rabbi and head of the rabbinical court of Zurich from 1934–1976. Author of *Chelkat Ya'akov*, a compendium of responsa on contemporary issues and medical ethics.

Though surgery is fraught with the potential for complications, since many have trodden upon the path of going to doctors, [we apply the rule that] "God protects the simple" (Psalms 116:6). Indeed, we see, thank God, that the overwhelming majority of patients who undergo surgery are healed.

Rabbi Mordechai Ya'akov Breish, *Chelkat Ya'akov, Choshen Mishpat* 31

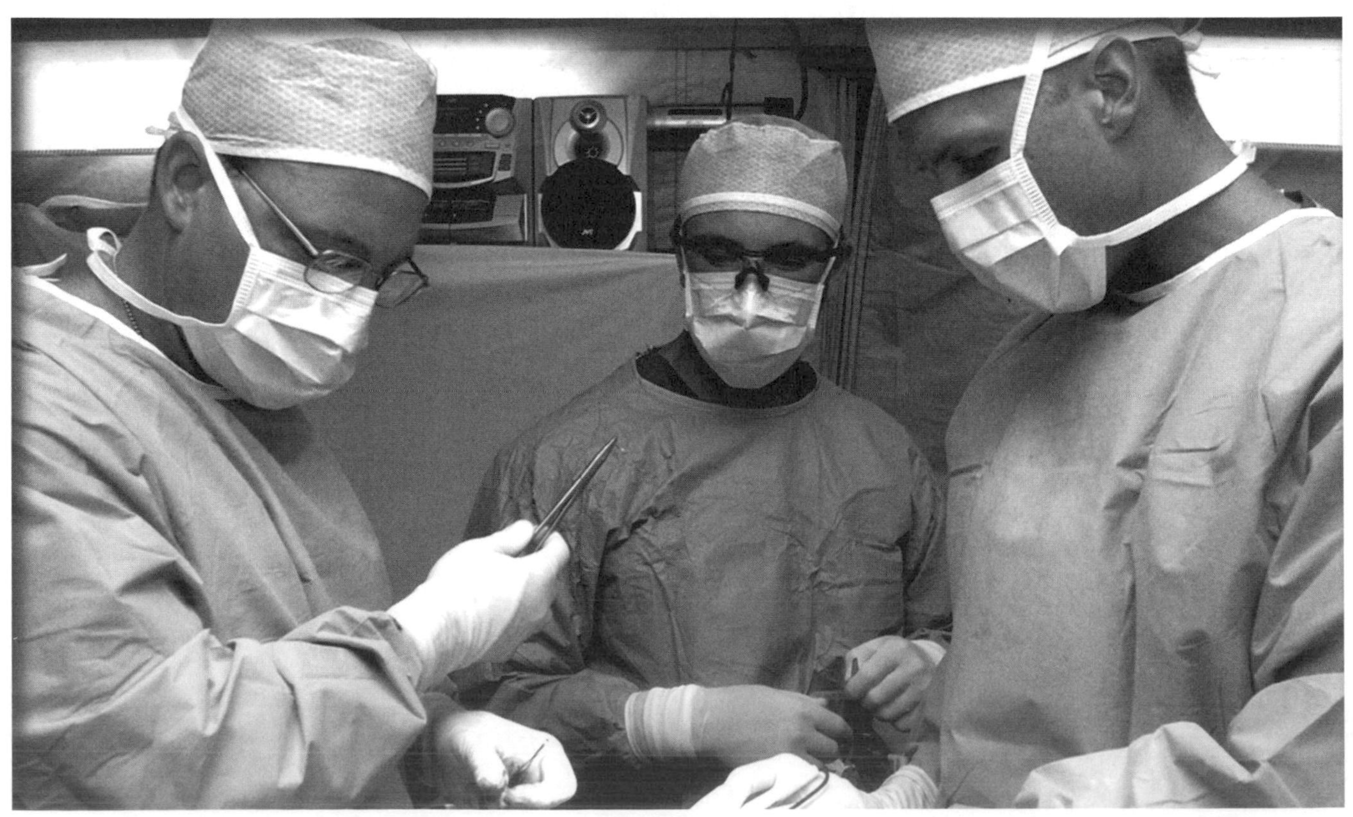

Cremation

Text 13a

כִּי הֹלֵךְ הָאָדָם אֶל בֵּית עוֹלָמוֹ, וְסָבְבוּ בַשּׁוּק הַסֹּפְדִים . . .
וְיָשֹׁב הֶעָפָר עַל הָאָרֶץ כְּשֶׁהָיָה, וְהָרוּחַ תָּשׁוּב אֶל הָאֱלֹקִים אֲשֶׁר נְתָנָהּ.
קהלת יב,ה-ז

Man goes to his everlasting home, and the mourners go about in the street. . . .

And the dust returns to the earth as it was, and the spirit returns to God Who gave it.

Ecclesiastes 12:5–7

Text 13b

כִּי קָבוֹר תִּקְבְּרֶנּוּ בַּיּוֹם הַהוּא.
דברים כא,כג

ou shall surely bury him on the same day.

Deuteronomy 21:23

Text 14a

מצוה לקיים דברי המת.

תלמוד בבלי, תענית כא,א

t is a mitzvah to uphold the wishes of the deceased.

Talmud, Ta'anit 21a

Text 14b

אם צוה שלא יספדוהו אין סופדין אותו.

משנה תורה, הלכות אבל יב,א

f [the deceased] instructed that he should not be eulogized, then he is not to be eulogized.

Maimonides, *Mishneh Torah*, Laws of Mourning 12:1

Text 14c

אבל אם צוה שלא יקבר אין שומעין לו.

משנה תורה, שם

f, however, he requested not to be buried, we disregard the request.

Maimonides, ibid.

The Soul of the Matter

Learning Activity 5

Which of the following is the most accurate characterization of Judaism?

a. an ethnicity

b. a way of life

c. a belief system

d. a state of being

e. b and c

Text 15

״חטא ישראל״ (יהושע ז,יא). אמר רבי אבא בר זבדא, אף על פי שחטא, ישראל הוא.
תלמוד בבלי, סנהדרין מד,א

Israel has sinned" (Joshua 7:11). Rabbi Abba bar Zavda explained: Even though he sinned, he is still called "Israel."

Talmud, Sanhedrin 44a

Key Points

1. Although all religions have similarities, they are not interchangeable.

2. Satan is an angel who fulfills God's will by enticing people to transgress. In doing so, he gives man the freedom to choose between good and evil.

3. Judaism regards marital union as the most holy act. The divine image is complete during intimacy when man and woman reunite as one.

4. Human life takes precedence over mitzvah observance because the *mitzvot* were created to serve the Jewish people.

5. If a Jew is asked to murder, worship idols, or perform sexually prohibited acts, he should give up his life rather than do so.

6. A person's body is not his own property; rather it belongs to God. For this reason, it is forbidden to harm oneself in any way.

7. Tattooing one's body is forbidden in Judaism; however, a person with a tattoo can be buried in a Jewish cemetery.

8. Cremation is a rejection of one of the fundamentals of Jewish faith, namely the resurrection of the dead that will take place in the time of the redemption.

9. Being Jewish is one's essential identity; it is not something we choose. However, we can decide on the degree to which we will actively engage in our Judaism.

Additional Readings

Judaism and Cosmetic Surgery

by **Daniel Eisenberg, M.D.**

The first successful partial face transplant from a donor was performed November 27, 2005 in Amiens, France. The recipient had lost her nose, lips, and chin after being mauled by her dog. The injuries left her grotesquely deformed, making it virtually impossible for her to interact normally with others. Muscles, blood vessels, nerves, and other tissues were transplanted from a "brain dead" donor in order to fashion a "hybrid" face that neither resembled the donor nor the recipient's original face. Since that time, several more face transplants have been performed, including a near total face transplant at the Cleveland Clinic in December, 2008.

These surgical procedures marked a new milestone in transplantation, adding new questions to the usual list of ethical issues involved in transplantation. Unlike kidney, liver, lung, or other vital organ transplants, which are life-saving procedures, the recent face transplants bring transplantation into the realm of plastic surgery.

From a Jewish perspective, the face transplant raises two sets of questions. There are the technical questions regarding transplant[1] and a more fundamental set regarding the approach of Judaism to vanity and plastic surgery.

Let us leave aside the issues of cadaveric transplantation and brain death involved in the recent face transplant cases and ask the more basic question of how far an individual may go to improve his/her appearance? Clearly the face transplant patients' surgeries were not prompted by mere vanity, as these patients were horribly disfigured. But, we must still ask if even routine plastic/cosmetic surgery is permitted at all? What are the possible concerns that may arise for one contemplating plastic surgery?

Cosmetic versus Reconstructive Surgery

Plastic surgery may be divided into cosmetic and reconstructive surgery. The former is performed for enhancement of one's physical appearance (such as rhinoplasty, liposuction, or breast augmentation). The latter is performed to correct a defect, whether congenital (from birth) or acquired (suffered in a car accident, for instance). These two indications for surgery may overlap and there is not necessarily a clean line that separates deformity from normal appearance. As has often been repeated, beauty is in the eye of the beholder.

Judaism treats the subjective sense of the individual very seriously when a person feels unattractive. What about a self-perceived cosmetic defect, one that is neither a true congenital defect nor the result of an injury? How much importance does Judaism place on self-esteem and self-consciousness?

The History of Plastic Surgery

The oldest descriptions of plastic surgery date back to 2600-year-old Sanskrit texts and ancient Egyptian papyri. These documents describe nose, ear, and lip reconstructions utilizing surgical flaps and skin grafts. Nevertheless, the term "plastic surgery" to describe reconstructive surgery was not introduced until 1818.[2]

Despite the long history of plastic surgery, no responsa were written about surgery performed for cosmetic surgery until the latter half of the 20th century. This is hardly surprising, since prior to the mid 19th century, all surgery was limited by the inability to adequately

[1] See Eisenberg, D, "Organ and Tissue Donation," JME, Vol. VI, No. 2 (Oct. 2008).

[2] http://www.emedicine.com/plastic/topic433.htm

ameliorate the pain of the surgery itself and the high morbidity and mortality of surgery in general.

This all changed due to important advances made in the second half of the 19th century. Building upon the work of Ignaz Philipp Semmelweis (who argued that hand washing would decrease hospital infections) and Louis Pasteur (who proved that bacteria cause infection), Joseph Lister introduced the concept of antiseptic surgery in the late 19th century, significantly decreasing the risk of surgical infection. Ether, the first form of general anesthesia, was publicly utilized for the first time on October 16, 1846, in an operating theater at the Massachusetts General Hospital, ushering in the age of modern anesthesia.[3] With these two breakthroughs came rapid advances in surgical techniques, and advancements in both reconstructive and cosmetic surgery, particularly between the first and second world wars.

The contemporary era of plastic surgery was ushered in by World War I. Due to the nature of trench warfare, which protected the soldier's lower body but exposed the head and neck to destructive new explosive devices, thousands of soldiers returned from war with horrible facial deformities. In order to aid these soldiers to integrate back into society, where they were finding difficulty finding jobs and spouses, several countries, including the United States, created special medical programs and hospitals dedicated to treating these injuries. World War II led to further advances in cosmetic surgery, largely for the same reason.[4]

As Max Thorek (the founder of the International College of Surgeons) pointed out, even modern cosmetic surgery was the direct result of war:

"If soldiers whose faces had been torn away by bursting shells on the battlefield could come back into an almost normal life with new faces created by the wizardry of the new science of plastic surgery, why couldn't women whose faces had been ravaged by nothing more explosive than the hand of the years find again the firm clear contours of youth."[5]

Thus was born the era of widespread "plastic" surgery.

The Earliest Responsum

As plastic surgery developed and the options for cosmetic enhancement grew, formal halachic discussion began. In 1961, Rabbi Immanuel Jakobovits, considered by many to be the father of the discipline of Jewish medical ethics,[6] addressed the American Society of Facial Plastic Surgery at a symposium entitled "Religious Views on Cosmetic Surgery."[7] Rabbi Jakobovits, later

---

3 http://www.etherdome.org/Our_Stor/Our_Stor.html

4 Backstein, R and Hinek, A, War and Medicine: The Origins of Plastic Surgery, University of Toronto Medical Journal, vol. 82, no. 3, (May 2005)

5 Tackla M. Phoenix from the flames: plastic surgery emerges out of the horrors of World War I. Cosmetic Surgery Times. Oct. 1, 2003. Cited by Backstein and Hinek, ibid.

6 Rabbi Jakobovits is considered by many to be the father of modern Jewish medical ethics as a specialized area of study, due to the publication in 1959 of his doctoral thesis in book form, entitled "Jewish Medical Ethics." For the first time, the breadth of Jewish attitudes toward crucial medical issues was available to the general public and healthcare workers in readable English. As Dr. Fred Rosner describes it:

> "Rabbi Jakobovits' now classic book is the first comprehensive treatise on the subject of Jewish medical ethics. Tracing the development of Jewish and other religions' views on medico-moral problems from antiquity to the present day, the book is profusely annotated by references to the original sources in religious, medical, legal and historical literatures. The book contains discussions of classic subjects in Jewish medical ethics such as abortion, artificial insemination, birth control, euthanasia, autopsies, eugenics, sterilization, treatment of patients on the Sabbath, and more. In addition, several chapters are devoted to the physician in Jewish religious law—his studies and privileges, his license and legal responsibilities, his professional charges and the admission of his evidence. The book is appropriately subtitled 'A comparative and historical study of the Jewish religious attitude to medicine and its practice.'" (Rosner, F, "Lord Immanuel Jakobovits: Grandfather of Jewish Medical Ethics," IMAJ 2001;3:304)

In 1981, Rabbi Jakobovits was knighted by Queen Elizabeth for his life of dedication.

7 Published in The Eye, Ear, Nose and Throat Monthly, New York, Feb/March 1962

Chief Rabbi of Great Britain, discussed the parameters of plastic surgery from a Jewish legal perspective.

After explaining that no responsa had yet been written on the topic, he dealt with the question of whether one may undergo plastic surgery for the purpose of improving one's physical appearance. As Rabbi Jakobovits eloquently described in his classic work, Jewish Medical Ethics:[8]

"The problem was considered under four headings: the theological implications of 'improving' God's work or 'flying in the face of Providence'; the possible risks to life involved in any operation; the Jewish objection to any mutilation of the body; and the ethical censure of human vanity, especially among males."

He concluded[9] definitively that plastic surgery for aesthetic enhancement is a form of arrogance and vanity (particularly for men) and is forbidden unless the patient meets certain criteria. He later wrote[10] as part of an overview of the Jewish approach to medicine:

"In the sparse rabbinic writings on the subject, these reservations could be discounted, provided the danger is minimal; and especially 1) if the operation is medically indicated, e.g. following an accident, or for grave psychological reasons; 2) if the correction of the deformity is designed to facilitate or maintain a happy marriage; or 3) if it will enable a person to play a constructive role in society and to earn a decent livelihood."

The four ethical concerns of Rabbi Jakobovits remained the pivotal issues in all future responsa and therefore bear further elucidation, as subsequent poskim have approached them in different ways.

8 Jakobovits, Immanuel, Jewish Medical Ethics: A Comparative and Historical Study of the Jewish Religious Attitude to Medicine and its Practice, 2nd Edition, Bloch Publishing Company, New York, 1975, p. 284.

9 Jakobovits, Immanuel, Noam 6:273 (Abridged in Sefer Assia 1:222-223).

10 Jakobovits, Immanuel, "Medicine and Judaism: an overview," Assia (English) 1980 Nov; 7(3-4):57-78.

Ethical Concerns

The first potential practical objection to plastic surgery is the Torah obligation to guard health[11] which might limit the surgical risks that one may accept as part of plastic surgery. In addition to the hazards associated with the surgery itself, anesthesia, particularly general anesthesia, presents a very small but real risk of death or incapacitation.

Beyond the blanket obligation to guard health, there is the particular prohibition of self-mutilation. Just as one may not injure someone else, one may not cause injury to oneself. The prohibition of injuring someone else is called *chavala* and is derived directly from the Biblical verse[12] that warns the court not to give a convicted criminal more lashes than legally mandated. The verse is interpreted to mean that if the court must not strike a criminal without justification, surely an ordinary individual may not strike or otherwise injure his neighbor.

The Talmud[13] discusses whether this prohibition applies to harming oneself, concluding that "one who injures himself even though it is forbidden, pays no damages. But if someone else injures him, they pay damages." Injuring oneself without a valid reason is called *chovel b'atzmo*. This proscription has limitations however. We are only barred from causing unnecessary injury to ourselves. The key question is what is considered necessary.

Risk and harming oneself are not the only issues. There are also philosophical considerations. Do we assert that God, as the ultimate craftsman Who fashions human beings, makes each person exactly as they should be and that our "remodeling" of ourselves is an affront to His judgment? That is, does the divine mandate to heal and obligation to seek medical treatment extend to plastic surgery?

The fourth issue applies predominantly to men. The Torah commands that a man not wear the clothing of a woman and that a woman not wear the clothing of a

11 Deuteronomy 4:9 & 4:15. See *Shulchan Aruch, Choshen Mishpat* 409:3 and 427:8.

12 Deuteronomy 25:3

13 *Baba Kama* 91b.

man.[14] This prohibition extends beyond mere clothing, but includes actions and activities that are characteristic of one of the sexes.[15] For instance, in most situations a man may not dye his white hairs back to black for purposes of improving his appearance since this is considered to be a feminine activity.[16] Is plastic surgery also considered a "feminine" activity?

A Variety of Approaches

In 1964, Rabbi Mordechai Yaakov Breish, Rabbi Menasheh Klein, and Rabbi Moshe Feinstein were each asked to rule on questions of cosmetic surgery for enhancement of appearance.

Rabbi Mordechai Yaakov Breish (1895-1976), author of the Chelkas Yaakov and a prominent posek [authority in Jewish law] in Switzerland, discussed the issues of risk and *chavala* (self-injury) when asked whether a woman may undergo cosmetic surgery to straighten and decrease the size of her nose in order to improve her chance of finding a suitable husband.[17]

He used a previous ruling of Rabbi Abraham of Sochachev, the 19th century author of the Avnei Nezer, as a starting point for his discussion of why it is permitted to enter into surgery or other dangerous situations, even when not absolutely necessary. The Avnei Nezer[18] had forbidden a child to have surgery to straighten a crooked leg due to the risk of the operation. Rabbi Breish points out several objections to this ruling.

So long as a doctor practices in an acceptable way, it is a mitzvah for a physician to treat even non-life-threatening illnesses even though he may injure or kill patients inadvertently.[19] That is the nature of the mandate to heal. Additionally, the Talmud allowed bloodletting as a preventative health mechanism, even though it was known to be somewhat dangerous. We also clearly see that one is not prohibited from entering into a dangerous situation voluntarily since we do not prohibit women from having babies, despite the risks associated with pregnancy and childbirth.[20]

Rabbi Breish also points out that the general population undergoes surgery for non-life-threatening conditions with a very low complication rate. He therefore invokes the concept of *Shomer Pesaim Hashem*,[21] that God watches over the simple, to defend low risk surgeries. He rules that from the perspective of risk, one may pursue plastic surgery as it is one of the activities that the general population finds to be acceptably safe.[22] To support his contention that one may injure oneself (independent of any associated risk) for treatment of a non-life-threatening malady, he brings two proofs. The Code of Jewish Law[23] warns a child not to remove a thorn, bloodlet, or amputate a limb from a parent, even for medical reasons, lest he transgress the capital offense of injuring a parent. Rabbi Moshe Isserles, in his gloss to the Code of Jewish Law, states that the child should only refrain if there is someone else present who can help the parent, for otherwise, the child should even amputate the limb if the parent is in pain. It seems clear that the prohibition is only to injure one's parent *unnecessarily*. But,

14 Deuteronomy 22:5

15 Shabbos 94b, Nazir 58b-59a, *Shulchan Aruch, Yoreh Deah* 182.

16 Maimonides, *Mishneh Torah, Hilchos Ovdei Kochavim* 12:10

17 *Chelkas Yaakov, Choshen Mishpat* 31

18 *Avnei Nezer Yoreh Deah* 321

19 Nachmanides, *Toras Ha'Adam, Inyan Ha'Sakana*. See also *Beis Yosef, Yoreh Deah* 241

20 Women are not required by the Torah to have children.

21 Psalms 116:6

22 The Torah has several *mitzvos* regarding personal safety. For instance, we are instructed to build a parapet around any flat roof, to prevent anyone from falling (Deuteronomy 22:8). Maimonides (*Mishneh Torah, Hilchos Rotzeach* 11:4) explains this to include any dangerous situation, such as an unguarded swimming pool. We must be proactive in eliminating all preventable risks, such as covering ditches on one's property (*Shulchan Aruch Choshen Mishpat* 427:6-7).

In addition to removing hazards, the Torah twice commands us to protect our health, safety and well being (Deuteronomy 4:9 & 4:15). For example, the Talmud forbids walking near a shaky wall, lest it fall and injure the passerby. Similarly, all dangerous pursuits are proscribed. Obviously, there is latitude in evaluating how much risk is acceptable. The Talmud asks in several places (for example, *Shabbos* 129b) why certain potentially dangerous actions are permitted. It answers that a person need not avoid small risks that are accepted by the rest of normal society without undue concern. This concept is called "*Shomer pasaim Hashem, dashu bay rabim*"

23 *Shulchan Aruch, Yoreh Deah* 241:3

the concept of bloodletting or amputation of a parent's limb *per se,* merely to relieve pain, despite the trauma involved, does not appear to be problematic!

The second proof is fundamental to our discussion of plastic surgery, particularly cosmetic surgery. The Talmud[24] states that a man may remove scabs from his body to alleviate pain, but not to improve his appearance.[25] At first glance, this may appear to exclude the possibility of plastic surgery. However, Tosofos,[26] commenting on this statement, promulgates a concept that demonstrates a very sensitive understanding of human nature and psychology. He writes: "If the only pain that he suffers is that he is embarrassed to walk among people then it is permissible, because there is no greater pain than this." Tosofos recognizes that there is no greater suffering than psychological pain and that it is very difficult to judge for someone else the degree of suffering they are experiencing as a result of a self-perceived defect.

Citing the psychological pain associated with the inability to find a spouse, Rabbi Breish ruled that the woman may have the cosmetic surgery.

That same year, Rabbi Moshe Feinstein (1895-1986) was asked the same question. His responsa first examines the parameters of the prohibition of *chavala*.[27] He points out that in his Mishneh Torah,[28] Maimonides clearly describes *chavala* as injury with malice. Rabbi Feinstein brings several examples of injury without the intention to do harm that Jewish religious literature finds acceptable.[29] His final ruling permits surgery when it is in the best interests of the patient, even if they are not sick and it does not treat an illness.[30] As a result, he permitted the woman to have cosmetic surgery since it was to her advantage and not being done to harm her.[31]

Also in 1964, Rabbi Menasheh Klein, author of Mishneh Halachos, dealt with the question of the permissibility of cosmetic surgery to correct various facial imperfec-

24 *Shabbos* 50b

25 Rashi comments that for a man to remove scabs for aesthetic reasons is feminine behavior.

26 *Shabbos 50b*, Opening phrase "*bishvil.*"

27 *Igros Moshe, Choshen Mishpat* 2:66

28 *Mishneh Torah, Chovel U'Mazik* 5:1. See *Shulchan Aruch, Choshen Mishpat* 420:31.

29 The four examples listed by Rabbi Feinstein are:

a. In the book of Kings I 20:35-36, a man is punished for refusing to hit a prophet. A discussion of the event is also recorded in Sanhedrin 89.

b. *Baba Kama* 91b describes that Rav Chisda would lift up his garment when walking through thorn bushes so that his legs would be scratched, but his clothes would not be hurt. He reasoned that his legs will repair themselves, but his clothes would not.

c. *Sanhedrin 84b* discusses the permission to do bloodletting on one's father if necessary based on the mitzvah, "*V'ahavta l're'acha kamocha*" ("Love your neighbor as yourself"). Rabbi Feinstein explains that we learn that one may cause an injury to his friend which is of a type that a reasonable person would want to have done to them, e.g. bloodletting. The Talmud does not even imply that bloodletting itself is halachically problematic, only that one must be careful when doing it on a parent. Injury as part of medical treatment is permitted and is only considered *chavala* when the intent is to injure or disgrace someone.

d. *Mishna Bechoros* 45a discusses one who removes an extra digit from his hand without any indication that such surgery is forbidden.

30 Nevertheless, see *Igros Moshe, Orach Chaim* 3:90 where Rabbi Feinstein argues that the Torah grants a mandate to heal only in cases of illness or injury, but not in order for a person to fulfill a mitzvah. Therefore, he rules that one may not have an intravenous line inserted before Yom Tov in order to allow fasting on Yom Kippur.

31 Rabbi Feinstein (*Igros Moshe, Choshen* Mishpat 2:65) took the same approach when asked whether dieting for the sake of improving a woman's appearance alone is permissible since the Talmud (*Baba Kamma* 91b) teaches that *chovel b'atzmo* (injuring oneself) is forbidden and Tosofos explains that this is even if the injury is for a purpose. Rabbi Feinstein first explains that dieting for medical reasons is certainly permitted. He then argues that if the hunger caused by dieting would cause true pain (which Rabbi Feinstein questions), it would be forbidden to diet for cosmetic purposes. But, Rabbi Feinstein argues that the real pain that ensues from dieting is merely the pain of abstaining from desirable food, which is not true suffering. Therefore, he argues that we must compare the pain of dieting against the pain of feeling unattractive. If the woman's pain from abstaining from enjoyable food is less than the pain that she feels from her appearance, the diet is permitted.

tions that mar a woman's appearance, such as a very long nose which makes it difficult for her to marry and which she feels makes her very unattractive.[32] Rabbi Klein utilizes an ingenious approach to evaluate the question. He points out that there is ample precedent for medical intervention to improve appearance dating back to Talmudic times.

The Mishna[33] discusses the case of a man who betroths a woman on the condition that she has no defect (*mum*) where a "*mum*" is defined as any defect that would bar a Cohen (Jewish priest) from serving in the Temple. Tosofos[34] states that if the woman had her blemish corrected by a physician before her engagement, the marriage is valid. Since many of the blemishes that would apply to a Cohen include cosmetic imperfections[35] of the face for which people today would desire elective plastic surgery and Tosofos permits these blemishes to be corrected by a physician, Rabbi Klein states that it appears that a man or woman may go to a doctor to correct a cosmetic defect merely for enhancement of their appearance. Rabbi Klein rejects the argument that plastic surgery entails any danger whatsoever based on information he received from physicians.

In a second responsum,[36] printed immediately following the previously discussed one, Rabbi Klein discusses plastic surgery and chemical peels in men with respect to the prohibition of a man performing female behaviors. He reiterates his previous ruling and adds that (minor) cosmetic procedures are forbidden for men if done strictly for aesthetic enhancement, but that the prohibition does not apply if the blemish causes the man enough embarrassment that he shuns social interaction. Rabbi Klein wisely points out that such a distinction requires a great deal of intellectual honesty.

In 1967, Rabbi Yitzchak Yaakov Weiss (1902-1989), head of the Eida Chareidis rabbinical court in Jerusalem and author of *Minchas Yitzchak*, dealt briefly with the issues of *chavala* and risk with respect to plastic surgery.[37] He takes the same approach to self-injury as Rabbi Feinstein, arguing that the prohibition of *chavala* only applies when the wound is inflicted with the intention of causing harm or degradation. He feels that cosmetic surgery would be permitted if not for the risk of surgery, which he believes to be a serious concern. He refers to one of his earlier responsa[38] which was directed to his in-law, Rabbi Breish, in which he forbids surgery for non-life-threatening conditions. While admitting that the line of reasoning of Rabbi Breish has merit, he disagrees, arguing that the permission of the Code of Jewish law to allow amputation of a limb is only in a life-threatening situation. He also agrees with Rabbi Breish that people desiring plastic surgery may be ill, but states that they are not endangered, and therefore is hesitant to allow elective plastic surgery, ending his 1967 responsa by saying the question requires further study.

Despite the generally strong support among halachic experts for the permissibility of reconstructive surgery for congenital defects and traumatic injuries, one dissenting opinion stands out with regard to cosmetic surgery merely to enhance one's appearance.

I am the Lord Your Healer[39]

There is an inherent tension in Judaism regarding the philosophical underpinnings of the mandate to heal. While the Torah clearly empowers the physician to treat illness, there is controversy regarding how far the permission extends.[40] While most Biblical commentators

32 *Mishneh Halachos* 4:246

33 *Kesubos* 72b

34 *Kesubos* 74

35 *Bechoros* and *Mishneh Torah, Be'as Hamikdash*, 8

36 *Mishneh Halachos* 4:247

37 *Minchas Yitzchak* 6:105

38 *Minchas Yitzchak* 1:28

39 Exodus 15:26

40 There is a great deal of controversy in Jewish halachic literature as to where we derive the mandate to heal. Depending on the origin of the permission to heal, a different set of parameters limiting medical treatment arise. While most authorities derive a very broad mandate there are a few very famous minority opinions that severely limit the scope of the authorization to provide medical care. Ibn Ezra (in his commentary to Exodus 21:19) is a notable example, writing that the command to heal "is a sign that permission has been granted to physicians to heal blows and wounds that are externally visible. But, all internal illnesses are in God's hand to heal." The Ibn Ezra's case is not a hard one to make. The Torah itself instructs that if we listen carefully and Jewish legal scholars interpret the Torah to grant a very broad license to heal, there is a consensus that the patient must be ill to allow the physician to treat the patient, particularly if the treatment is dangerous or requires injuring the patient in the process of healing.

This is one of the major concerns voiced by Rabbi Eliezer Yehuda Waldenberg (1917-2006), author of *Tzitz Eliezer*, a multivolume set of responsa, much of which deals with medical issues. First, Rabbi Waldenberg[41] objects to performing surgery on someone who is neither sick nor in pain.[42] He argues that such activities are outside the boundaries of the physician's mandate to heal (since he questions whether cosmetic surgery is truly included in the category of healing). He further asserts that the patient has no right to ask the physician to wound him or her for the purposes of merely enhancing beauty. Rabbi Waldenberg then makes the theological argument that as the ultimate artisan, God creates each person in His image, exactly as he or she should be, with nothing extra nor anything lacking. He therefore posits that cosmetic surgery that is not pursued to relieve pain or true illness is an affront to God and is forbidden.[43]

A Final Argument

The last major posek to voice an opinion is a fitting conclusion to our discussion of the various approaches of Jewish legal authorities to plastic surgery. Dr. Abraham Abraham reports[44] the opinion of Rav Shlomo Zalman Auerbach (1910-1995), the great Israeli posek, on the question of a person whose arm or finger had been traumatically amputated.

In response to those who forbid plastic surgery, Rabbi Auerbach discussed the question of whether an amputated limb could be reattached by surgery requiring general anesthesia, even if the patient had already been treated so that he was no longer in danger his life. He ruled that the surgery would certainly be permitted on a weekday[45] "since the surgery would not be considered an injury but a repair and treatment to save the limb. Why then should it be forbidden for someone to undergo plastic surgery in order to look normal?" In a published responsa,[46] Rabbi Auerbach writes:

If the plastic surgery is done to prevent suffering and shame caused by a defect in his looks (for instance a nose which is very abnormal) this would be permitted based on the Tosafot and the Gemara, since the purpose is to remove a blemish. However if the only reason is for beauty, this is not permitted.

---

to the mitzvot of the Torah "then any of the diseases that I placed upon Egypt, I will not bring upon you, for I am God, your Healer" (Exodus 15:26). This verse implies that God does not need man to cure the afflictions that He creates. The Ibn Ezra argues that the meaning of this Torah passage is that because God acts as the (sole) healer of all illness, we will not need physicians. See Eisenberg,,D, *"The Mandate to Heal,"* "http://www.aish.com/societyWork/work/The_Mandate_to_Heal.asp

41 Responsa *Tzitz Eliezer*, 11:41

42 See Responsa *Tzitz Eliezer*, 12:43 where Rabbi Waldenberg rules that truly elective surgery is never permitted.

43 Rabbi Waldenberg's approach is based on the accepted concept that there is no inherent right for man to practice medicine, but that direct permission was required from the Torah which carefully circumscribes the limits of medical practice (see *Tosofos, Bava Kamma* 85a, opening word, *"sh'nitna"*). The duty to save one's fellow man is well grounded in the Torah and the restrictions are discussed at length in our codes of Jewish law. The complexity of the philosophical tension between God's control of health and the role of the human healer is encapsulated by the enigmatic opening words of the Code of Jewish Law's discussion of the laws applying to physicians: "The Torah gives permission to the physician to heal; moreover, this is a mitzvah and it is included in the mitzvah of saving a life; and, if he withholds his services, he is considered a shedder of blood." (*Shulchan Aruch, Yoreh Deah* 336)

Why is permission specifically granted here? Because only here we may have thought that the action should be forbidden. Left to our own logic, we would have no choice but to assume that God makes people sick and God alone heals (see note 40). But, once the Torah clearly stated that healing is permitted, it immediately becomes a mitzvah—a religious obligation—like all other mitzvos. Therefore, the Code of Jewish Law quite appropriately states that "The Torah gives permission to the physician to heal; moreover, this is a mitzvah."

44 *Nishmat Avraham, Yoreh Deah*, p. 62, Mesorah Publications (English version)

45 "On *Shabbat* or *Yom Tov* this would not be permitted since there was only *danger to a limb* and one could not set aside Torah law for this." Ibid.

46 *Minchas Shlomo Tinyana* 86:3 quoted in *Nishmat Avraham*, ibid.

Rabbi Auerbach sums up the consensus of most legal experts in ruling that plastic surgery to allow someone to appear normal, and more importantly to view themselves as appearing normal is permitted. It is only when such surgery is performed merely for vanity that the rabbis have serious reservations. Clearly however, true reconstructive surgery and even surgery for an appearance that makes one feel embarrassed is not an issue of vanity. Such was clearly the case with the French face transplant recipient.

This leaves us with a very potent human message. We must always appreciate the self-constructed prisons in which some of our friends and acquaintances live and the empathy of our rabbis to their plight. Whether it is the torture of feeling unattractive or the feeling of hopelessness of a single friend who is losing hope that he/she will ever have a wife/husband and family, we must always look for ways to ease their pain.

Jewish Medical Ethics and Halacha 7, no.1 (Schlesinger Institute for Medical-Halachic Research, 2009):24-29.
(Also published on Dr. Eisenberg's website, www.jewishmedicalethics.com)
Reprinted with permission of the author and publisher

A Jewish Poet

by **Yehoshua November**

It is hard to be a Jewish poet.
You cannot say things about God
that will offend the disbelievers.
And you will always have to remind someone
it wasn't your people who killed their savior.
And Solomon and David are always laughing
over your shoulder
like a father and son ridiculing the unfavored brother.
And you cannot entice people with the sloping
parts of a woman's body
because you must always remain pure.
And every day you have to ask yourself why you're writing
when there is already the one great book.
It is hard to be a Jewish poet.
You cannot say anything about the disbelievers,
which might offend God.

Prairie Schooner 81, no. 1, ed. Hilda Raz (University of Nebraska Press, 2007):49. (Also appears in November's poetry book, God's Optimism [Main Street Rag, 2010])
Reprinted with permission of the author

An Intimate View on Intimacy

by **Rabbi Manis Friedman**

Conventional wisdom says that sexuality is a natural instinct. It's a very common and innocent human activity, it's what happens between a man and a woman, it's what people do and all we need to do is relax and enjoy it, right?

It seems so simple. But if it were so simple, why do we need to be reminded over and over again that it's natural, it's innocent, it's pleasurable, it's what we do, it's what happens, relax and enjoy it? In fact, the media has bombarded us with that message for so long and in so many different ways with such ingenuity that you have to wonder why the message hasn't been accepted. Why are we still so uncomfortable, so unsure, so mystified by our own sexuality?

In the world that the Almighty created, there are three conditions. First, there is the secular, weekday, mundane condition—ordinary, common things that we possess. Second, there is the holy, Divine condition—so heavenly that we don't have these things at all. These two parts, so far, are pretty easily accepted and understood. The difficult part is the third condition, the sacred. Although sacred means set aside and unavailable, the sacred is not totally unavailable. The sacred is that which is holier than the ordinary, but not so holy that we can't approach it at all. It's something in between what we have and what we cannot have.

Confused? Let's use a simple example. The Almighty grants us the blessing of children. So, we have children. Your children. My children. But when we say "my children," is that a possessive "my"? Do I own my children? The answer, of course, is no. They're not really mine. They don't belong to me. When I say "my wife," is that a possessive thing? Does "my husband" mean that which belongs to me? Of course not. And yet, we can use a term so familiar as "my" in referring to these things in life. That's the sanctity in life, and if we're not careful, in our arrogance, we can lay claim to things that will never belong to us and lose their sanctity.

So, where does sexuality fit in? By its very nature—not by divine decree, not by religious belief or dictate—sexuality belongs to the arena of the sacred. We experience it, but we cannot own it. We can go there, but we don't belong there. We can be sexual, but we cannot possess our own sexuality. The reason for it is very natural and very basic. To be intimate means to go into a place that is private, that is sacred, that is set aside. Sexuality means one person entering into the private, sacred part of another human being's existence.

You cannot own another person's intimacy. It's not available. Even if the person wants to give ownership. Can't do it. It's not sharable. It's one of those things in life that the Almighty gives us that we can never possess. I cannot possess my children. I cannot possess my spouse. I cannot possess my Creator. I can't even possess my life. I, certainly, cannot possess the other person's intrinsic, sacred and unsharable part.

Well, if it's that unavailable, if I can't possess it, then what connection, what relationship do I have with it?

This is the sanctity we can experience, but cannot own. And that is why the pleasure in intimate relations is more intense than any other pleasure. You can enjoy a good meal. You can enjoy good food, and it's great pleasure, but it's not the pleasure of sexuality because you possess the food. It's yours. You planted the vegetables, you grew them, you plucked them and you ate them. They're yours. There's no awe involved. The pleasure of sexuality is that it's a combination of having and not having. It's a combination of ordinary and other worldly at the same time. It's something that you are granted, but you cannot own and possess. And when you feel that combination, the pleasure of being in another person's intimate space while at the same time remembering that you don't belong there—it's not your place and can never be your place—that's what makes sexuality different.

The key word is familiarity. With the sacred, you cannot afford to become familiar. With the truly divine, there's no danger. It's out of your reach—forget about it. With the secular and mundane, well, you should become familiar. So where does familiarity breed contempt? Where is familiarity really destructive and unwelcome? In sanctity. If you become familiar, too familiar, with the intimacy of another person's life, whether physical, emotional or mental, then you've compromised the sanctity.

In our tell-all world, visualizing the destructiveness of familiarity might be difficult. But you don't call your parents by their first name... because that's too familiar. We don't use the Almighty's name in vain... because it's too familiar. And for our grandparents and our great-grandparents, intimate relations was a sacred thing not to be talked about... because that would be too familiar. The relationship between a husband and wife was restricted to behind closed doors. It was a sacred thing, something you don't squander, share, or even speak about. That's why our grandparents could not talk about their relationship. They weren't keeping secrets—they were keeping something sacred.

Today, human sexuality is something you're supposed to become familiar with. We claim to already be familiar with our sexuality and we are ashamed to admit that we are not. We've removed the sanctity, all because we thought our uptight parents were keeping a secret from us. The media continues to bombard us with these brilliant, subtle messages of the "naturalness" and "openness" of human sexuality, and it's not convincing us. Try as we might, we cannot ignore what our bubbes and zaides knew: the marriage bed is a sacred thing and the only way it works is when you treat it with sanctity.

Still need proof? Look at those same bubbes and zaides a little closer. Those two people, who have been married fifty, sixty, seventy years, are still a little bashful with each other. They still blush with each other. They still excite each other. That is human sexuality. That is sanctity. And that is the last word on intimacy.

Authors' Acknowledgments

The distance between the conception of a course and its expert execution is vast.

We thank **Dr. Chana Silberstein**, editor in chief and dean of curriculum for JLI, for embracing the concept of this course in its most nascent form and for shepherding it so brilliantly through every one of its many stages. It is the work of Dr. Silberstein, **Rabbi Naftali Silberberg,** and the other members of the flagship editorial team, that brought our effort to completely new heights. The mark of their scholarship and creativity is found on every page.

We humbly thank our Creator for the opportunity to have, in some small way, added to the flame of Torah learning that JLI has ignited. As chasidim, *shluchim* of the Rebbe, and longtime JLI affiliates (and in the case of Rabbi Avrohom Sternberg, an executive committee member of JLI), this work has intersected with so much of what we hold near and dear.

With boundless gratitude, we dedicate the work we did together on this project to our beloved parents, **Rabbi Menachem Nochum** and **Rebbetzin Esther Sternberg**, our first, most important, and continuous teachers of Torah, who through personal example and depth of conviction have raised us and our children to love the Torah and the *Notein HaTorah*.

ואני, זאת בריתי אותם אמר ה'—רוחי אשר עליך, ודברי אשר שמתי בפיך, לא ימושו מפיך ומפי זרעך ומפי זרע זרעך, אמר ה', מעתה, ועד עולם (ישעיהו נט,כא)

In awe, we salute JLI's executive director **Rabbi Efraim Mintz** for how far he has brought the Rohr JLI under his expert stewardship. To the indefatigable chairman, **Rabbi Moshe Kotlarsky**, and the visionary *Zevulun* of JLI, **Mr. George Rohr** and family, we wish continued *nachas* and unending return on your investment.

Finally, we thank our students of all years past whose questions and insights were the impetus for this course. It is to you that we owe our continued growth and inspiration.

Mrs. Rivkah Slonim
Binghamton, NY

Rabbi Avrohom Y. H. Sternberg
New London, CT

Acknowledgments

The Rohr Jewish Learning Institute has long desired to offer a gateway course, an entry into Jewish learning that would invite, intrigue, and inspire those who have not yet had the opportunity to engage in much Jewish learning. However, introductory courses often face the challenge of being a mile long and an inch deep: in the effort to ensure that every topic is at least touched upon, little time is left for probing deeply and exploring the issues that make learning edifying and worthwhile.

It is with great pleasure, therefore, that we launch the present course, ***Fascinating Facts: Exploring the Myths and Mysteries of Judaism***. While we have made no effort to be comprehensive, the course is fast-paced and engaging, an eclectic assortment of tidbits designed to surprise and inform both those with and without prior Jewish knowledge while introducing fundamental principles that can guide and inform future Jewish study.

We are grateful, first and foremost, to our course authors, **Rabbi Avrohom Sternberg** and **Mrs. Rivkah Slonim**, who first suggested this innovative paradigm. Based on their extensive experience as community educators and classroom instructors, they have crafted this breathtaking panoramic view of Judaism while ensuring that each lesson has numerous focal points of interest. They have their fingers on the pulse of the audience, and their well-honed instincts have guided each stage of this course's development.

The JLI Editorial Board has provided many useful suggestions to enhance the course and ensure its suitability for a wide range of students. Many thanks to **Rabbi Yosef Loschak**, **Rabbi Yossi Nemes**, **Rabbi Shraga Sherman**, and **Rabbi Aryeh Weinstein** for their thoughtful review at various stages of course production.

We are greatly indebted to the flagship editorial team whose constant efforts ensure that our courses follow a rising trajectory of growth. **Rabbi Naftali Silberberg**, who served as lead editor on this course, nurtured and cultivated the spirit of the course while preserving its unique characteristics. Rabbi Silberberg's careful attention to clarity and tone highlighted the course's natural warmth, empathy, and gentle humor. **Rabbi Mordechai Dinerman** reviewed the logic and structure of the material, and his incisive analysis resulted in many improvements to the document. We are also grateful to **Ms. Neria Cohen** for her editorial contributions and careful review of the document.

Rabbi Avrohom Bergstein thoughtfully researched the wide range of subject matter touched upon in this course and provided many sources to aid the instructor. Rabbi Bergstein also designs the Powerpoint presentations that accompany each lesson and crafts the lesson maps that serve as a powerful guide to lesson preparation. We also thank **Rabbi Yehuda Shurpin** for his research assistance.

We are proud to partner this semester with the **Kohelet Foundation**, an organization devoted to dramatically improving the effectiveness and affordability of American Jewish day schools. We are grateful to the president of the Kohelet Foundation, **Mr. David Magerman**, who has spearheaded the notion of supporting Jewish day schools through engaging parents in Jewish learning. His pioneering efforts are transforming the future of Jewish education. We are also much indebted to the director of the Kohelet Foundation, **Mrs. Holly Cohen**, who has worked closely with JLI to ensure an exemplary program.

Mrs. Lea-Perl Shollar developed the Parent Pages that accompany the course, allowing Kohelet parents to share their learning with their children. In addition, Mrs. Shollar is our JLI blog master, bringing rich supplementary perspectives to our student-learning community via Twitter, Facebook, and our JLI blog.

A particular mention is due **Ms. Chava Zviklin**, our flagship production manager, who carefully weaves together the many strands that make up the fabric of our flagship operation. Her research, editorial, and managerial skills have played a critical role in our smooth operation. We wish her a warm *mazal tov* upon her upcoming wedding. May the merits of her holy work bring the young couple much blessing and happiness for many years to come.

JLI's efficient and talented production team is responsible for the outstanding quality of our printed materials. **Rabbi Mendel Sirota**, production manager, sets perfection as JLI's baseline standard. He orchestrates the myriad tasks that are necessary to our overall operation, including posting and personalizing marketing materials, overseeing the delivery of our books, and ensuring that our affiliates receive all support materials in a timely manner. **Mrs. Rachel Witty**, our proofreader, meticulously prepares our manuscript for print. **Nachman Levine**, our layout designer and research editor, brings to our work not only an artistic eye but also a scholarly one.

Thank you, **Spotlight Design**, for proving that you *can* judge a book by its cover. Finally, we would like to acknowledge the efforts of **Shimon Leib Jacobs**, who oversees our printing and shipping.

We extend our thanks to **Rabbi Zalman Abraham**, director of marketing, as well as the members of our JLI marketing board, **Rabbi Simcha Backman**, **Rabbi Ronnie Fine**, **Rabbi Ovadia Goldman**, **Rabbi Mendel Halberstam**, and **Rabbi Yehudah Shemtov**.

The hardworking support staff at JLI Central is critical to our success and growth. JLI's administrative staff, **Mrs. Chana Dechter**, **Mrs. Musie Kesselman**, **Mrs. Fraydee Kessler**, **Mrs. Chana Shaffer-Minkowitz**, and **Mrs. Mindy Wallach** attend to the many details that hone our professional edge to perfection. **Mrs. Shaina Basha Mintz**, **Mrs. Nechama Shmotkin**, and **Ms. Musie Karp** oversee our accounts. **Rabbi Mendel Bell**, webmaster *par excellence*, ensures the integrity of our online environment. **Rabbi Levi Kaplan** directs our international division and adapts our material for our Hebrew-speaking and Spanish-speaking markets. **Rabbi Mendel Popack**, director of JLI Academy, is the organizing force behind our annual JLI conference and is devoted to providing our affiliates with the development tools they need. **Dubi Rabinowitz**, chief operating officer, invites us to constantly rethink our roles and to reconfigure ourselves for efficiency and results.

We are immensely grateful for the encouragement of our chairman, and vice-chairman of Merkos L'Inyonei Chinuch—Lubavitch World Headquarters, **Rabbi Moshe Kotlarsky**. We are blessed to have the unwavering support of JLI's principal benefactor, **Mr. George Rohr**, who has fully invested in our work and has been instrumental in the monumental expansion of the organization.

JLI's dedicated executive board—**Rabbi Chaim Block**, **Rabbi Hesh Epstein**, **Rabbi Yosef Gansburg**, **Rabbi Shmuel Kaplan**, **Rabbi Yisrael Rice**, and **Rabbi Avrohom Sternberg**—devote countless hours to the ongoing development of JLI. Their dedicated commitment and sage direction have helped JLI continue to grow and flourish.

We owe a particular debt of thanks to **Rabbi Yisrael Rice**, chairman of our flagship division, whose patient and thoughtful guidance has been an exceptional source of support throughout a period of rapid development.

The constant progress in JLI is a testament to the visionary leadership of our director, **Rabbi Efraim Mintz**, who is never content to rest on his laurels and who boldly encourages continued innovation and change.

Finally, JLI represents an incredible partnership of more than 300 *shluchim* who give of their time and talent to further Jewish adult education. We thank them for generously sharing their thoughts, feedback, questions, and teaching experiences. They are our most valuable critics and our most cherished contributors.

Inspired by the call of the **Lubavitcher Rebbe** of righteous memory, it is the mandate of the Rohr JLI to allow all Jews throughout the world to experience and take part in the Torah learning that is their heritage. May this course succeed in fulfilling that sacred charge.

On behalf of the Rohr Jewish Learning Institute,

Chana Silberstein, PhD

Ithaca, New York
Chai Elul, 5771

The Rohr Jewish Learning Institute

An affiliate of
Merkos L'Inyonei Chinuch
The Educational Arm of
The Chabad Lubavitch Movement
822 Eastern Parkway, Brooklyn, NY 11213

Rabbi Yisroel Altein
Pittsburgh, PA

Rabbi Yechiel Baitelman
Richmond, BC

Rabbi Chaim Brikman
Seagate, NY

Rabbi Berel Bell
Montreal, QC

Rabbi Hesh Epstein
Columbia, SC

Rabbi Zalman Aaron Kantor
Mission Viejo, CA

Rabbi Levi Kaplan
Brooklyn, NY

Rabbi Dr. Shmuel Klatzkin
Dayton, OH

Rabbi Yakov Latowicz
Ventura, CA

Rabbi Yosef Loschak
Goleta, CA

Rabbi Levi Mendelow
Stamford, CT

Rabbi Benzion Milecki
Dover Heights, AU

Rabbi Yossi Nemes
Metairie, LA

Rabbi Reuven New
Boca Raton, FL

Rabbi Dr. Shlomo Pereira
Richmond, VA

Rabbi Shalom Raichik
Gaithersburg, MD

Rabbi Benny Rapoport
Clarks Summit, PA

Rabbi Nochum Schapiro
Sydney, AU

Rabbi Shraga Sherman
Merion Station, PA

Rabbi Avraham Steinmetz
S. Paulo, BR

Rabbi Avrohom Sternberg
New London, CT

Rabbi Aryeh Weinstein
Newton, PA

Rabbi Motti Wilhelm
Portland, OR

Multimedia Development

Rabbi Avrohom Bergstein
Ms. Neria Cohen
Rabbi Chesky Edelman
Moshe Raskin
Mrs. Leah-Perl Shollar
Rabbi Levi Teldon

Administration

Mrs. Chana Dechter
Mrs. Chana Shaffer-Minkowitz
Rabbi Mendel Sirota
Mrs. Mindy Wallach

Affiliate Support

Mrs. Musie Kesselman
Mrs. Fraydee Kessler
Rabbi Mendel Sirota
Mrs. Mindy Wallach

Online Division

Rabbi Mendel Bell
Rabbi Dovid Ciment
Rabbi Mendel Sirota

Marketing and Branding

Rabbi Zalman Abraham
Director

Marketing Committee

Rabbi Simcha Backman
Glendale, CA

Rabbi Ronnie Fine
Montreal, QC

Rabbi Ovadia Goldman
Oklahoma City, OK

Rabbi Mendy Halberstam
Miami Beach, FL

Rabbi Reuven New
Boca Raton, FL

Rabbi Yehuda Shemtov
Yardley, PA

Marketing Consultants

Scott Dubin
Dubin Strategy and Consulting LLC
Toronto, ON

JJ Gross
New York, NY

Warren Modlin
MednetPro, Inc.
Alpharetta, GA

Alan Rosenspan
Alan Rosenspan & Associates
Sharon, MA

Alan M. Shafer
Alliant Marketing Solutions
Stamford, CT

Gary Wexler
Passion Marketing
Los Angeles, CA

Graphic Design

Spotlight Design
Brooklyn, NY

Friedman Advertising
Los Angeles, CA

Yossi Graphic Design
Brooklyn, NY

Publication Design

Nachman Levine
Detroit, MI

Printing

Shimon Leib Jacobs
Point One Communications
Montreal, QC

Shipping

Mary Stevens
Nixa, MO

Accounting

Ms. Musie Karp
Mrs. Shaina B. Mintz
Mrs. Nechama Shmotkin

JLI Departments

Dubi Rabinowitz
Chief Operating Officer

JLI Flagship

Rabbi Yisrael Rice
Chairman
S. Rafael, CA

Dr. Chana Silberstein
Dean of Curriculum
Ithaca, NY

Rabbi Mordechai Dinerman
Associate Editor

Rabbi Naftali Silberberg
Developmental Editor

Mrs. Leah-Perl Shollar
Instructional Designer

Rabbi Avraham Bergstein
Instructional Support

Rabbi Mendel Sirota
Production Manager

Ms. Chava Zviklin
Managing Editor

Mrs. Rachel Witty
Proofreader

Nachman Levine
Research Editor

Department of Continuing Education

Mrs. Mindy Wallach
Director

Ms. Musie Karp
Registrar

Mrs. Rivka Sternberg
Administrative Support

Dr. Michael Akerman, MD
Consultant
Continuing Medical Education
Associate Professor of Medicine,
SUNY–Downstate Medical Center

JLI For Teens

in partnership with CTeeN: Chabad Teen Network

Rabbi Chaim Block
Chairman
San Antonio, TX

Rabbi Benny Rapoport
Director
Clarks Summit, PA

Mrs. Gani Goodman
Administrator

Rabbi Beryl Frankel
Director, CTeeN
Yardley, PA

JLI International Desk

Rabbi Avrohom Sternberg
Chairman
New London, CT

Rabbi Elya Silfen
Coordinator

Rabbi Yossi Baitsh
Administrator, JLI Israel

Rabbi Yitzchak Marton
Regional Representative
Israel

Rabbi Nochum Schapiro
Regional Respresentative
Australia

Rabbi Hirshel Hendel
Regional Representative
Spanish Division

JLI Teacher Training

Rabbi Berel Bell
Director
Montreal, QC

myShiur:

Advanced Learning Initiative

Rabbi Shmuel Kaplan
Chairman
Potomac, MD

Rabbi Levi Kaplan
Director

Rosh Chodesh Society

Rabbi Shmuel Kaplan
Chairman
Potomac, MD

Mrs. Shaindy Jacobson
Director

Mrs. Musie Kesselman
Administrator

Steering Committee
Mrs. Chanie Bukiet
Mrs. Simcha Fine
Mrs. Sara Lieberman
Mrs. Michla Schanowitz
Mrs. Bronya Shaffer

National Jewish Retreat

Rabbi Hesh Epstein
Chairman
Columbia, SC

Rabbi Mendy Weg
Founding Director

Rabbi Boruch Cohen
Director

Bruce Backman
Coordinator

Mrs. Shaina B. Mintz
Administrator

Sinai Scholars Society

in partnership with Chabad on Campus

Rabbi Menachem Schmidt
Chairman
Philadelphia, PA

Rabbi Yitzchok Dubov
Director

Executive Committee
Rabbi Moshe Chaim Dubrowski
Rabbi Efraim Mintz
Rabbi Menachem Schmidt
Dr. Chana Silberstein
Rabbi Nechemia Vogel
Rabbi Eitan Webb

TorahCafe.com

Online Learning

Rabbi Levi Kaplan
Director

Mrs. Miri Birk
Adminisrator

Rabbi Simcha Backman
Golan Ben-Oni
Rabbi Leibel Karp
Consultants

Rabbi Mendy Elishevitz
Rabbi Mendel Bell
Onstream Media
Website Development

Rabbi Getzel Raskin
Director of Filming and Editing

Menachem Amos
Ms. Fraidy Bell
Avrohom Shimon Ezagui
Yehoshua Hayward
Yosef Kramer
Yehuda Shaffer
Akiva Silberstein
Yosef Schmalberg
Mendel Serobranski
Filming Crew

Moshe Raskin
Chaya Rosenfeld
Joelle Wilshinsky
Video Editing

Torah Studies

Rabbi Yossi Gansburg
Chairman
Toronto, ON

Rabbi Meir Hecht
Director

Rabbi Moshe Teldon
Administrator

Steering Committee
Rabbi Yaacov Halperin
Rabbi Nechemia Schusterman
Rabbi Ari Sollish

JLI Academy

Rabbi Hesh Epstein
Chairman

Rabbi Mendel Popack
Director

Dr. Gill Heart
Consultant

Steering Committee
Rabbi Yoel Caroline
Rabbi Mordechai Grossbaum
Rabbi Levi Mendelow

Beis Medrosh L'Shluchim

in partnership with Shluchim Exchange

Rabbi Sholom Zirkind
Administrator

Rabbi Mendy Rabin
Coordinator

Rabbi Mendel Margolin
Producer

Steering Committee
Rabbi Simcha Backman
Rabbi Mendy Kotlarsky
Rabbi Efraim Mintz

JLI Central

Founding Department Heads

Rabbi Zalman Charytan
Acworth, GA

Rabbi Mendel Druk
Cancun, Mexico

Rabbi Menachem Gansburg
Toronto, ON

Rabbi Yoni Katz
Brooklyn, NY

Rabbi Chaim Zalman Levy
New Rochelle, NY

Mrs. Chana Lightstone
Brooklyn, New York

Rabbi Elchonon Tenenbaum
Napa Valley, CA

Rohr JLI Affiliates

Share the **Rohr JLI** experience with friends and relatives worldwide

ALABAMA

Birmingham
Rabbi Yossi Friedman
205.970.0100

ARIZONA

Chandler
Rabbi Mendel Deitsch
480.855.4333

Flagstaff
Rabbi Dovie Shapiro
928.255.5756

Glendale
Rabbi Sholom Lew
602.375.2422

Phoenix
Rabbi Zalman Levertov
Rabbi Yossi Friedman
602.944.2753

Scottsdale
Rabbi Yossi Levertov
Rabbi Yossi Bryski
480.998.1410

ARKANSAS

Little Rock
Rabbi Pinchus Ciment
501.217.0053

CALIFORNIA

Agoura Hills
Rabbi Moshe Bryski
818.991.0991

Bel Air
Rabbi Chaim Mentz
310.475.5311

Brentwood
Rabbi Boruch Hecht
Rabbi Mordechai Zaetz
310.826.4453

Burbank
Rabbi Shmuly Kornfeld
818.954.0070

Calabasas
Rabbi Eliyahu Friedman
818.585.1888

Carlsbad
Rabbi Yeruchem Eilfort
Rabbi Michoel Shapiro
760.943.8891

Chatsworth
Rabbi Yossi Spritzer
818.718.0777

Contra Costa
Rabbi Yaakov Kagan
Rabbi Dovber Berkowitz
925.937.4101

Encino
Rabbi Joshua Gordon
Rabbi Eli Rivkin
818.758.1818

Folsom
Rabbi Yossi Grossbaum
916.608.9811

Glendale
Rabbi Simcha Backman
818.240.2750

Huntington Beach
Rabbi Aron Berkowitz
714.846.2285

Irvine
Rabbi Alter Tenenbaum
Rabbi Elly Andrusier
949.786.5000

Laguna Beach
Rabbi Elimelech Gurevitch
949.499.0770

Lomita
Rabbi Eli Hecht
Rabbi Sholom Pinson
310.326.8234

Long Beach
Rabbi Abba Perelmuter
562.621.9828

Los Angeles
Rabbi Leibel Korf
323.660.5177

Marina del Rey
Rabbi Danny Yiftach
Rabbi Mendy Avtzon
310.859.0770

Newport Beach
Rabbi Reuven Mintz
949.721.9800

North Hollywood
Rabbi Nachman Abend
818.989.9539

Northridge
Rabbi Eli Rivkin
818.368.3937

Pacific Palisades
Rabbi Zushe Cunin
310.454.7783

Pasadena
Rabbi Chaim Hanoka
626.564.8820

Rancho Cucamonga
Rabbi Sholom B. Harlig
909.949.4553

Rancho Palos Verdes
Rabbi Yitzchok Magalnic
310.544.5544

Rancho S. Fe
Rabbi Levi Raskin
858.756.7571

Redondo Beach
Rabbi Dovid Lisbon
310.214.4999

Sacramento
Rabbi Mendy Cohen
916.455.1400

S. Barbara
Rabbi Yosef Loschak
805.683.1544

S. Clemente
Rabbi Menachem M. Slavin
949.489.0723

S. Cruz
Rabbi Yochanan Friedman
831.454.0101

S. Diego
Rabbi Motte Fradkin
858.547.0076

S. Francisco
Rabbi Peretz Mochkin
415.571.8770

S. Monica
Rabbi Boruch Rabinowitz
310.394.5699

S. Rafael
Rabbi Yisrael Rice
415.492.1666

Simi Valley
Rabbi Nosson Gurary
805.577.0573

Stockton
Rabbi Avremel Brod
209.952.2081

Studio City
Rabbi Yossi Baitelman
818.508.6633

Temecula
Rabbi Yitzchok Hurwitz
951.303.9576

Thousand Oaks
Rabbi Chaim Bryski
805.493.7776

Tustin
Rabbi Yehoshua Eliezrie
714.508.2150

Ventura
Rabbi Yakov Latowicz
Mrs. Sarah Latowicz
805.658.7441

West Hills
Rabbi Avrahom Yitzchak Rabin
818.337.4544

Yorba Linda
Rabbi Dovid Eliezrie
714.693.0770

COLORADO

Aspen
Rabbi Mendel Mintz
970.544.3770

Boulder
Rabbi Pesach Scheiner
303.494.1638

Denver
Rabbi Yossi Serebryanski
303.744.9699

Highlands Ranch
Rabbi Avraham Mintz
303.694.9119

Longmont
Rabbi Yaakov Dovid Borenstein
303.678.7595

Vail
Rabbi Dovid Mintz
970.476.7887

Westminster
Rabbi Benjy Brackman
303.429.5177

CONNECTICUT

Glastonbury
Rabbi Yosef Wolvovsky
860.659.2422

Greenwich
Rabbi Yossi Deren
Rabbi Menachem Feldman
203.629.9059

New London
Rabbi Avrohom Sternberg
860.437.8000

Orange
Rabbi Sheya Hecht
Rabbi Adam Haston
203.795.5261

Simsbury
Rabbi Mendel Samuels
860.658.4903

Stamford
Rabbi Yisrael Deren
Rabbi Levi Mendelow
203.3.CHABAD

West Hartford
Rabbi Yosef Gopin
Rabbi Shaya Gopin
860.659.2422

Westport
Rabbi Yehuda L. Kantor
Mrs. Dina Kantor
203.226.8584

DELAWARE

Wilmington
Rabbi Chuni Vogel
302.529.9900

FLORIDA

Aventura
Rabbi Laivi Forta
Rabbi Yakov Garfinkel
305.933.0770

Bal Harbour
Rabbi Dov Schochet
305.868.1411

Boca Raton
Rabbi Moishe Denberg
Rabbi Zalman Bukiet
561.417.7797

Boynton Beach
Rabbi Yosef Yitzchok Raichik
561.732.4633

Bradenton
Rabbi Menachem Bukiet
941.388.9656

Coral Gables
Rabbi Avrohom Stolik
305.490.7572

Deerfield Beach
Rabbi Yossi Goldblatt
954.422.1735

Delray Beach
Rabbi Sholom Ber Korf
561.496.6228

East Boca Raton
Rabbi Ruvi New
561.417.7797

Fort Lauderdale
Rabbi Yitzchok Naparstek
954.568.1190

Fort Myers
Rabbi Yitzchok Minkowicz
Mrs. Nechama Minkowicz
239.433.7708

Hollywood
Rabbi Leizer Barash
954.965.9933

Kendall
Rabbi Yossi Harlig
305.234.5654

Key Biscayne
Rabbi Yoel Caroline
305.365.6744

Key West
Rabbi Yaakov Zucker
305.295.0013

Naples
Rabbi Fishel Zaklos
239.262.4474

North Miami Beach
Rabbi Moishe Kievman
305.770.1919

Orlando
Rabbi Yosef Konikov
407.354.3660

Parkland
Rabbi Mendy Gutnik
954.796.7330

Pinellas County
Rabbi Shalom Adler
727.789.0408

Sarasota
Rabbi Chaim Shaul Steinmetz
941.925.0770

Satellite Beach
Rabbi Zvi Konikov
321.777.2770

South Palm Beach
Rabbi Leibel Stolik
561.889.3499

South Tampa
Rabbi Mendy Dubrowski
813.287.1795

Sunny Isles Beach
Rabbi Alexander Kaller
305.803.5315

Tallahassee
Rabbi Schneur Zalmen Oirechman
850.523.9294

Venice
Rabbi Sholom Ber Schmerling
941.493.2770

Walnut Creek
Rabbi Zalman Korf
954.374.8370

Weston
Rabbi Yisroel Spalter
954.349.6565

West Palm Beach
Rabbi Yoel Gancz
561.659.7770

West Pasco
Rabbi Yossi Eber
727.376.3366

GEORGIA

Alpharetta
Rabbi Hirshy Minkowicz
770.410.9000

Atlanta
Rabbi Yossi New
Rabbi Isser New
404.843.2464

Atlanta: Intown
Rabbi Eliyahu Schusterman
Rabbi Ari Sollish
404.898.0434

Gwinnett
Rabbi Yossi Lerman
678.595.0196

Marietta
Rabbi Ephraim Silverman
Rabbi Zalman Charytan
770.565.4412

IDAHO

Boise
Rabbi Mendel Lifshitz
208.853.9200

ILLINOIS

Champaign
Rabbi Dovid Tiechtel
217.355.8672

Chicago
Rabbi Meir Hecht
312.714.4655

Gurnee
Rabbi Sholom Ber Tenenbaum
847.782.1800

Glenview
Rabbi Yishaya Benjaminson
847.998.9896

Highland Park
Mrs. Michla Schanowitz
847.266.0770

Naperville
Rabbi Mendy Goldstein
630.778.9770

Northbrook
Rabbi Meir Moscowitz
847.564.8770

Peoria
Rabbi Eli Langsam
309.692.2250

Skokie
Rabbi Yochanan Posner
847.677.1770

Wilmette
Rabbi Dovid Flinkenstein
847.251.7707

INDIANA

Indianapolis
Rabbi Mendel Schusterman
317.251.5573

KANSAS

Overland Park
Rabbi Mendy Wineberg
913.649.4852

LOUISIANA

Metairie
Rabbi Yossi Nemes
504.454.2910

MARYLAND

Baltimore
Rabbi Elchonon Lisbon
410.358.4787

Rabbi Velvel Belinsky
Classes in Russian
410.764.5000

Bethesda
Rabbi Bentzion Geisinsky
Rabbi Sender Geisinsky
301.913.9777

Columbia
Rabbi Hillel Baron
Rabbi Yosef Chaim Sufrin
410.740.2424

Gaithersburg
Rabbi Sholom Raichik
301.926.3632

Potomac
Rabbi Mendel Bluming
301.983.4200

Silver Spring
Rabbi Berel Wolvovsky
301.593.1117

MASSACHUSETTS

Amherst
Rabbi Shmuel Kravitsky
413.835.0085

Hyannis
Rabbi Yekusiel Alperowitz
508.775.2324

Longmeadow
Rabbi Yakov Wolff
413.567.8665

Sudbury
Rabbi Yisroel Freeman
978.443.3691

Swampscott
Mrs. Layah Lipsker
781.581.3833

MICHIGAN

Ann Arbor
Rabbi Aharon Goldstein
734.995.3276

Grand Rapids
Rabbi Mordechai Haller
616.957.0770

Novi
Rabbi Avrohom Susskind
248.790.6075

West Bloomfield
Rabbi Kasriel Shemtov
248.788.4000

Rabbi Elimelech Silberberg
Rabbi Avrohom Wineberg
248.855 .6170

MINNESOTA

Minnetonka
Rabbi Mordechai Grossbaum
952.929.9922

Rochester
Rabbi Dovid Greene
507.288.7500

S. Paul
Rabbi Shneur Zalman Bendet
651.278.8401

MISSOURI

S. Louis
Rabbi Yosef Landa
314.725.0400

MONTANA

Bozeman
Rabbi Chaim Shaul Bruk
406.585.8770

NEBRASKA

Omaha
Rabbi Mendel Katzman
402.330.1800

NEVADA

Henderson
Rabbi Mendy Harlig
Rabbi Tzvi Bronstein
702.617.0770

Summerlin
Rabbi Yisroel Schanowitz
Rabbi Tzvi Bronstein
702.855.0770

NEW JERSEY

Basking Ridge
Rabbi Mendy Herson
908.604.8844

Cherry Hill
Rabbi Mendy Mangel
856.874.1500

Clinton
Rabbi Eli Kornfeld
908.623.7000

Fort Lee
Rabbi Meir Konikov
201.886.1238

Franklin Lakes
Rabbi Chanoch Kaplan
201.848.0449

Hillsborough
Rabbi Shmaya Krinsky
908.874.0444

Holmdel
Rabbi Shmaya Galperin
732.772.1998

Madison
Rabbi Shalom Lubin
973.377.0707

Manalapan
Rabbi Boruch Chazanow
732.972.3687

Medford
Rabbi Yitzchok Kahan
609.953.3150

Mountain Lakes
Rabbi Levi Dubinsky
973.551.1898

North Brunswick
Rabbi Levi Azimov
732.398.9492

Old Tappan
Rabbi Mendy Lewis
201.767.4008

Randolph
Rabbi Avraham Bechor
973.895.3070

Rockaway
Rabbi Asher Herson
Rabbi Mordechai Baumgarten
973.625.1525

Sparta
Rabbi Shmuel Lewis
973.726.3333

Teaneck
Rabbi Ephraim Simon
201.907.0686

Tenafly
Rabbi Mordechai Shain
Rabbi Yitzchak Gershovitz
201.871.1152

Toms River
Rabbi Moshe Gourarie
732.349.4199

West Orange
Rabbi Mendy Kasowitz
973.731.0770

Woodcliff Lake
Rabbi Dov Drizin
201.476.0157

NEW MEXICO

S. Fe
Rabbi Berel Levertov
505.983.2000

NEW YORK

Albany
Rabbi Yossi Rubin
518.482.5781

Bedford
Rabbi Arik Wolf
914.666.6065

Binghamton
Mrs. Rivkah Slonim
607.797.0015

Brighton Beach
Rabbi Zushe Winner
Rabbi Avrohom Winner
718.946.9833

Brooklyn
Mrs. Shimona Tzukernik
718.493.2859

Dix Hills
Rabbi Yaakov Saacks
631.351.8672

Dobbs Ferry
Rabbi Benjy Silverman
914.693.6100

East Hampton
Rabbi Leibel Baumgarten
631.329.5800

Great Neck
Rabbi Yoseph Geisinsky
516.487.4554

Ithaca
Rabbi Eli Silberstein
607.257.7379

Kingston
Rabbi Yitzchok Hecht
845.334.9044

Larchmont
Rabbi Mendel Silberstein
914.834.4321

NYC Tribeca
Rabbi S. Zalman Paris
646.510.3109

NYC West Side
Rabbi Yisrael Kugel
212.799.0809

NYC Gramercy Park
Rabbi Naftali Rotenstreich
212.924.3200

NYC Kehilath Jeshurun
Rabbi Elie Weinstock
212.774.5636

Ossining
Rabbi Dovid Labkowski
914.923.2522

Port Washington
Rabbi Shalom Paltiel
516.767.8672

Riverdale
Rabbi Levi Shemtov
718.549.1100

Rochester
Rabbi Nechemia Vogel
585.271.0330

Roslyn
Rabbi Yaakov Reiter
516.484.8185

Sea Gate
Rabbi Chaim Brikman
Mrs. Rivka Brikman
718.266.1736

Staten Island
Rabbi Moshe Katzman
Rabbi Shmuel Bendet
718.370.8953

Rabbi Nachman Segal
718. 761.4483
Classes taught in Hebrew

Stony Brook
Rabbi Shalom Ber Cohen
631.585.0521

West Hempstead
Rabbi Yossi Lieberman
Rabbi Mordechai Dinerman
516.596.8691

NORTH CAROLINA

Asheville
Rabbi Shaya Susskind
828.505.0746

Charlotte
Rabbi Yossi Groner
Rabbi Shlomo Cohen
704.366.3984

Greensboro
Rabbi Yosef Plotkin
336 617 8120

Raleigh
Rabbi Aaron Herman
919.637.6950

Rabbi Pinchas Herman
Rabbi Sholom Ber Estrin
919.847.8986

OHIO

Beachwood
Rabbi Yossi Marosov
216.381.4736

Blue Ash
Rabbi Yisroel Mangel
513.793.5200

Columbus
Rabbi Areyah Kaltmann
Rabbi Levi Andrusier
614.294.3296

Dayton
Rabbi Nochum Mangel
Rabbi Dr. Shmuel Klatzkin
937.643.0770

Toledo
Rabbi Yossi Shemtov
419.843.9393

OKLAHOMA

Oklahoma City
Rabbi Ovadia Goldman
405.524.4800

Tulsa
Rabbi Yehuda Weg
918.492.4499

OREGON

Ashland
Rabbi Avi Zwiebel
541.482.2778

Portland
Rabbi Moshe Wilhelm
Rabbi Mordechai Wilhelm
503.977.9947

PENNSYLVANIA

Ambler
Rabbi Shaya Deitsch
215.591.9310

Bala Cynwyd
Rabbi Shraga Sherman
610.660.9192

Clarks Summit
Rabbi Benny Rapoport
570.587.3300

Devon
Rabbi Yossi Kaplan
610.971.9977

Lancaster
Rabbi Elazar Green
717.368.6565

Newtown
Rabbi Aryeh Weinstein
215.497.9925

Philadelphia: Center City
Rabbi Yochonon Goldman
215.238.2100

Pittsburgh
Rabbi Yisroel Altein
412.422.7300 ext. 269

Pittsburgh: South Hills
Rabbi Mendy Rosenblum
412.278.3693

Reading
Rabbi Yosef Lipsker
610.921.2805

Rydal
Rabbi Zushe Gurevitz
215.572.1511

RHODE ISLAND
Warwick
Rabbi Yossi Laufer
401.884.7888

SOUTH CAROLINA
Columbia
Rabbi Hesh Epstein
803.782.1831

TENNESSEE
Chattanooga
Rabbi Shaul Perlstein
423.490.1106

Knoxville
Rabbi Yossi Wilhelm
865.588.8584

Memphis
Rabbi Levi Klein
901.766.1800

Nashville
Rabbi Yitzchok Tiechtel
615.646.5750

TEXAS
Dallas
Rabbi Peretz Shapiro
Rabbi Moshe Naparstek
972.818.0770

Fort Worth
Rabbi Dov Mandel
817.263.7701

Houston
Rabbi Moishe Traxler
713.774.0300

Houston: Rice University Area
Rabbi Eliezer Lazaroff
Rabbi Yitzchok Schmukler
713.522.2004

Plano
Rabbi Mendel Block
Rabbi Yehudah Horowitz
972.596.8270

S. Antonio
Rabbi Chaim Block
Rabbi Yossi Marrus
210.492.1085

UTAH
Salt Lake City
Rabbi Benny Zippel
801.467.7777

VERMONT
Burlington
Rabbi Yitzchok Raskin
802.658.5770

VIRGINIA
Alexandria/Arlington
Rabbi Mordechai Newman
703.370.2774

Fairfax
Rabbi Leibel Fajnland
703.426.1980

Norfolk
Rabbi Aaron Margolin
Rabbi Levi Brashevitzky
757.616.0770

Richmond
Rabbi Dr. Shlomo Pereira
804.740.2000

Tysons Corner
Chapter founded by
Rabbi Levi Deitsch, OBM

Rabbi Chezzy Deitsch
703.829.5770

WASHINGTON
Bellevue
Rabbi Mordechai Farkash
Rabbi Sholom Ber Elishevitz
425.957.7860

Olympia
Rabbi Cheski Edelman
360.584-4306

Seattle
Rabbi Elazar Bogomilsky
206.527.1411

Spokane County
Rabbi Yisroel Hahn
509.443.0770

WISCONSIN
Mequon
Rabbi Menachem Rapoport
262.242.2235

Milwaukee
Rabbi Mendel Shmotkin
414.961.6100

PUERTO RICO
Carolina
Rabbi Mendel Zarchi
787.253.0894

ARGENTINA
BUENOS AIRES
Belgrano-Olleros
Rabbi Mendy Birman
54.11.4774.5071

Palermo Nuevo
Rabbi Mendy Grunblatt
54.11.4772.1024

Recoleta
Rabbi Hirshel Hendel
54.11.4807.7073

Villa del Parque
Rabbi Yosef Itzjok Levy
54.11.4504.1908

AUSTRALIA
Bondi
Rabbi Pinchas Feldman
Rabbi Eli Feldman
612.9387.3822

Brisbane
Rabbi Chanoch Sufrin
617.3843.6770

Double Bay
Rabbi Yanky Berger
612.9327.1644

Dover Heights
Rabbi Benzion Milecki
612.9337.6775

Melbourne
Rabbi Schneier Lange
613.9522.8222

Rabbi Shimshon Yurkowicz
613.9822.3600

North Shore
Rabbi Nochum Schapiro
Mrs. Fruma Schapiro
612.9488.9548

Sydney
Rabbi Levi Wolff
612.9389.5622

Victoria
South Yarra
Rabbi Yehuda Hoch
03.9613.0738

BRAZIL
Rio de Janeiro
Rabbi Yehoshua Goldman
Rabbi Avraham Steinmetz
55.21.3543.3770

S. Paulo
Rabbi Avraham Steinmetz
55.11.3081.3081

CANADA
ALBERTA
Calgary
Rabbi Mordechai Groner
403.238.4880

Edmonton
Rabbi Ari Drelich
Rabbi Mendy Blachman
780.851.1515

BRITISH COLUMBIA
Richmond
Rabbi Yechiel Baitelman
604.277.6427

Victoria
Rabbi Meir Kaplan
250.595.7656

MANITOBA
Winnipeg
Rabbi Avrohom Altein
Rabbi Shmuel Altein
204.339.8737

ONTARIO
London
Rabbi Eliezer Gurkow
519.434.3962

Niagara Falls
Rabbi Zalman Zaltzman

Ottawa
Rabbi Menachem M. Blum
613.823.0866

Toronto Area
BJL
Rabbi Leib Chaiken
416.916.7202

Greater Toronto
Regional Office & Thornhill
Rabbi Yossi Gansburg
905.731.7000

Lawrence/Eglinton
Rabbi Menachem Gansburg
416.546.8770

Mississauga
Rabbi Yitzchok Slavin
905.820.4432

Richmond Hill
Rabbi Mendel Bernstein
905.770.7700

York Mills
Rabbi Levi Gansburg
647.345.3800

York University
Rabbi Vidal Bekerman
416.856.4575

QUEBEC
Montreal
Rabbi Ronnie Fine
Rabbi Leibel Fine
514.342.3.JLI

Town of Mount Royal
Rabbi Moshe Krasnanski
514.739.0770

Ville S. Laurent
Rabbi Schneur Zalmen Silberstein
514.808.1418

COLOMBIA

Bogota
Rabbi Yehoshua B. Rosenfeld
Rabbi Chanoch Piekarski
571.635.8251

DENMARK

Copenhagen
Rabbi Yitzchok Lowenthal
45.3316.1850

GERMANY

Berlin
Rabbi Yehuda Tiechtel
4930.212.808.30

GREECE

Athens
Rabbi Mendel Hendel
30.210.520.2880

GUATEMALA

Guatemala City
Rabbi Shalom Pelman
502.2485.0770

ISRAEL

Ashdod
Rabbi Yosef Friedman
052.4240675

Balfurya
Rabbi Noam Bar-Tov
054.5804770

Be'er Sheva
Rabbi Avrohom Cohen
08.6233197

Caesarea
Rabbi Chaim Meir Lieberman
054.6212586

Even Yehuda
Rabbi Pinchos Noyman
054.7770707

Ganei Tikva
Rabbi Gershon Shnur
054.5242358

Giv'atayim
Rabbi Pinchus Bitton
052.6438770

Holon
Rabbi Yerachmiel Gorelik
03.6530300

Jerusalem
Rabbi Eliyahu Canterman
Classes in English
054.6823737

Karmiel
Rabbi Mendy Elishevitz
054.5213073

Kiryat Bialik
Rabbi Pinny Marton
050.6611768

Kiryat Motzkin
Rabbi Shimon Eizenbach
050.9020770

Maccabim Re'ut
Rabbi Yosef Yitzchak Noiman
054.9770549

Meitar
Rabbi Shneor Kurtz
054.5391770

Nes Ziyona
Rabbi Pinchos Feldman
054.4977092

Netanya
Rabbi Schneur Brod
054.5797572

Omer
Rabbi Menachem Feldman
050.2223770

Ramat HaSharon
Rabbi Meir Abiyov
054.5639278

Ramat Yishai
Rabbi Shneor Wolosow
052.3245475

Tel Aviv
Rabbi Menachem Gerlitzky
054.7765565

Zikhron Ya'akov
Rabbi Yosef Yitzchak Freiman
054.6631770

NETHERLANDS

Den Haag
Rabbi Shmuel Katzman
31.70.347.0222

PANAMA

Panama City
Rabbi Ari Laine
Rabbi Gabriel Benayon
507.223.3383

SINGAPORE

Singapore
Rabbi Mordechai Abergel
656.337.2189

SOUTH AFRICA

Cape Town
Rabbi Mendel Popack
Rabbi Pinchas Hecht
27.21.434.3740

Johannesburg
Rabbi Dovid Hazdan
Rabbi Shmuel Simpson
27.11.728.8152

Rabbi Dovid Masinter
Rabbi Ari Kievman
27.11.440.6600

SWEDEN

Stockholm
Rabbi Chaim Greisman
468.679.7067

SWITZERLAND

Lugano
Rabbi Yaakov Tzvi Kantor
091.921.3720

Luzern
Rabbi Chaim Drukman
414.1361.1770

UNITED KINGDOM

Edgeware
Rabbi Leivi Sudak
Rabbi Yaron Jacobs
44.208.905.4141

Leeds
Rabbi Eli Pink
44.113.266.3311

London
Rabbi Gershon Overlander
Rabbi Dovid Katz
44.208.202.1600

VENEZUELA

Caracas
Rabbi Yehoshua Rosenblum
58.212.264.7011

NOTES

NOTES

NOTES

The Jewish Learning Multiplex

Brought to you by the Rohr Jewish Learning Institute

In fulfillment of the mandate of the Lubavitcher Rebbe, of blessed memory, whose leadership guides every step of our work, the mission of the Rohr Jewish Learning Institute is to transform Jewish life and the greater community through the study of Torah, connecting each Jew to our shared heritage of Jewish learning.

While our flagship program remains the cornerstone of our organization, JLI is proud to feature additional divisions catering to specific populations, in order to meet a wide array of educational needs.

THE ROHR JEWISH LEARNING INSTITUTE,
a subsidiary of *Merkos L'Inyonei Chinuch*,
is the adult education arm of the Chabad-Lubavitch Movement.